Armenia's Velvet Revolution

Armenia's Velvet Revolution

*Authoritarian Decline and Civil
Resistance in a Multipolar World*

Edited by
Laurence Broers and Anna Ohanyan

I.B. TAURIS

LONDON • NEW YORK • OXFORD • NEW DELHI • SYDNEY

I.B. TAURIS
Bloomsbury Publishing Plc
50 Bedford Square, London, WC1B 3DP, UK
1385 Broadway, New York, NY 10018, USA

BLOOMSBURY, I.B. TAURIS and the I.B. Tauris logo are trademarks of
Bloomsbury Publishing Plc

First published in Great Britain 2021

Cover design by Namkwan Cho (nam-design.co.uk)
Cover image: Armenian opposition leader Nikol Pashinyan, 2018.
(© VANO SHLAMOV/AFP/Getty Images)

ISBN: HB: 978-1-7883-1718-4
PB: 978-1-7883-1717-7
ePDF: 978-1-7883-1720-7
eBook: 978-1-7883-1719-1

Typeset by Deanta Global Publishing Services, Chennai, India
Printed and bound in Great Britain

To find out more about our authors and books visit www.bloomsbury.com and
sign up for our newsletters.

Contents

Illustrations

Figure

Tables

Contributors

Pavel K. Baev is a research professor at the Peace Research Institute Oslo.

Laurence Broers is Caucasus Programme Director at peacebuilding organization Conciliation Resources and an associate fellow at the Royal Institute for International Affairs at Chatham House. He is the author of *Armenia and Azerbaijan: Anatomy of a Rivalry* (2019).

Kristin Cavoukian holds a doctorate in political science from the University of Toronto.

Salpi Ghazarian is Director of the Institute for Armenian Studies at the University of Southern California.

Richard Giragosian is the founding director of the Regional Studies Center, an independent think-tank located in Yerevan, Armenia, and serves as both a visiting professor at the College of Europe's Natolin Campus and a senior expert at Yerevan State University's Centre for European Studies.

Anna Ohanyan is a two-times Fulbright scholar (2012–13) and the Richard B. Finnegan Distinguished Professor of Political Science and International Relations at Stonehill College in Massachusetts. She is the author of *Networked Regionalism as Conflict Management* (2015) and the editor of *Russia Abroad: Driving Regional Fracture in Post-Communist Eurasia and Beyond* (2018).

Yevgenya Jenny Paturyan is an assistant professor in the Political Science and International Affairs Program at the American University of Armenia (AUA), Yerevan.

Jonathan Pinckney is a programme officer with the programme on non-violent action, U.S. Institute of Peace, and is the author of *From Dissent to Democracy: The Promise and Perils of Civil Resistance Transitions* (2020). He received his PhD in 2018 from the Josef Korbel School of International Studies at the University of Denver.

Tamar Shirinian is a postdoctoral teaching fellow in the Department of Anthropology at the University of Tennessee, Knoxville. Her research interests are in the tensions between political economy and gender and sexuality, especially in how anxieties around sexual perversion in post-socialist contexts are giving rise to new nationalisms and forms of the geopolitical.

Mikayel Zolyan is a historian and political analyst from Armenia.

Foreword

On 14 April 2018, my son and I were in a car heading from Mush to Van, then from Van to Kars – in Turkey. My grandparents are from somewhere in that region – I'll never know exactly where – and so, I make this journey for many reasons, including a search for a place to belong. On the road, near Ani, within physical view of Armenia but at a border that remains closed, I was following, with amazement and incredulity, live reports of a new sort of protest gaining ground on the other side of the border in Armenia. My source was CivilNet.am, streaming on my mobile phone.

In March 2018, a few hundred people had joined Nikol Pashinyan, a journalist turned activist, on a walk across Armenia. The day before my drive to Kars, they had arrived in Yerevan as exemplary students of the tactics of civil disobedience, staying two steps ahead of authorities who were alternately confident and confused. Pashinyan and his cohort of supporters were prepared to disrupt daily life in order to bring about serious political change. Pashinyan called his movement 'My Step' – a step towards a bold and clearly articulated intent: to bring down the solidly entrenched head of government, Serzh Sargsyan, and with him a countrywide economic and political monopoly. Pashinyan invited each individual Armenian to 'take your step' and join the movement. On 13 April, his first day in Yerevan, hundreds had turned into thousands. This felt different. My son and I changed course, leaving Kars behind, and drove, via Georgia, to Armenia.

What was happening in Armenia was also a search to belong – to belong to a society with a responsive government elected by the people, a society with responsible citizens accepting of their role in building an egalitarian, prosperous and desirable country. This quest for political identification, which had begun earlier in the decade, was reaching a culmination of sorts. There had been repeated expressions of political and social frustration prior to this. Yet as the first generation to have been born after the collapse of the Soviet Union – the first genuinely post-Soviet generation – matured, it was these young people, in their twenties, who were visibly leading and setting the tone of the demonstrations and demands. They wanted a hand in building the democracy they had been promised, a democracy that offered them choices and that took their thoughts and needs into account, and where economic opportunity and political access were available to everyone. They reacted to perceived injustice in specific government decisions by creating ad hoc collectives that brought people to the street. They registered successes –

small and large. And they learned and taught others that in the absence of functioning, accountable public institutions, these popular demonstrations were necessary. Their message was that the street was the only 'institution' that would help them build that secure, hopeful, inclusive society to which they would want to belong.

Oddly, Armenia's news media did not cover these civic actions. Just as it had not covered the history-changing events of 1988. Then, in the waning days of the Soviet empire, countrywide protests, with tens of thousands, hundreds of thousands and, on a few occasions, perhaps as many as one million Armenians were overlooked on the Soviet Armenian airwaves in favour of Verdi's operas. Instead of news outlets, the best instruments of information dissemination were the massive gatherings in the centre of Yerevan. At first, these demonstrations condemned environmental excesses. Once chemical production plants were shut down, the public understood the power of such mobilization. Soon after, protesters gathered in solidarity with the Armenian population of Nagorny Karabakh in the neighbouring republic of Azerbaijan, who, following Soviet Communist Party General Secretary Mikhail Gorbachev's calls for openness, demanded self-determination. Later, the rallies articulated calls for independence. Throughout, these mass meetings were unbelievable manifestations of sophisticated, deep political understanding. Questions and answers sounded throughout the massive meetings, and people gathered and dispersed peacefully. In the absence of responsible media, a nascent civil society created its own public square. Appropriately enough, it was the Matenadaran, Yerevan's repository of ancient manuscripts and learning, that was the site of these gatherings and that became the public agora.

Although twenty difficult years had passed since these never-before-seen mass protests that culminated in a collapsed USSR and an independent Republic of Armenia, some things had remained woefully unchanged. In 2011 and 2012, too, television continued to ignore every event of social or political consequence that did not have a government-sanctioned or government-orchestrated public relations value. Live television did not exist. The first time these demonstrations were covered live was by the online bilingual news channel CivilNet, which went live in 2011 by reporting on Armenia's first-ever local elections, as they happened. I had co-founded CivilNet, and its parent organization Civilitas, just a few years earlier, and its twenty-something-year-old staff was deeply aware of its role in making history.

By 2018, online media was already an important political civil society player. I was not the only one watching developments on my phone, hundreds or thousands of miles away. The international media, too, was following closely, as were governments and opposition groups around the world. In an era when the opportunity available to citizens to drastically alter the nature and composition of their government seemed to have diminished almost everywhere in the world, this seemingly simple and quickly escalating movement in Armenia merited attention. The scale of the opportunities this presented echoed around the world. Understanding this phenomenon is clearly the motivation behind this book.

In the previous twelve months, Western media outlets had published around a half-dozen articles about Armenians. They were either about the conflict over Karabakh between Armenians and Azerbaijan or about the consequences of the 1915 Armenian Genocide by the Ottoman Empire. None were about Armenia's complicated domestic challenges. In April 2018, journalists were sent to report on Armenia and its people. Some came seeking understanding through the lens of geopolitics, but quickly realized that they were confronted by an entirely domestic movement of citizens seeking a peaceful path to regime change. The puzzle that demanded explanation was not about great powers or foreign interference, but about how a near-solitary walk, over a couple of weeks, could transform into a national, non-violent movement carrying out decentralized acts of disruption and gaining thousands, and very quickly, hundreds of thousands of supporters. In Yerevan, and around the world, the challenge was to understand and explain this counter-intuitive, innovative, teachable and learnable 'revolution'. That was the overarching significance of 'the Velvet' for the world, not just for Armenians but for those invested in peaceful change everywhere.

As the international community watched, Nikol Pashinyan preached non-violence; expounded on the difference between fact and disinformation; communicated the tenets of personal agency; elaborated the scope of Armenia's capacity to self-govern, self-determine and develop domestic policy independent of foreign direction or influence; and acknowledged, even welcomed, the potential of a new diaspora, one formed post-independence, that relied on outspoken and self-propelled individuals. Each day, the number of participants multiplied in number, engaged in autonomous actions throughout the city, paralysed movement and operations, and stayed two steps ahead of authorities perplexed by the new tactics. The message and direction came from the centre, but the principals were those who had amassed on-the-ground skills and organizing proficiency. The climax was reached on 23 April when President-turned-Prime Minister Serzh Sargsyan resigned.

This volume explores and explains the social and political environment as well as the civic and political processes that capped the three-week-long crusade. Each author reviews an aspect of civil society's involvement, and invariably concludes with a question about what is to come. Will this be a complete revolution – not just an abrupt change of power, but also of organization and structure? Will the experiment that led to political transformation be followed by an equally bold vision for governance? These are the fundamental questions that must be asked if we are to understand the depth and reach of 'the Velvet', and they are explored in this volume. Is it possible that this 'revolution' is an aberration – merely a release of political steam and tensions? Or is this a fundamental turning point in Armenia's state-building project where power is consolidated by a new sort of government, no longer claiming a dual monopoly over politics and economy?

As bold as the methods of achieving political power were, the way to enhance that power and bring change to institutions, economic structures and the electorate's psyche and confidence – all that will depend on ambitious governance based on a bold vision. This book delves into the still-new and still-incredible revolution and its progression, and can offer tools for designing a strategy for a continuing revolution in governance. This will involve not just a bold vision but also institutions able to explore, design, amend and implement policy. The media, experiencing less government pressure than in the past, has still not reinvented itself. With a handful of exceptions, dozens of 'news' outlets, almost entirely online, continue to be 'sponsored' and to produce the content appropriate to that sponsor's political or economic agendas. Thus, the natural objective and essential oversight function is lacking, as is accessible media as a sounding board for new policies.

Nevertheless, new policies are expected of a government – and a society – that calls itself revolutionary. From education to social protections to fiscal, monetary and trade policy, new outputs require new inputs. Nowhere is that more urgent and evident than in the economy. International organizations will continue to look at macroeconomic indicators to judge the pace and degree of growth and to register stability. The public, that is, the electorate, will look at jobs, wages and basic rights such as healthcare and shelter. The gap between macroeconomic measurements of growth and fundamental on-the-ground evidence of inequality and stagnation will need to be addressed with labour, tax and economic policies as bold and as non-traditional as the Velvet itself, if the political transformation is to be consolidated.

Such a transformation is necessary, evident and possible in healthcare where instead of granular steps that will lead to small and incremental improvements, bold policies can be introduced – and welcomed – for the provision of patient-centred, high quality, equitable and accessible health care and the transformation of Armenia's health care system and culture to focus on building health rather than treating disease – essential in a country where demographic statistics demonstrate urgent social needs.

Finally, similarly tough choices await the education sector – the nurturing ground for democratic citizens ready to take on civic responsibility. The options facing the government are updating and cleaning up existing textbooks, curricula and tests where the vision and the goals are unclear, or taking on the challenge of reforms that are as much intellectual and conceptual as they are educational. Can the government insist on holistic and equitable education, critical thinking skills and lifelong learning as the tools necessary for a country still consolidating its democratic institutions? Will education be redesigned to instil an ethos geared towards the progress of the self – equipped for a knowledge-based economy, together with a progressive society – an essential but bold ideal in a post-Soviet society that long ago discarded the 'collective'?

Reviewing and renewing outdated educational and social service systems will not produce notably different outcomes. Instead, Armenia, and a diaspora clamouring for a chance to belong, has the opportunity to leap over existing systems and traditions and to embrace the new – in education, in health care, in labour and tax policy, just as it did in replacing an outdated political power structure with a new one.

The authors contributing to this volume help us understand how that happened, and how that may happen again.

Salpi Ghazarian
Director
USC Institute of Armenian Studies
Los Angeles

Acknowledgements

We are truly grateful to all those in Armenia and beyond who shared experiences, insights and contacts that have informed our chapters in this volume: Karena Avedissian, Richard Giragosian, Vahe Grigoryan, Armen Grigoryan, Natalie Harutyunyan, Alexander Iskandaryan, Stephen F. Jones, Katy Pearce, Isabella Sargsyan, Nune Sargsyan, Anahit Shirinyan, Tim Straight, Gevorg Ter-Gabrielyan and Maria Titizian. None bears responsibility for any error herein.

We are thankful to Salpi Ghazarian not only for writing the volume's foreword but also for many years of promoting activism and connectivity bridging Armenia and the American Armenian community.

In the course of the dramatic political transitions in Armenia of the first decade of the twenty-first century, many in the worldwide Armenian diaspora have also been inspired and mobilized from afar. The Armenian-American community of the Boston area, and the National Association for Armenian Studies and Research (NAASR) in particular, have been exemplary in providing an environment for community discussion and debate on the transformative developments in Armenia and its neighbourhood. We are indebted to Marc Mamigonian and Sarah Ignatius of NAASR for their support of this work. Stonehill College in Massachusetts and Eurasia International University in Armenia have also been instrumental in providing much-needed administrative and logistical support towards making our endeavour successful. We owe a special shout-out to the Artbridge, Green Bean and Square One cafés in Yerevan, where one or other editor spent many working hours, inspired by excellent coffee and superb service. And we also thank all of our loved ones who have been patient with us throughout this work, indulging our long travels, research trips and speaking engagements.

Finally, we are particularly grateful to Dr Concepción Barrio for making possible the face-to-face conversations that helped set us on the path towards this volume. It is to her, and to the memory of her husband, Prof James Ajemian, that this book is dedicated. Jim's lifelong support of his students and his caring mentorship have made this world a more compassionate and a peaceful place. Born into a family of survivors of the Armenian Genocide, a legacy that affected him deeply, Jim dedicated his life to the study and practice of human rights and restorative social work. He changed the lives of many, both near and far. His teaching touched tomorrow, and his values elevated many. Armenia's Velvet Revolution would have heartened him beyond measure, and his memory will continue to guide our work.

L.B. and A.O.
London and Boston,
5 April 2020.

Introduction

An unlikely transition?

Laurence Broers

In April 2018, Armenia experienced a remarkable popular uprising against the leadership of Serzh Sargsyan and his ruling Republican Party of Armenia (RPA). In a rapid sequence of events that took domestic and international observers completely by surprise, a non-violent protest movement under the leadership of opposition politician Nikol Pashinyan brought the country to a standstill. Driven by widespread disillusionment with socioeconomic decline, persistent insecurity and authoritarian encroachment, the uprising forced Sargsyan's resignation as prime minister on 23 April, to be replaced by Pashinyan in a parliamentary vote two weeks later. In the months that followed, Armenia's new leadership led the country into a precipitous programme of liberalization, political and socioeconomic reform, and criminal investigations of the outgoing elite, while maintaining – despite the foregoing – the country's delicate and deeply asymmetric relationship with Russia. The events of April–May 2018 came to be known as Armenia's 'Velvet Revolution', a term that explicitly related Armenia's experience to the civil resistance movements in Central and Eastern Europe in the late 1980s, rather than the historically and geographically more proximate 'colour revolutions' in the post-Soviet space.

This volume tells the story of how a popular protest movement, showcasing civil disobedience as a political strategy, overcame unpromising circumstances to dislodge an entrenched but decaying authoritarian regime. Situating the events in Armenia in their national, regional and global contexts, the essays here evaluate the causes driving Armenia's unexpected democratic turn, the reasons for regime vulnerability and the factors mediating a non-violent outcome. Looking outwards, this collection assesses the contradictions facing democratic transition in the South Caucasus, a fractured neighbourhood pulled towards a Russian geopolitical orbit, and coinciding with a moment of strategic uncertainty as democratization efforts across the globe confront a post-American world order and growing multipolarity. Contributors also consider the Velvet Revolution as window on gendered social norms in Armenia and its impact on community structures in the Armenian diaspora. We begin, however, with a narrative of what actually happened in April 2018.

The events of April–May 2018

The immediate trigger for Armenia's Velvet Revolution was a constitutional transition from a presidential to a parliamentary system of rule. In February 2013, President Serzh Sargsyan was elected to his second, and according to the Armenian constitution final, term. From that moment, what would happen at the end of his presidency, and who would succeed Sargsyan, became critical questions in Armenian politics. Later that year, Sargsyan appeared to offer an answer by announcing a transition to a parliamentary system of rule. In a process featuring minimal public consultation, a series of amendments to the Armenian constitution were drafted and then put to a national referendum on 6 December 2015. The amendments envisaged a far-reaching transformation of Armenia's political system. The presidency would become a largely ceremonial post elected by a parliamentary college system for one seven-year term only, while a prime minister, nominated by parliamentary majority, would hold executive power. Parliament, reduced from 131 to 101 seats, would be elected through a proportional representation system, a measure allegedly aimed at fostering the institutionalization of political parties. Amid public concerns regarding the conduct of the vote and small-scale protests against it, the amendments were approved by 63 per cent, with a turnout of 50.8 per cent.

The prevailing assumption about the parliamentary transition, both locally and abroad, was that its main aim was to secure President Sargsyan's political future beyond the end of his second term. Sargsyan had attempted to distance himself from unseemly motives by announcing before the December 2015 referendum that he would seek neither the role of prime minister nor parliamentary speaker. However, in his continued role as leader of the RPA, Sargsyan would have continued to exert considerable influence over any handpicked successor. Over the following two years, a number of candidates for this role appeared: notably Karen Karapetyan, former mayor of the Armenian capital, Yerevan, and employee of the Russian gas giant Gazprom, appointed prime minister in September 2016; and Vigen Sargsyan, a loyal aide (but no relation) to Serzh Sargsyan, appointed minister of defence also in September 2016.

In April 2017, the first parliamentary elections under the new amendments appeared to indicate that whoever Sargsyan's choice would be, resistance would be minimal. The ruling RPA won the elections with 49.2 per cent, while its coalition partners Prosperous Armenia and the Armenian Revolutionary Federation (ARF) won 27.4 per cent and 6.6 per cent, respectively. The 'traditional' opposition, the Armenian National Congress (previously the Armenian National Movement) led by the first president of independent Armenia, Levon Ter-Petrossian, fared poorly, garnering only 1.7 per cent. The Congress appeared to cede its place to a newer oppositional grouping, the *Yelk* (meaning 'way out' in Armenian) alliance, which secured 7.8 per cent. The election, which passed off without public protests or contestation of the results by the opposition, indicated that the RPA and its coalition partners would be firmly in control of the parliament just as Armenia shifted to a parliamentary system in April 2018.

Until the end of 2017, Sargsyan's intentions regarding the key new role of prime minister remained unclear. In January 2018, he nominated former prime minister and ambassador to Britain Armen Sarkissian to the newly configured post of president. Sarkissian was duly elected by a parliamentary vote on 2 March. As Armenia moved towards its parliamentary transition in April, Sargsyan's silence on his preferred successor fed long-standing suspicion that he would take the prime ministerial role himself. Under the new constitutional amendments, the Armenian government was required to resign on 9 April, pending the nomination of candidates for the prime ministerial role, and the swearing in of the eventual winner on 17 April. On 11 April, President Sargsyan finally announced that he would, after all, seek the RPA's nomination as prime minister, reneging on his earlier pledge to the contrary. What made him do so remains the subject of speculation, but the effect of his announcement was immediate and drastic. Events rapidly escalated out of his control.

Twelve days before Sargsyan's announcement, Nikol Pashinyan had begun a two-week march across Armenia to generate protest against the coming transition, beginning in Vardanants Square in Armenia's second city, Gyumri. Pashinyan, forty-two years old, was leader of a small opposition party, Civil Contract, and had previously been an associate of Ter-Petrossian in the Armenian National Congress. For many years, he had edited *Haykakan Zhamanak* ('Armenian Times'), a liberal newspaper known for its exposés of elite corruption and deeply unflattering portraits of Armenia's numerous 'oligarchs'. Pashinyan later became known for rousing oratory, playing a key role in Ter-Petrossian's 2008 election campaign against Serzh Sargsyan. That campaign had come to a violent close on 1 March 2008 when troops fired on Ter-Petrossian supporters protesting Sargsyan's victory. Ten people – eight protesters and two servicemen – died in the violence. It was the worst incident of post-electoral violence in the history of the post-Soviet South Caucasus, casting a long shadow over Sargsyan's tenure as president. In the aftermath, an arrest warrant was issued for Pashinyan, who went into hiding for over a year. In 2009, Pashinyan turned himself in, and though sentenced to seven years' imprisonment, he was released early in 2011. Pashinyan entered parliament through the Armenian National Congress in 2012, and remained a visible presence at public protest events in the years that followed. In 2013, he founded Civil Contract, initially as a non-governmental organization (NGO) and later as a political party in 2015. Pashinyan was re-elected to parliament in the April 2017 election through *Yelk'*. Accompanied by a small band of supporters, his 120-kilometre march proceeded under the slogan *K'ayl ara*, meaning 'take a step' in Armenian.

Pashinyan's march arrived in Yerevan on 13 April, and coalesced rapidly with local protest movements that had begun on 12 April. Pashinyan's *K'ayl ara* slogan melded with local movements gathered under the slogan *Merzhir Serzhin!* ('Reject Serzh!') to call on citizens to 'take a step' by calling on Sargsyan to resign. As a RPA congress in the town of Tsaghkadzor approved Serzh Sargsyan's nomination as prime minister on 14 April, Pashinyan's supporters seized the public radio, and over the following days, what had hitherto been small-scale marginal protests gathered pace across the capital. On 17 April, Sargsyan was sworn in as Armenia's prime minister as protests were spreading to Gyumri, Vanadzor and other cities across the country. By 20 April, the numbers of people mobilizing daily were reaching hundreds of thousands, bringing Yerevan and other city centres to a standstill; almost 200 protesters were arrested in the capital that day alone. Featuring very high levels of youth participation, what was essentially a highly decentralized pattern of protest was coordinated through daily Facebook livestreams from Pashinyan himself and evening rallies of crowds at Yerevan's Republic Square. These generated iconic images of crowds with mobile phones held aloft with their torches lit against the warm tuff-stone façades of Armenian architect Alexander Tamanyan's mid-twentieth century ensemble.

On 22 April, Prime Minister Sargsyan met Pashinyan for a 'public dialogue' in front of the press at the Marriott Hotel. The meeting, which pitted the taciturn and awkward Sargsyan against the media-savvy and charismatic Pashinyan, lasted less than five minutes, yet had a transformative, galvanizing effect on the Armenian public. Sargsyan appeared to issue a threat by asking Pashinyan if he had not learnt the lesson of 1 March 2008, before abruptly leaving the room. Pashinyan and some of his associates were arrested shortly after. The public reaction to what was widely perceived as an oblique threat of another violent dispersal of crowds was immediate: massive, non-violent protest on the nation's streets far exceeding the numbers gathering over the previous fortnight. Sending shockwaves through regime and society alike, members of the Armenian army's prestigious peacekeeping battalion marched in uniform with protesters, suggesting that Sargsyan did not enjoy the complete loyalty of the army. The next day, 23 April, after just one week in office, Prime Minister Sargsyan tendered his resignation, including an enigmatic mea culpa – 'Nikol Pashinyan was right, I was wrong' – in his statement. Whatever lay behind this, it finally and unambiguously identified a successor to his rule: Nikol Pashinyan. People kissed, hugged and danced in the streets, and one day later, on 24 April, the date commemorated by Armenians as the beginning of the Armenian Genocide in 1915, the annual procession of more than 100,000 people to the memorial site at Tsitsernakaberd on a hilltop overlooking Yerevan passed off in a mood of catharsis.

The agenda for change did not, of course, remain limited to merely 'rejecting Serzh'. Behind Serzh Sargsyan lay the deep structures of the RPA regime and its pervasive informal networks. If Sargsyan had resigned, the parliament remained the same as had been elected in April 2017, and, correspondingly, was dominated by the RPA and its coalition partners. Over the following week, there was intense speculation on the possible voting constellations for and against Pashinyan's candidacy as prime minister scheduled for 1 May. Following a marathon debate, Pashinyan failed to be elected prime minister by forty-five votes to fifty-five against. Despite losing the vote, Pashinyan headed directly for the podium on Republican Square as if for a victory speech, and pledged a return to mass civil disobedience. This duly resumed on 2 May, locking down Zvartnots airport, roads, schools and universities, and even the country's borders. In a re-run of the vote on 8 May, Pashinyan was elected prime minister by fifty-nine votes to forty-two. He subsequently appointed a new cabinet, characterized by a large number of ministers in their thirties, and even some in their twenties. It was, emphatically, a *post*-Soviet executive: young, inexperienced and untainted by political office in the last years of the Soviet Union or the sovereign but corrupt Armenian governments that succeeded it.

Over the following six months, a challenging period of cohabitation ensued between Pashinyan and his executive on the one hand, and the still RPA-dominated parliament. While Pashinyan was committed to new parliamentary elections under a new electoral code, the new constitution made it difficult for him to call them. After a strong result in Yerevan municipal elections on 23 September 2018, in which his 'My Step' bloc won 81 per cent, and maintaining crowd pressure on an obstructive parliament, Pashinyan eventually negotiated and set a date for new parliamentary elections on 9 December. In order to trigger the elections according to the terms of the new constitution, he formally resigned on 16 October. His 'My Step' alliance won the elections, deemed free and fair by international observers, with 70.4

per cent of the vote. Two other parties, the Bright Armenia party, previously allied with My Step, and the Prosperous Armenia party, an incongruous *ancien régime* holdover, entered parliament. Neither the RPA nor their former coalition partner, the ARF, passed the threshold for representation. Armenia had entered a new era.

Domestic constraints on a democratic breakthrough

To many observers, Armenia was an unlikely candidate for a democratic opening. Once regarded as one of the more promising Soviet successor states for reform, after twenty-five years of independence Armenia was widely seen as a durable but stagnating regime, locked in a draining conflict with oil-rich Azerbaijan and dependent on Russian patronage. Like most of the world's states Armenia featured a 'hybrid' regime combining formal democratic institutions with pervasive authoritarian control.

Until 2018, it was often difficult to remember that Armenia had once been a front runner in terms of liberalization and reform during the final years of Soviet rule. Armenia had witnessed the accession of one of the first non-communist administrations in the Soviet Union, when the Armenian National Movement under the leadership of Levon Ter-Petrossian was elected into office in 1990. Yet from the mid-1990s, Armenia's domestic politics were predominantly understood through the paradigm of 'failed transition' (Bremmer and Welt 1997; Payaslian 2011). Armenia was correspondingly invisible in the literature on post-Soviet transitions, appearing as a negative case in comparative studies of transition outcomes and as a rather typical example of non-democratic, or 'patronal', regime development in Eurasia (Hale 2015). An alternative research tradition nevertheless highlighted what Giorgi Derluguian and Ruben Hovhannisyan (2018) call the 'Armenian anomaly': a persistent tradition of popular mobilization against authoritarian governance (Andreasyan and Derluguian 2015; Ishkanian 2015).

In the light of these contradictory trends, I find Steven Levitsky and Lucan Way's seminal theory of 'competitive authoritarianism' to be the most productive in interpreting regime development in post-Soviet Armenia (Levitsky and Way 2010). Their theory describes regimes that are 'competitive in that opposition parties use democratic institutions to contest seriously for power, but they are not democratic because the playing field is heavily skewed in favor of incumbents. Competition is thus real but unfair' (Levitsky and Way 2010: 5). Armenia between 1996 and 2018 exhibited many of the characteristic features of a competitive authoritarian regime, such as a vibrant multiparty system, fiercely contested electoral campaigns, heavily manipulated electoral results, frequently though not universally violated civil liberties and extensive deployment of the administrative resources of the state in support of incumbent power.

Yet in another example of Armenian anomalousness, Armenia's competitive authoritarian regime proved surprisingly robust. Competitive authoritarian regimes may endure, but they are by nature unstable. Many such regimes in post-Soviet Eurasia experienced contested transitions to a more democratic status, while others consolidated into more authoritarian regimes, or underwent repeated power transitions without democratizing. Armenia's political regime, however, appeared to successfully withstand both the tide of 'colour revolutions' that swept through the post-Soviet space in the 2000s (Hess 2010; Zolyan 2010), and subsequent waves of domestic protest in 2011, 2013 and 2015. Compared to neighbouring Georgia, for example, whose political regime was unseated twice in 2003–4 and 2012–13, under presidents Robert Kocharian (1998–2008) and Sargsyan (2008–18) Armenia appeared to have secured regime stability despite facing significantly larger protests (Levitsky and Way 2010: 207–13; Fumagalli and Turmanidze 2018). A 2017 study found that under Kocharian and Sargsyan's leadership, the ruling RPA apparently struck a sufficient balance between legitimation, repression and co-optation to retain power (Shubladze and Khundadze 2017). A first critical question posed by the Velvet Revolution, then, was why a seemingly durable authoritarian system, one that had appeared impervious to domestic mobilization and transnational 'waves' of protest, collapsed – and collapsed so quickly. There is clearly a story about authoritarian decline in Armenia's political system that has been missed and that this volume aims to illuminate.

A second factor that tempered expectations of political change in Armenia was the previous history of coercion that had quelled earlier waves of popular mobilization. Competitive authoritarianism assumed a particularly coercive form in Armenia, as violence was repeatedly used to disperse protesting crowds – most notoriously on 1 March 2008. As a lawyer representing victims of the March 2008 violence, Vahe Grigoryan, observed to this author, there was 'carte blanche' for any regime in Armenia to use weapons to quell protest (see Chapter 3). Insurgent violence *against* the state has also been a prominent feature of Armenian politics, most recently in July 2016, when a radical oppositional group, known as the *Sasna Tsrer* (the 'daredevils of Sassoun', a term evoking a medieval Armenian epic), took control of a local police station, including several hostages. Two policemen, and a citizen bringing the insurgents food, died before the crisis was resolved. Given these unhappy precedents, the Velvet Revolution's foregrounding of civil disobedience and regime restraint signalled a watershed moment in terms of peaceful change. Over the second half of April 2018, Armenia witnessed a veritable festival of civil disobedience and peaceful protest. Families with toddlers in prams, dancing teenagers and impromptu citizen collectives blocked roads, surrounded government buildings and literally brought the country to a standstill. Aside from some minor scuffles with law enforcement agencies, Sargsyan ceded power without a shot being fired. Why did non-violent varieties of protest win out in Armenia over them? And why did a threatened regime not resort to violence, as it did in March 2008? Answers to these questions can help us to situate the Velvet Revolution within the wider literature validating the strategic value of non-violent disobedience (Chenoweth and Stephan 2012).

Alongside the interconnected factors of authoritarian endurance and the threat of coercion, a long-standing dichotomy between democracy and security in Armenian political culture was a third factor making a democratic breakthrough appear unlikely. Since 1988, before their independence from the Soviet Union, Armenia and Azerbaijan have been locked in a struggle for sovereignty in Nagorny Karabakh (de Waal 2013). A full-scale war in 1992–4 claimed more than 25,000 lives, and ended in an Armenian military victory. The status quo has increasingly been challenged since the mid-2000s, as oil revenues have enabled Azerbaijan to rearm, leading to a regional arms race. Armenia has confronted a growing power asymmetry, combined with increasing frontline violence that has generated a climate of pervasive insecurity. Escalating sharply in 2014, frontline violence culminated in a 'four-day war' of 2–5 April 2016, which saw Azerbaijan recapture territory for the first time since the 1994 ceasefire and with heavy combined losses of some 200 fatalities (Broers 2016).

This context led to a commonplace privileging of security over democracy in Armenia, and rhetorical strategies depicting a zero-sum relationship between the two (Ghaplanyan 2018). Armenian citizens mobilizing for democratic change have been repeatedly 'demobilized' by political elites using 'rallying effects' to depict such challenges to their power as a threat to national security (Broers 2019). The Velvet Revolution overturned this strategy, despite plausible fears that Azerbaijan could seek to take advantage of internal turmoil in Armenia. Another important question that the Velvet Revolution poses, then, concerns the mitigation of national security constraints when attempting democratic change in the context of long-term conflict. How can politicians and activists in such contexts counter discourses of securitization and reframe the debate about security?

Overcoming entrenched authoritarianism, the threat of coercion and the use of national security discourse to demobilize demand for democracy constituted a triple bottleneck that the Velvet Revolution overcame in the domestic arena. No less challenging is the regional and international context for a democratic transition in Armenia.

International constraints on democratic transition

The South Caucasus has emerged as perhaps the most fractured of the post-Soviet regions (Ohanyan 2018). Domestic outcomes in the region's states have a wider geopolitical resonance due to conflicting vectors of actual and aspirational security alliances, competing Eurasian and European projects in hegemonic regionalism, and beyond them, the wider rivalry between Russia and Euro-Atlantic powers for influence over the 'shared neighbourhood' between them (Averre 2009; Simão 2017; Broers 2018). The struggle for influence in the shared European neighbourhood took off in the mid-2000s with the onset of the colour revolutions in 'in-between states': civic uprisings that saw alliances between former elite factions and liberal civil societies oust authoritarian rulers through the contestation of flawed elections (Bunce and Wolchik 2011; Ó Beacháin and Polese 2010). Scripted through the prism of Eurasian geopolitics, the colour revolutions (or 'fruit and flower revolutions' to their detractors) pitted Westernizing modernizers against Moscow-friendly traditionalists. Geopolitical entrepreneurship and domestic reform agendas were firmly intertwined in this storyline, actively promoted by colour revolutionaries such as Georgian president Mikheil Saakashvili. Combined with the appearance of mass protest against Vladimir Putin's rule in Moscow in 2011–12, the colour revolutions sharpened the contours of the 'near abroad' as an arena in which Moscow perceived existential interests to be at stake (Toal 2017).

Armenia's predicament in this situation has been particularly challenging. Both of its longest borders, with Azerbaijan and Turkey, are closed due to the conflict in Nagorny Karabakh and the conflicted history of the Armenian Genocide in Ottoman Turkey. Increasing dependence on Russia in order to sustain an enduring rivalry with Azerbaijan has locked Armenia within Russian-led regional integration and security structures, and severely curtailed Yerevan's ability to develop linkages with other partners (Giragosian 2018). Yet Armenia also sought partnership in the spheres of institution-building, trade and development with Euro-Atlantic actors, where several of the largest and most influential Armenian diaspora communities were also located. Armenian policy-makers sought to reconcile the country's conflicted geopolitical agendas through the schema of 'complementarity'. This implied a harmonious compartmentalization of Armenia's linkages, with security and some institutional linkages vectored towards Russia, and other linkages vectored towards Europe. Complementarity, as Alexander Iskandaryan has aptly put it, 'does not enable a country to make many friends, but allows it to avoid making enemies' (Iskandaryan 2013: 6). This limited scope of ambition appeared appropriate for a landlocked state dependent for access to the outside world on a border with Georgia, a friendly but equally vulnerable state to the north, and a small and geographically extremely remote border to the south with Iran, a state regarded by many Euro-Atlantic actors as an international pariah and whose relations with the United States in particular are prone to repeated crisis.

Complementarity, as an actual policy solidifying multilateral linkages rather than just a rhetorical strategy, remained largely nominal through the 2000s as Russian linkages predominated. Armenia was a founder signatory of the Collective Security Treaty in 2002 and member of the Collective Security Treaty Organization (CSTO), the Russia-led security alliance. Yerevan also signed a number of bilateral treaties with Russia in the late 1990s, embedding Armenia within a Russian extended deterrent. In 2010, an effort to re-calibrate and reinvigorate complementarity by negotiating an association agreement with the European Union (EU) was undertaken, briefly making Armenia the EU's 'unexpected ideal neighbour' (Delcour and Wolczuk 2015). But after three years of quiet, unadvertised progress in negotiations between Yerevan and Brussels, geopolitical deference to Russia was emphatically reasserted in September 2013, when Armenia renounced the association agreement and announced it would be joining the Russian-led Eurasian Economic Union (EAEU) instead (Grigoryan 2014; Ohanyan 2015; Ter-Matevosyan et al., 2017). The national security imperative, the fate of millions of Armenian migrant labourers in Russia (and of their remittances) and the hopelessness of normative convergence with the EU were adduced as reasons justifying the démarche.

In the light of this setting, the unlikelihood of democratic transition for as long as Armenia was in a Russian geopolitical orbit had long been a prevailing assumption both inside the country and among external observers of the South Caucasus. The popular script of the colour revolutions conflated democratization with pro-Western leanings, which Armenia's enduring insecurity did not permit and for which it had already been punished in 2013. Furthermore, the deep structural penetration of Armenia's economy by Russian business interests conceded by Presidents Kocharian and Sargsyan created extensive vested interests in the domestic arena with no incentives to reform or liberalize.

On multiple levels, then, the Velvet Revolution threw down a gauntlet to the received wisdom that Armenia's geopolitics were incompatible with democratic change. As a vivid demonstration of the power of street protest, the Velvet Revolution embodied the very kind of popular mobilization causing antipathy and alarm in Moscow. It recalled a more troubled moment in relations between Moscow and Yerevan, when Armenia was one of the most rebellious republics in Mikhail Gorbachev's Soviet Union of the late 1980s. As a tightly disciplined movement championing non-violence, the Velvet Revolution upended the domination of realist paradigms asserting a hard definition of security. Nikol Pashinyan and his supporters articulated a different vision, of security through liberalization, strengthening institutions and peaceful transformation of goals. And its emphasis on rooting out corruption set the Velvet Revolution on a path of inevitable collision with the heavily Russian-oriented oligarchic space populated by RPA grandees, the Prosperous Armenia party, and their clients and affiliates.

To be sure, the extent to which Russia really seeks to diffuse an authoritarian model of governance in the post-Soviet space is a topic of lively debate (Ambrosio 2010; Way 2015). Moscow has seen its efforts to influence elections in even such small and supposedly manageable clients as the unrecognized or partially recognized republics of Abkhazia and Transdniestria embarrassingly backfire. There is evidence to suggest that so long as its clients renounce aspirations for formal membership of Euro-Atlantic structures, Moscow may be agnostic on the regime types they exhibit. Where that line lies, however, appears to be an empirical question in each case, inviting the questions of how the Velvet Revolution negotiated damaging geo-politicizing framings, and how the revolution was perceived and acted on by Moscow. Beyond these questions lies the longer-term question of whether the Velvet Revolution will transform the Armenian foreign policy context and enable new relations, or whether the project to liberalize Armenia will remain constrained by its immediate international environment.

This tension was evident in the Velvet Revolution's explicit rejection of geopolitical branding. Its leaders pledged no changes in the country's foreign policy and stressed its domestically driven agenda. Yet beyond Russia's likely or possible reaction, the global conjuncture hardly appeared conducive to a democratic transition. Scholars had long since dismissed the school of transition politics – 'transitology' – and have elaborated alternative theories explaining colour revolutions and other attempted civic uprisings as largely epiphenomenal to deeply embedded cycles of power transition that nevertheless yielded authoritarian continuity (Hale 2015). If competitive authoritarianism, as Levitsky and Way argued (2010: 34), had emerged as a response to the unipolar post–Cold War global order, characterized by Western liberal hegemony and declining resources for authoritarianism, that unipolar moment had been eclipsed by a global turn towards populist authoritarianism, Euro-Atlantic introspection, an uncertain and unpredictable relationship between President Donald Trump and President Vladimir Putin, and the emergence of a fragmenting, multipolar world. Regionally, backsliding on reform despite successive popular uprisings in Ukraine and an uncertain record in neighbouring Georgia pointed to the elusiveness of real democratic change in Eurasia.

Unfolding against a precarious, multipolar context offered both opportunities and risks. On the one hand, it allowed Nikol Pashinyan to avoid accusations of undue international interference or demonstration effects as drivers of events in Armenia. Armenia's transition could be clearly understood and recognized as a domestic achievement, garnering plaudits such as *The Economist*'s commendation as its 'country of the year' in 2018 (*The Economist* 2018). On the other hand, the Velvet Revolution, a movement for liberal democracy, clean government and civic inclusivity, unfolded at a time when these were no longer seen as inevitable or hegemonic around the world. Whether ideals of inclusivity, equality and human rights protections can translate into real social change in Armenia, against a rising regional and global tide of right-wing populism, remains uncertain. With the Velvet Revolution, Armenia moved decisively into its own post-truth era characterized by vicious culture wars, as associates of the former RPA regime retained control over most of the republic's media space, and ostensibly 'new' groups with old regime ties appeared, such as 'Adekvad' ('adequate') and 'Civic Consciousness'. These groups promoted anti-Western propaganda, disseminated conspiracy theories and hate speech, and mimicked fact-checking and civic monitoring practices to attack Armenia's new government at every opportunity (Grigoryan 2018). The capacity of these groups to mobilize and receive support from outside of Armenia, in an ironic reversal of the Velvet Revolution's own modus operandi, augurs a long-term struggle over social values, equality and freedoms in Armenia.

Chapter guide

Bringing together an authoritative collective of authors, this volume situates the events in Armenia both in their national-historical context and within theoretical and practical debates on democratic transitions, social movements, civil disobedience and Eurasian geopolitics.

In the opening chapter Anna Ohanyan situates Armenia's Velvet Revolution in a global comparative context. She argues for a wider perspective on the events in Armenia than a focus on regime politics in Eurasia allows, and brings in comparative insights from transition politics in the Middle

East and Latin America. Ohanyan explores what she terms the 'interaction effect' between two core variables in mediating transition outcomes across these disparate spaces: the patterns of popular mobilization and the degree to which the state is institutionalized or what she refers to as 'stateness'. She thus conceives of transition as a 'dual-track' process, unfolding at the level of civil society and popular agency, on the one hand, and the institutional capacity of state institutions to coerce, co-opt and subsequently stabilize contentious politics when they do erupt, on the other. Despite a deep democratic deficit and an often vigorously contested competitive authoritarian system, the Armenian state had experienced a relatively long period of stable state-building prior to the Velvet Revolution. At the same time, Ohanyan, argues, a deeply nested network of civil society actors and movements developed alongside Armenia's authoritarian regime. In April 2018, these interacted to produce a conjuncture between a highly experienced civil society enriched by years of strategic learning and a relatively high degree of institutional stability in the state, allowing the Velvet Revolution to be enacted with an unlikely smoothness and coherence. Based on these findings, Ohanyan argues that the Velvet Revolution has much more in common with the gradualist and cumulative transitions taking place in Latin America in the 1970s and 1980s than with either the colour revolutions of the post-Soviet space or most of the scenarios that unfolded in the Arab Spring.

Mikayel Zolyan then situates the Velvet Revolution in the historical context of Armenia's post-Soviet trajectory. He argues that the fact of the protests of April 2018 was not in itself surprising, but what seemed unlikely was that these protests would ever succeed, as a multitude of previous protest movements had largely ended in vain. As he shows, however, repeated failure was, in this case, a productive process. On the one hand, authoritarianism in Armenia was never able to quell surges of demand for political participation, embedding protest – particularly after contested elections – as a prominent feature of post-Soviet Armenian political culture. Zolyan argues that this was a key factor preventing a crude extension of Serzh Sargsyan's tenure and motivating the considerably riskier transition to a parliamentary system – which eventually yielded the opening for the Velvet Revolution. On the other hand, Armenia's protest culture developed in multiple ways, from the more institutionalized activities of NGOs and associations to the more spontaneous and networked structure of 'civic initiatives' that did not pose overtly political challenges to the regime, but succeeded in popularizing a vivid culture, especially among the youth, of creative and innovative civil resistance.

Zolyan discusses two precursors to the Velvet Revolution that he sees as the 'writing on the wall': the 'Electric Yerevan' protests against energy price rises in 2015 and the violent seizure of a police station in a Yerevan suburb by the *Sasna Tsrer* group a year later in July 2016. Electric Yerevan demonstrated the potential for innovative, youth-driven and peaceful mass protest, while also illustrating the need for political leadership if such protests were to be effective. The *Sasna Tsrer* incident, which claimed the lives of three people but attracted widespread support for the aims – if not the methods – of the group behind the hijacking, illustrated both the extent to which Armenia's regime had lost legitimacy and the limited horizons of armed struggle as a response. In its combination of disciplined leadership, non-violent methods and innovative appeal to the youth, the Velvet Revolution subsumed the lessons of both Electric Yerevan and *Sasna Tsrer*.

In his contribution, Laurence Broers examines the trajectory of Armenian authoritarianism and why it became vulnerable. He argues that a vibrant nationalist tradition, a political elite fractured since the perestroika era and limited economic resources for patronage conditioned at times vigorous competitiveness in the Armenian political arena. Drawing on Johannes Gerschewski's framework of the three 'pillars of stability' underpinning authoritarian rule, Broers argues that incumbents throughout the 1998–2018 period met the challenge of competition through strategies balancing between: legitimacy deriving from the Karabakh conflict and claims to provide for national security; repression enacted by a large and loyal security apparatus inherited from war with Azerbaijan in the 1990s; and the co-optation of emerging elite factions. Although authoritarian rule endured, this came at the cost of repeated use of coercion to quell mass mobilizations. The institutionalization of the RPA as a catch-all ruling party and coalitions with co-opted economic actors ('oligarchs') and nationalists were responses to this problem, and appeared through the mid-2010s to have met with some success.

To capture the dynamics of authoritarian decline, Broers parses the Velvet Revolution as a terminal destabilization of the three pillars of legitimacy, repression and co-optation. Legitimation failure flowed from President Sargsyan's own bloody accession to power in March 2008, the compromising of his national security credentials during the 'four-day war' with Azerbaijan in April 2016 and a long-term context of ineffective policy-making. Coercion failure flowed from the widely perceived costs of having used this strategy in 2008, a limited yet significant professionalization of Armenia's security sector under Sargsyan's presidency, and the suddenness and scale of protests in April 2018. Conversely, Broers argues that complacency in the regime flowed from the apparent success of Sargsyan's co-optation strategies. These had seemingly yielded a loyal parliament with a negligible opposition in the 2017 election, just as Armenia was shifting to a parliamentary system. Thus, while Broers agrees with Ohanyan and Zolyan that the Velvet Revolution (or something like it) was a strategic inevitability given Armenia's history of protest and political economy, he argues that in April 2018, it came as a devastating tactical surprise, under conditions in which the traditional remedy of coercion was no longer available.

Jenny Paturyan asks in her chapter to what extent can the strength of the mobilization in April–May 2018, its self-organization and its peaceful nature be attributed to Armenian civil society? She traces three decades of civil society activism in Armenia, beginning with mass mobilization in support of the unification of Nagorny Karabakh and Armenia in the late 1980s and in response to the 7 December 1988 earthquake in Armenia. These waves of mobilization were followed by demobilization and disappointment, as the reality of Armenian independence failed to live up to ideals. Through democracy assistance, a professionalized NGO sector appeared in Armenia, which although effective in monitoring and advocacy roles had a limited reach into wider constituencies in society. From the latter half of the 2000s, a new form of civic activity appeared in Armenia: the so-called civic initiatives that presented a different model to the activities of NGOs by being informal, decentralized, networked and often single-issue in scope and aims. Paturyan argues that civic initiatives became 'the default mode of struggle for many young people', operating innovatively, accessibly and spontaneously through social media and informal activist spaces (see Avedissian 2020).

These different forms of civic activism converged in the Velvet Revolution, where civil society brought strategic learning from earlier episodes of mobilization, coordinated and disseminated information, and contributed tactics of networked resistance and inspiring celebratory frames appealing to a wide bandwidth in society. Paturyan warns, however, that the aftermath of the Velvet Revolution presented Armenian civil society of different kinds with new challenges. Some activists transitioned into public office, resulting in a depletion of human and social capital. Working with a putatively 'friendly' government, now staffed in some cases by former colleagues, evokes challenging issues for civil society of how to define and express criticism and distance. Paturyan expresses concern that a historical pattern of mass mobilization and high ideals derailed by disappointment in the actual democratic dividends achieved may repeat itself. As she concludes, 'We can hardly afford another lapse into cynicism, another generation lost to activism, and another twenty years of stagnation in our public life.'

Jonathan Pinckney's chapter focuses on one of the Velvet Revolution's most distinctive features: its foregrounding of non-violent resistance as its primary tactical repertoire. Armenia's Velvet Revolution joins a series of more than 100 major non-violent movements for peaceful change since 1945.

It connects with a ground-breaking body of scholarship arguing that political transitions initiated by non-violent resistance tend to lead to more democratic outcomes than the alternatives. Resistance in such scenarios involves the mass and systematic withdrawal of cooperation from a system of power, but the avoidance of any physical violence in doing so. Drawing on Ackerman and DuVall's framework of the 'three engines' of non-violent resistance, Pinckney demonstrates how unity, strategic planning and non-violent discipline were all effectively deployed during the Velvet Revolution. Positive and inclusive framing of the movement's agenda and encouragement of participation from the broadest possible cross-section of society contributed to unity. Strategic planning was evident in the decentralized strategy of resistance, avoiding concentration – and confrontation – with security forces that had proved so disastrous for earlier rounds of mass mobilization in Armenia. As Pinckney points out, the very term 'Velvet Revolution' reflected a strategic frame appealing to both regime and society to refrain from violence. Protestor discipline in avoiding violence, whether active or reactive, upheld this appeal from the side of the crowds. As Pinckney argues, 'Armenia demonstrates the possibility of combining the energy of tech-savvy youth activists with the institutional connections and hierarchy of opposition parties for a powerful blend of parliamentary and street politics.'

While Pinckney echoes Paturyan's concerns about post-revolutionary disillusionment, he is cautiously optimistic on the transformational potential of the Velvet Revolution. He notes how public mobilization remained high in the post-revolutionary period, yet oriented towards positive goals of building institutional accountability rather than bringing institutions down. He cites the mobilization against the environmental impacts of the Amulsar gold mine as a case in point. Pinckney's analysis chimes also with Ohanyan's when he observes that Nikol Pashinyan has strived to keep his pursuit of political goals within institutional confines, working with the state rather than against it.

Moving to Armenia's external relations, Richard Giragosian's contribution discusses the challenges to Armenia's Velvet Revolution posed by geography, geopolitics and multipolarity. As Giragosian argues, the Velvet Revolution coincided with the definitive arrival of a new global conjuncture, namely, the superseding of American hegemony and the emergence of a multipolar order. This presents Yerevan with both opportunities and risks. On the one hand, Armenia has an opportunity to expand and develop its long-standing foreign policy of complementarity, which envisages the advancement of linkages in diverse yet complementary geopolitical directions. In Armenia's recent history, complementarity has often been more a constrained agenda rather than an actual policy. Giragosian sees new scope for that to change if

Armenian diplomacy demonstrates sufficient determination and creativity. But multipolarity also confronts any new Armenian diplomatic initiatives with risks. One particularly salient risk, as Giragosian shows, is an uncertain and unpredictable relationship with the United States. He identifies a 'crisis of confidence' characterizing ties between Yerevan and Washington, occasioned by the Donald Trump administration's antipathy to Armenia's long-standing efforts to develop relation with Iran, Yerevan's humanitarian deployments to Syria and, more broadly, the uncertainties surrounding the relationship between Presidents Trump and Putin. Even if, as Giragosian suggests, the Armenian-US crisis of confidence will blow over, Armenia will face steep challenges in isolating the scope and content of its desired regional ties from the brash red lines and higher-order agendas of global powers.

While the Revolution shook up long-standing approaches to Armenia's intractable foreign policy challenges, Giragosian argues that it also offered new resources, such as domestic legitimacy, renewed international interest and a new element of soft power. He relates the new conjuncture that Armenia faces with a wider imperative for a 'small state strategy' recognizing both the limits and dangers to Armenia of realist and 'hard power' approaches. Giragosian offers a series of recommendations as to how Yerevan might build out its approach to small state diplomacy, including a more creative emphasis on economic statecraft, innovating new roles for Armenia as a bridge between European and Eurasian economic blocs, engaging China and making more creative use of the soft power potential within the Armenian diaspora.

As already noted, the Velvet Revolution disrupted a long-standing assumption that democratic transition is all but excluded within a Russian geopolitical orbit. As Pavel Baev observes at the beginning of his chapter, what made the Revolution unique among those enacted in post-communist Eurasia since 1989 was the imperative of preserving the military-security alliance with Russia. As Baev notes, however, assiduous assurances of Armenia's unwavering commitment to its ties with Russia have not earned Nikol Pashinyan the Kremlin's trust. Baev situates the Velvet Revolution in the context of three constituent elements in Russia's perspectives on the South Caucasus: its diminishing abilities to project geopolitical power into the region; its aversion to street protest and 'revolutionary' change of any kind; and its instrumentalization of economic, and especially energy, linkages to assure political loyalty among clients dependent on Russian gas supplies. Armenia's Velvet Revolution appeared as an unwelcome return of the 'Eurasian street' just as concerns in Moscow about protests in the 'near abroad' had dissipated.

Yet Russia's reaction was uncharacteristically hesitant and ambivalent. Rather than strategic reasoning or pragmatism, however, Baev attributes this to timing. In the early months of 2018, President Vladimir Putin and his team were distracted with managing Putin's re-election to the Russian presidency on 18 March, and beyond that, the forthcoming hosting of the World Cup in June. Apparent Russian quiescence should therefore be understood as 'a major oversight in risk assessment', forcing Moscow to accept a 'colourless' revolution in Armenia as an exception from its otherwise unwavering policy of opposing civil uprisings. To be sure, Baev argues that Armenian exceptionalism is facilitated by its unquestioned geopolitical loyalty to Moscow. But that exceptionalism is tied in the Kremlin's perspective to the expectation that Pashinyan's government will regress to what it sees as the 'natural' Eurasian default of a personalized authoritarian regime. A significantly more challenging and disagreeable prospect for Moscow, Baev argues, would be an Armenia that breaks with the pattern of authoritarian retrenchment and persists with democratic reforms. Under those circumstances, the odds for preserving the alliance would become all but prohibitive.

The extent to which the Velvet Revolution could deliver real equality and inclusivity is addressed by Tamar Shirinyan in her chapter from the perspective of gendered hierarchies. Drawing on in-depth interviews with the members of *Aghchiknots'* (literally meaning 'girls' place' in Armenian), a Facebook chat uniting a group of women activists, Shirinyan analyses the Velvet Revolution as a theatre for the contestation of political patriarchy. She argues that the Armenian nation may be understood as a 'nation-family', in which gendered hierarchies stemming from kinship norms determine rights and eligibility to exercise political agency. While the Velvet Revolution was not a feminist movement, it produced myriad encounters and contentious moments through which feminist goals were advanced and enacted. As Shirinyan demonstrates with rich ethnographic material, contradictory trends were at work here. On the one hand the Velvet Revolution's call to universality and inclusivity implied that public space and political action were no longer the preserve of masculine agency. Yet in the process of mobilizing and taking to the streets, women activists continually found themselves interrupted and confronted by men reasserting masculine propriety over female action. Even within the protest movement, political patriarchy reasserted itself to produce gendered hierarchies disrupting an inclusive vision of social trust.

Nevertheless, across countless encounters, the women of the *Aghchiknots'* group felt 'that we were crossing over onto the other side of the boundary of what it meant to be a woman', challenging both 'appropriate behaviours' for women as defined by men and the overarching male claim to 'political fatherhood'. Shirinyan's interviewees attest to the inspirational impact of individual moments of resistance to political patriarchy during the Velvet Revolution, the personal realization of the numbers of feminist and queer activists present during the events and the awareness of a wider horizon of solidarity than is normally visible under conditions of stable patriarchy. Yet Shirinyan concludes that the space and time for the contestation of propriety, paternalism and patriarchy proved to be liminal, pending renewed patriarchal closure. She observes that Prime Minister Pashinyan appointed only two women among twenty ministerial positions in his new cabinet. The Velvet Revolution's legacy for equality and inclusivity consequently remains uncertain: while the re-consolidation of power appeared to go hand-in-hand with a re-consolidation of patriarchy, the Revolution had also produced new subjects, and new subjectivities, 'less willing to submit to the previous world's regulations of their bodies, voices, and access to public space'.

Kristin Cavoukian considers the complex entanglements of democratic transition and the politics of the Armenian diaspora. She notes that since Armenia's independence (and even before that) the Armenian diaspora has generally acted as a conservative and risk-averse force in domestic politics. Perennially concerned with external threats, diasporic mobilization has tended to fall in behind the existing power structure in Armenia and to mobilize around development and national security issues as the incumbent regime defines them, rather than connecting with domestic efforts to democratize Armenia. This tendency was further reinforced by a process that Cavoukian terms 'identity gerrymandering', a rhetorical strategy aiming to dilute potentially more critical voices of diaspora communities in Western states by elevating a more pliant post-Soviet diaspora, above all the substantial Armenian community in Russia. The Velvet Revolution challenged many basic postulates of an Armenian diasporic identity by avoiding the identification of an external enemy or 'other', and by trenchantly identifying instead Armenia's own regime in this role. Given that many diasporans retained justifiable fears regarding the impact of domestic turmoil on Armenia's overall situation, initial reactions were tepid. Whether in Western states or Russia, establishment organizations such as the ARF (also a coalition partner to the ruling RPA in Armenia), the Armenian Assembly of America or the Union of Armenians of Russia, all greeted the protests of April 2018 with silence or cautionary statements. Cavoukian argues that, indeed, the Velvet Revolution exposed schisms within communities between established institutions that preserved a guarded distance from the protests in Armenia, and individuals, smaller groups and diasporic youth who broke with community organizations to support the protests in Armenia as they unfolded.

Only after Sargsyan's resignation did the diaspora establishment join the Velvet bandwagon. Repercussions of the events in Armenia, however, led to further irritants for the Armenia–diaspora relationship, including the arrest on charges of embezzlement of senior officials in the Hayastan All-Armenian

Fund, one of the most trusted fundraising institutions channelling diasporic funds to domestic development, and the abolition of the Ministry of the Diaspora. Cavoukian argues, however, that specific institutional arrangements are less important than wider attitudinal shifts regarding roles and expectations in the homeland-diaspora relationship. As she puts it, the 'Velvet Revolution opposed and exposed the corruption of the regime toward its own citizenry, but its aftermath presented an opportunity to reassess the degree to which the state-diaspora relationship was itself problematic, and in turn facilitated the regime's corrupt practices.' She sees a diminished role for diaspora Armenians in the future of Armenia as both inevitable and not in itself a negative development. Rather there is scope for diaspora communities to 'prioritize direct, unmediated engagement with individuals, intellectuals, and civil society groups in the home state', rather than to seek to influence the homeland with one voice.

Revolutions, famously, never end. As of this writing, the struggle in – and for – Armenia is still being waged. In a concluding chapter, Anna Ohanyan reflects on both the prospects and the lessons of the Velvet Revolution, or what she refers to simply as 'the Velvet'. She identifies four factors that she sees as critical to the Velvet's future trajectory. Internally, these are the depth and resilience of 'authoritarian reserves', meaning residual spaces, institutions and networks still operating according to the rules of the *ancien régime*, and the capacity of an effective multiparty system to emerge and channel contested politics within state institutions. She warns that self-restraint within Nikol Pashinyan's ruling bloc is a key variable, yet exercising that restraint in the face of external challenges will be extremely challenging. Externally, the surrounding context of regional fracture poses specific challenges to consolidating democracy in Armenia. Ohanyan argues that domestic political fractures offer opportunity to the Kremlin to sabotage the democratization project. The enduring rivalry with Azerbaijan imposes another 'wild card'. Ohanyan observes that the relationship between democratization and ongoing or resumed conflict is highly complex, and simple cause-effect relationships should not be assumed. Resumed large-scale violence may not necessarily derail the democratization project completely, and democratization may even contribute to the capacity of states to defend themselves. Nevertheless, continuing insecurity casts long-term constraints over the scope and pace of the project to liberalize Armenia. On the positive side, Ohanyan notes the emergence of a 'democratic dyad' between Armenia and Georgia. She brings evidence that local clustering among democracies can generate liberal outcomes at regional and global levels. Armenia and Georgia, two neighbours with an extraordinarily intertwined history yet little to offer one another in the post-Soviet era, have a historic opportunity to re-calibrate their relationship.

Ohanyan concludes that for the global policy landscape in supporting democratic change, the Velvet offers important lessons. Too often the 'transitology' toolkit has seen change as a top-down phenomenon and has reacted ineffectively to liberal politics emanating from below. Western support and tolerance of 'low-intensity democracies' – in other words, hybrid or competitive authoritarian regimes – has thwarted more radical change that could actually challenge the inequalities of wild neoliberalism and oligopolies. Ohanyan calls for more calibrated foreign policies towards aspiring democratizers caught in-between competing geopolitical powers, and makes concrete recommendations to this end. As she observes, as the liberal democratic order finds itself in retreat across the world, the fate of aspiring democracies in the world's margins assumes a new importance.

As of this writing in early April 2020, the Covid-19 pandemic is engulfing Armenia, the South Caucasus and the entire world, with unpredictable results for global governance, the world economy and regional geopolitics. Perhaps fortuitously, Armenia entered the pandemic having recently just undergone a major stress-test through the Velvet Revolution. Yet the impacts of the pandemic, from the shutting down of communications, to economic depression, to pressures on civil liberties, will create a formidable additional set of challenges overturning a multitude of prior assumptions and expectations. Beyond lives lost, the coronavirus crisis will impact deeply on the balance among the world's great powers, on discourses of sovereignty and on global narratives on the resilience and capabilities of different regime types – in ways that will cascade ambiguously into fractured regional settings such as the South Caucasus. It is too early to speculate on the long-term consequences of Covid-19, and indeed on the Velvet Revolution's medium to long-term trajectory. What is more certain is that the popular demand for participation and representation characterizing Armenian political culture will not subside. If and when this demand is frustrated, we should not be surprised if once again our eyes are drawn to the Armenian street as a theatre of public mobilization, civil resistance and a carnivalesque challenge to authoritarian practice.

References

Ambrosio, T. (2010) Constructing a Framework of Authoritarian Diffusion: Concepts, Dynamics, and Future Research. *International Studies Perspectives*, 11: 375–92.

Andreasyan, Z. and Derluguian, G. (2015) Fuel Protests in Armenia. *New Left Review*, 95 (September–October): 29–48.

Avedissian, K. (2020). New Media and Digital Activism: Comparing Armenia and Chechnya. In: Yemelianova, Y. and Broers, L., eds, *Routledge Handbook of the Caucasus*. London and New York: Routledge, 416–27.

Averre, D. (2009) Competing Rationalities: Russia, the EU and the 'Shared Neighbourhood'. *Europe-Asia Studies*, 61 (10): 1689–713.

Bremmer, I. and Welt, C. (1997) Armenia's New Autocrats. *Journal of Democracy*, 8 (3): 77–91.

Broers, L. (2016) *The Nagorny Karabakh Conflict. Defaulting to War*. Chatham House Research Report. London: Royal Institute for International Affairs.

Broers, L. (2018) The South Caucasus: Fracture Without End? In: Ohanyan, A., ed., *Russia Abroad: Driving Regional Fracture in Eurasia and the Middle East*. Washington DC: Georgetown University Press, 81–102.

Broers, L. (2019) *Armenia and Azerbaijan: Anatomy of a Rivalry*. Edinburgh: Edinburgh University Press.

Bunce, V. J. and Wolchik, S. L. (2011) *Defeating Authoritarian Leaders in Postcommunist Countries*. Cambridge: Cambridge University Press.

Chenoweth, E. and Stephan, M. (2012) *Why Civil Resistance Works: The Strategic Logic of Nonviolent Conflict*. New York: Columbia University Press.

Delcour, L. and Wolczuk, K. (2015) The EU's Unexpected 'Ideal Neighbour'? The Perplexing Case of Armenia's Europeanisation. *Journal of European Integration*, 37 (4): 491–507.

Derluguian, G. and Hovhannisyan, R. (2018) The Armenian Anomaly: Toward an Interdisciplinary Interpretation. *Demokratizatsiya: The Journal of Post-Soviet Democratization*, 26 (4): 441–64.

The Economist. (2018) The Economist's Country of the Year 2018. *The Economist*, 22 December. https://www.economist.com/leaders/2018/12/22/the-economists-country-of-the-year-2018 (accessed 23 November 2019).

Fumagalli, M. and Turmanidze, K. (2018) *Authoritarian Stability in the South Caucasus: Voting Preferences, Autocratic Responses and Regime Stability in Armenia and Georgia*. London and New York: Routledge.

Ghaplanyan, I. (2018) *Post-Soviet Armenia: The New National Elite and the New National Narrative*. London and New York: Routledge.

Giragosian, R. (2018) Small States and the Large Costs of Regional Fracture: The Case of Armenia. In: Ohanyan, A., ed., *Russia Abroad: Driving Regional Fracture in Post-communist Eurasia and Beyond*. Washington DC: Georgetown University Press, 103–17.

Grigoryan, A. (2014) Armenia: Joining under the Gun. In: Starr, S. F. and Cornell, S. E., eds, *Putin's Grand Strategy: The Eurasian Union and Its Discontents*. Washington DC and Stockholm: Central Asia and Caucasus Institute, 98–109.

Grigoryan, A. (2018) 'Armenia First': Behind the Rise of Armenia's Alt-Right Scene. *Open Democracy*, 02 September. https://www.opendemocracy.net/en/odr/armenia-first-behind-the-rise-of-armenias-alt-right-scene/ (accessed 02 February 2020).

Hale, H. E. (2015) *Patronal Politics: Eurasian Regime Dynamics in Comparative Perspective*. Cambridge: Cambridge University Press.

Hess, S. (2010) Protests, Parties and Presidential Succession: Competing Theories of Color Revolutions in Armenia and Kyrgyzstan. *Problems of Post-Communism*, 57 (1): 28–39.

Ishkanian, A. (2015) Self-Determined Citizens? New Forms of Civic Activism and Citizenship in Armenia. *Europe-Asia Studies*, 67 (8): 1203–27.

Iskandaryan, A. (2013) Armenia's Foreign Policy: Where Values Meet Constraints. In: Palonkorpi, M. and Iskandaryan, A., eds, *Armenia's Foreign and Domestic Politics: Development Trends*. Yerevan: Caucasus Institute and Aleksanteri Institute, 6–17.

Levitsky, S. and Way, L. A. (2010) *Competitive Authoritarianism: Hybrid Regimes After the Cold War*. Cambridge: Cambridge University Press.

Ó Beacháin, D. and Polese, A. (2010) *The Colour Revolutions in the Former Soviet Republics: Successes and Failures*. New York and London: Routledge.

Ohanyan, A. (2015) *Networked Regionalism as Conflict Management*. Stanford: Stanford University Press.

Ohanyan, A., ed. (2018) *Russia Abroad: Driving Regional Fracture in Post-Communist Eurasia and Beyond*. Washington DC: Georgetown University Press.

Payaslian, S. (2011) *The Political Economy of Human Rights in Armenia: Authoritarianism and Democracy in a Former Soviet Republic*. London: I.B. Tauris.

Shubladze, R. and Khundadze, T. (2017) Balancing the Three Pillars of Stability in Armenia and Georgia. *Caucasus Survey*, 5 (3): 301–22.

Simão, L. (2017) *The EU's Neighbourhood Policy towards the South Caucasus: Expanding the European Security Community*. New York: Palgrave Macmillan.

Ter-Matevosyan, V., Drnoian, A., Mkrtchyan, N. and Yepremyan, T. (2017) Armenia in the Eurasian Economic Union: Reasons for Joining and its Consequences. *Eurasian Geography and Economics*, 58 (3): 340–60.

Toal, G. (2017) *Near Abroad: Putin, the West, and the Contest over Ukraine and the Caucasus*. Oxford: Oxford University Press.

de Waal, T. (2013) *Black Garden: Armenia and Azerbaijan Through Peace and War*. 2nd edn. New York: New York University Press.

Way, L. A. (2015) The Limits of Autocracy Promotion: The Case of Russia in the 'Near Abroad'. *The European Journal of Political Research*, 54 (4). https://doi.org/10.1111/1475-6765.12092 (accessed 16 August 2019).

Zolyan, M. (2010) Armenia. In Ó Beacháin, D. and Polese, A., eds, *The Colour Revolutions in the Former Soviet Republics: Successes and Failures*. New York and London: Routledge, 83–100.

1

Velvet is not a colour

Armenia's democratic transition in a global context

Anna Ohanyan

Introduction

Velvet is not a colour. And Armenia's Velvet Revolution, contrary to a narrative widely circulating at the time of the events in Yerevan in April–May 2018, differed sharply from the post-Soviet 'colour Revolutions'. These were largely top-down, elite-driven 'revolutions' across the post-communist space (and beyond), while Armenia's Velvet[1] was decentralized, socially rooted and resulted from several years and successive rounds of experimentation with diverse strategies of political change. Armenia's transition had a specific signature – non-violent, civil disobedience on a mass scale – which was dispersed, disciplined and peaceful. It unfolded patiently and incrementally through the existing institutions and laws of the state rather than in opposition to them. This pathway to change stands in contrast to the more prevalent elite-driven, 'big bang' colour revolutions to date in Eurasia, which unfolded against backdrops of significantly higher levels of state fragility and institutional weakness than was the case in Armenia.

The discussion on the nature of Armenia's democratic transition is more than a scholarly exercise. Throughout the Velvet Revolution, incumbent forces and the governing elites sought to portray the Velvet as being precisely a colour revolution. The framing of events in Armenia as analogous to Georgia's 'Rose' and Ukraine's 'Orange' revolutions implied that they were the product of intervention by outside powers and would lead, inevitably, to political instability. In fact, the Armenian movement's leaders and participants went out of their way to highlight the organic, grassroots nature of the movement, and its focus on internal issues of governance and rights rather than grand geopolitical orientations. In short, managing and framing this movement as organic and home-grown rather than as imported and manufactured were central for maintaining an overwhelmingly peaceful and sustained large-scale mobilization. This strategy succeeded in keeping both people involved and engaged, and external powers restrained.

The scholarly significance of parsing the Velvet Revolution is nevertheless very important. Traditionally, political developments in Armenia have been analysed through the temporal and spatial frames of post-Soviet Eurasia. I argue in this chapter that these frameworks of analysis may obscure more than they reveal about the Velvet Revolution, and that indeed the events in Armenia marked a significant break with traditional trends and patterns in post-communist Eurasia. The blinkered comparison of the Velvet to the colour revolutions in the post-Soviet space exaggerates the agency of (primarily Western) international actors and the power of Soviet legacies at the expense of the local agency of society, and non-Soviet legacies and trajectories. This approach concentrates disproportionately on external factors and the international context at the expense of internal and societal forces in mediating outcomes of authoritarian retrenchment, as well as democratic transition down the road. Indeed, the end of Cold War bipolarity, the hegemony of liberal democracy and Western democracy promotion strategies in 1990s–2000s, along with the post-communist colour revolutions that began with the overthrow of Slobodan Milošević in Serbia in 2000, elevated the international context from a mere background factor to the overall determining condition in Eastern Europe, the former Soviet Union, and in parts of Asia and Africa (Stone et al. 2013; Pevehouse 2002; Levitsky and Way 2005).

In this chapter, I call for an adjustment of our frameworks of analysis. A more colour-blind approach, so to speak, requires an assessment of state as well as societal forces facilitating authoritarian decline and leading to the democratic opening in Armenia. There is, of course, a rich literature focusing on both structure and agency of societal actors in the outcomes of regime politics in post-Soviet Eurasia. Here, however, I argue that it is the *interaction* between popular agency, manifesting in patterns of mobilization bubbling up from below, and structural forces (such as the levels of economic inequality, institutional design of the legislature, the specific type of authoritarianism in the country, etc.), that best explains why and how the Velvet occurred at this particular moment in Armenia's history.

The 'patterns of mass mobilization' are indicators of the power of agency, that is, people power and civic depth in Armenia, while at the structural level, the factors that mattered most are the level of state cohesion, the extent to which the state is institutionalized as well as its coercive power. Combined under the rubric of *stateness*, these dimensions include the organizational power of the governing regime as the dominant political actor (Levitsky and Way 2010). Yet they also signal the broader institutional effects on statehood that emerged, perhaps unintentionally, from the relatively stable entrenchment of authoritarian rule in the decades prior to the Velvet Revolution. The strategic interaction between these two factors, popular agency and stateness, over the years has been ongoing, producing mutual learning, attempts at co-optation and coercion by the government, and bargaining and push back by social forces. And it is this interaction that is often under-theorized and misunderstood by the scholarship on democratic transitions and hybrid regimes.

Armenia is a country where mass-scale mobilization has been recorded to be the highest in the post-Soviet space over the past few decades, against the backdrop of its 'Potemkin democracy': 'devoid of the most fundamental, rudimentary ingredients of procedural and substantive democracy in its practical aspects' (Payaslian 2011: 287). Yet while the regime had successfully pushed back against public unrest on previous occasions, the interaction between agency and structure proved to be politically consequential in April 2018, and the regime caved in. I argue that it is the interaction effect between different patterns of popular mobilization in Armenia and the quality of stateness over the years that has generated variable outcomes at different times. This interaction effect becomes particularly explicit when the comparative analysis of other attempts at democratic transition are considered later in the chapter. This framework underpins a core contention of my argument, which is that the Velvet Revolution unfolded along two tracks: on one level in civil society through mass-based mobilization, and on another through elite negotiations and institutional bargaining. This signature 'dual-track transition' became possible because of the strategic interactions and learning over the past three decades between social forces and ruling elites, producing a conjuncture conducive to non-violent change.

Specifically, I argue that in terms of its duality in democratic transition, and the interaction between structural factors and agency, Armenia's Velvet Revolution resembles the Latin American democratic transitions from the 1970s and the 1980s much more than the more recent colour revolutions in the post-communist space, or the Arab Spring in the Middle East and North Africa (MENA). My argument thereby transcends the spatial and temporal bias that tends to dominate the existing analysis on Armenia, which often groups the country with post-Soviet Eurasia, with the end of the Cold War as a key temporal referent. The approach introduced here is one of interactivity and dynamism between the agency of civil society, which has a chequered history of strength and weakness predating Armenia's Soviet roots, and the structural conditions of statehood and political economy. A broader, more global comparative analysis of the Armenian case, transcending its Soviet contours, is essential to produce a fuller picture of the political transition in the country.

From people to parliament:
The dual transition of Armenia's Velvet

The post-Soviet framework in which Armenia has been analysed has been rather deterministic in terms of geography and culture. Cultural explanations, such as clientelism and informality, have been privileged in the dominant frameworks exploring regime dynamics. Hale, for instance, has explained the prospects of political change in terms of the dynamics of power pyramids controlled by centralized clientelistic groups (Hale 2012, 2015). According to Hale, 'After an initial period of turmoil, the political history of (non-Baltic) post-Soviet countries can thus largely be seen as a history of the emergence of single-pyramid systems' (Hale 2012: 73). The Velvet Revolution showed that the single-pyramid system, described by Hale, was a house of cards in Armenia, lacking institutional durability and vulnerable to internal collapse and social backlash. Culture is malleable, after all. The structural factors favoured by other scholars, such as the relative distance to the West (Levitsky and Way 2010), are also challenged by the Velvet Revolution. The ahistorical nature of structural factors is a conceptual challenge, which omits the power of diasporic groups as transnational actors with direct and indirect effects on Armenia's political culture. Historically rooted civic legacies (see Chapters 2 and 4 in this volume) illustrate the ethno-centric nature of studies on civil society in political science, which have offered few tools to connect the civic legacies in Armenia's Soviet and pre-Soviet political histories with their more contemporary manifestations.

Against this backdrop, the framework presented in this chapter attempts to capture the dramatic changes and transitions occurring both within civil society and government/state institutions, the strategic interaction between which is a defining moment of the Velvet Revolution. Reflecting the conceptualization of a 'dual-track transition' introduced earlier, I make two main arguments. First, the Velvet Revolution differs from the colour revolutions and the Arab Spring uprisings in terms of the *modes of public mobilization*. The Velvet Revolution deployed a non-violent disobedience strategy, which required and rested on sustained, broad-based and grassroots-level mass mobilization. In doing so, it utilized deep capacities in civil society that had accumulated over the previous decade. As noted, in this dimension, the movement echoed democratic transitions in Latin America in the late 1970s and early 1980s, and parts of Asia, rather than the post-communist colour revolutions or the Arab Spring.

Second, and in contrast to many other cases of popular uprisings, such as those in the Arab Spring, this was a deeply 'institutional' revolution, as it worked within the existing institutional parameters of the state, thereby crafting a politically stable path for itself in the long-term. Working with, as opposed to against the state (Ohanyan 2018), the Velvet Revolution unfolded gradually. This perspective necessitates a long view of the Velvet Revolution as a process unfolding over the duration of 2018, rather than just the headline events of April and May. For eight months, newly elected prime minister Nikol Pashinyan was an institutional hostage of sorts to a parliament still controlled by the previous ruling party, the Republican Party of Armenia (RPA). This uneasy cohabitation persisted until new elections were called on 9 December 2018. *Institutional stateness* is the Velvet Revolution's second core dimension, and one that has been theoretically significant in the study of democratization and authoritarianism within comparative politics. My conception of institutional stateness incorporates, but is not co-extensive with, Levitsky and Way's concept of 'organizational power', which they used to analyse the composite capacities of the state in terms of coercion, party strength and economic control, establishing hyper-incumbency advantage (Levitsky and Way 2010: 54–70).

Institutional stateness in the Armenian case refers to the stability and consolidation of state governance over the years preceding the Velvet Revolution. To be sure, the democratic deficit in Armenia was real and systemic. Yet in its efforts to consolidate its rule via shallow and co-opted democratic institutions, the authoritarian regime in Armenia succeeded in building a durable and in many ways stable competitive authoritarian system. This also contributed to the institutional stability of the state, which played out in favour of the Velvet Revolution once it erupted. This is a different setting from the 'Rose' and 'Orange' revolutions in Georgia and Ukraine, respectively. Armenia's Velvet Revolution was challenging a deeply entrenched hybrid regime in a setting of institutional stability, rather than an institutionally weak state, which was the case with Georgia and Ukraine in 2003–4. Despite being shallow and co-opted, Armenia's democratic institutions were nevertheless subversive institutions creating vulnerability to grassroots mobilization from below.

Over the past few decades, repeated interactions between mobilizing civil society and opposition political parties on the one hand, and the state on the other, generated repeated interaction effects feeding strategic and organizational learning. Whether in terms of large-scale demonstrations in support of Nagorny Karabakh's secession from Azerbaijan in the late 1980s, or post-election protests in 2008, mass mobilization became a recurrent feature of Armenian politics (see Chapter 2). Yet, as Levitsky and Way point out (2010), if Armenia registered the highest levels of political mobilization in the post-Soviet space, it was also among the more 'stable' competitive authoritarian regimes where the ruling regime maintained a solid grip on power (see Chapter 3). Levitsky and Way rightly conclude that mass mobilization is insufficient to dislodge an authoritarian regime. While mass mobilization in the twilight years of the Soviet Union, driven by the Karabakh movement, human rights concerns and environmentalism, registered significant successes, post-election mass mobilizations later on were less successful. Against this backdrop, how and why did this Velvet round of mass mobilization succeed in producing authoritarian breakdown, while the previous waves of post-electoral protests failed to do so, is an important question to ask.

I find answers in the interaction of the structural dimensions of the state with the agency of bottom-up mass-based mobilization. As I argue below, the math of the revolution (large numbers that grew from non-violent civil disobedience) and its political chemistry (a certain composition of social forces and economic factors) worked to produce the peaceful democratic breakthrough in the country. The patterns of mass mobilization in the form of 'people power' (Chenoweth and Stephan 2012), the agency behind the revolution, was an effective strategy of transition that produced the necessary numbers to overwhelm the security forces in the streets. 'Doing the math' was a matter of strategy. Principled non-violence helped to grow the number of participants around the country. And the 'chemistry' of the Velvet Revolution refers to the structural composition of civil society and the state. The layered nature of the civil society and civic legacies, discussed further, produced the necessary organizational depth within the social forces driving the revolution peacefully and incrementally. I also argue that the civic depth achieved over the years has been a response to the institutional developments within the state, which includes, but is not limited to, the narrower elite politics and authoritarian regime survival strategies widely covered in the literature on post-Soviet transitions.

With people power as its signature, the Velvet Revolution highlights the centrality of individual agency within the post-communist space. This has been a region described in terms of deterministic forces, from weak civil societies (Foa and Ekiert 2016) and culturally deterministic clientelistic networks (Hale 2012) to geopolitical powers and wars that sapped any democratic potential inside aspirant democratizers (e.g. Grigas 2016). Combined with authoritarian resurgence worldwide, few had foreseen a democratic transition executed with the politically most progressive and sophisticated technologies of collective action: mass-scale, non-violent disobedience. The subsequent sections provide a comparative analysis of the patterns of mass mobilization and the social forces driving them, and the parallel changes within the institutions of the state in the context of the Velvet Revolution.

The patterns of mass mobilization: From Bahrain to Brazil

The nature of mass mobilization has been a central strategic variable in the study of authoritarian breakdowns and democratic transitions, albeit connected with the structural factors pertaining to the nature of authoritarian regimes. Bunce and Wolchik (2018) confirm that the type of an authoritarian regime can shape the contours and content of contentious politics challenging it. Specifically, the varied levels of repression within authoritarian states shape the strategies utilized by democratic forces. The tighter the levels of repression, the more limited the menu of contentious strategies is for the reformers and the more drastic their content. Higher levels of repression push democratic forces into the streets in mass-scale popular uprisings. The authors further argue that in Arab Spring revolutions in the MENA region, in countries with high levels of repression (such as Syria, Libya and Egypt), there were very few tools for democratic forces to utilize, other than mass-scale uprisings.

The alternatives of contesting deeply entrenched authoritarian regimes through elections, inter-elite pacts or even smaller-scale post-election protests, as observed in the post-Soviet world, were underdeveloped in the MENA region during the Arab Spring. While delivering mixed results in terms of the number and depth of democratic transitions, the Arab Spring succeeded in challenging the myth of 'Arab exceptionalism' – the belief that democratic values are alien to the region, that Islam and democracy are incompatible, and that the third wave of democratization bypassed this region (Cavatorta 2019). But the Arab Spring also exposed the dire shortage of deep capacities in civil society as a major factor in the failure to consolidate the democratic opening it had created. With the exception of Tunisia, the mass mobilizations and political uprisings in Bahrain, Egypt, Libya and Syria lacked a partner in strong political parties and civil society leadership, both to manage the movements as well as to consolidate the opening they provided. Mass mobilization in Egypt was strong and successful in pushing for President Hosni Mubarak's resignation, but too weak and shallow to take on the highly institutionalized power of the military. The gulf between secular liberal and religious forces, with the latter dominated by the Muslim Brotherhood, also weakened the prospects of democratic consolidation. Citing Tunisia's successful democratic transition, scholars have pointed out the need for alliances between secular liberals and Islamist parties, which was the case in Tunisia, for successful democratic transitions and their consolidation (Stepan and Linz 2013; Angrist 2013). Indeed, broad-based alliances are credited for splitting authoritarian elites, and enabling democratic transitions, as was the case during the Velvet Revolution.

Despite the region-wide weakness of civil society and authoritarian entrenchment, differences between the levels of civil society development and the institutionalization of authoritarianism existed across the Middle East. It is these differences that explain the varied outcomes from the Arab Spring, which ranged from full democratic transition in Tunisia to civil war in Libya. Libya, where the Arab Spring resulted in violence, state collapse and civil war, stood out in the region for the most restrictive legal framework for civil society organizations. Region-wide pressure on civil society organizations pre-dated the Muammar Gaddafi regime that seized power in 1969, and with the important exception of tribal structures, society lacked any history of public associations and grassroots self-governance (Bribena 2017). While crushing any attempts to establish formal civil society organizations, Gaddafi governed by co-opting tribal leaders, who otherwise would have been important sources of social capital and public mobilization. The lack of civil society was painfully exposed during the Arab Spring, when the regional swelling of public protests was left without a cushioning network of civil society institutions. In contrast to Libya, autocrats in Tunisia and Egypt tolerated and managed a certain level of civic organization. While mostly focused on narrow social and cultural issues, and highly choreographed by the government, these civil society groups are credited with cultivating civic traditions and habits, mobilizing the masses in the streets and supporting negotiating processes with governing elites (Deane 2013). In the case of Egypt, development and religious associations accounted for more than half of the nearly 30,000 civil society organizations (Hassan 2011).

Overall, even in cases where regimes in the Middle East liberalized in the 1970s–1980s, top-down mechanisms were largely utilized, and the reversals of those gains in the 1990s quickly followed. With top-down reforms, the autocrats in the region created highly controlled civic spaces and managed the minimal structures of civil society, partly to strengthen their legitimacy in Western eyes. Sources of funding from the United States and European Union (EU) have stressed democracy promotion in the region, but have done so unevenly and inconsistently. In contrast to the perception of the Western-led 'exporting democracy' narrative, the Middle East is a case where Western donors' democracy assistance has actually strengthened the hands of authoritarian regimes (Snyder 2018). The low levels of donor dependence and the strategic significance of the countries for the United States has shaped the ability of autocrats to negotiate democracy-tied aid, drastically diluting its intended impact on civil society development.

In addition, the aftermath of the Arab Spring uprisings has unfolded within highly securitized settings (Battaloglu and Farasin 2017). Democracy was viewed as a security threat, which fragmented broad-based alliances in support of democracy, as observed in Egypt for example. The changes in foreign aid giving by the West resulted in a weaker emphasis on democracy promotion, and a greater focus on security and military aid. In addition, the oil wealth in many cases has allowed for proportionally large security apparatuses, and the threat of Islamist terrorism has been leveraged as a justification for intrusive security governance and stalling on democratization. The gap between governments and societies, which has been central to political cultures in the regional states, has remained relatively undisturbed in the aftermath of the Arab Spring.

Contrasting with MENA's experience is that of the Latin American human rights networks in the 1970s and the 1980s, which evolved into political movements capable of influencing governing elites. For instance, during Argentina's Dirty War of 1976–83, the coordinated mobilization of victims' groups, business associations, labour and human rights activists, and other civic groups played an important role in pushing the military regime to restore electoral politics. Civil society played a similarly significant role in pushing for Brazil's democratic transition under its military regime. Facing severe economic crisis, and grassroots and incremental civil society mobilization, Brazil's military regime prepared for the peaceful transition of power to reformers (Pio 2013). A wave of social mobilization in the manufacturing heartland of the country, in the São Paulo area, enabled the political takeover of the trade unions by the reformers, who then started to organize strikes and mass gatherings, challenging the old corporatist structures of the state. This path of parallel tracks of social mobilization and contestation of power through the ballot box is a pattern that repeated itself in Armenia, over thirty years after delivering democratic transitions in many Latin American countries.

In addition to socioeconomic drivers of social mobilization, severe violations of human rights in Brazil also stimulated several civil society actors to mobilize, with a distinctly transnational mode of organizing. Amnesty International's denouncement of torture in Brazil, issued in 1969, was followed by the Vatican's Pontifical Commission for Justice and Peace, condemning human rights violations. This catalysed and strengthened domestic networks of human rights activists that, facing constraints at home, consistently sought out contacts with global networks. The Catholic Church, the Brazilian Bar Association and the Brazilian Press Association are among the most active civil society organizations, some of which utilized global connections to produce domestic change (Pio 2013).

Similar to many Latin American democratic transitions in the 1970s and the 1980s, the Velvet Revolution was driven by social forces, rather than the top-down elites and the externally supported NGO sector characteristic of the post-Soviet colour revolutions (Jones 2006; Cheterian 2008; Broers 2005). This reality has been largely invisible in post-Soviet scholarship, much of which interpreted Armenia's nascent civil society through the reductive lens of the communist legacy. The evidence of weak civil society participation in the post-communist world, observed for example by Howard (2003), was explained in terms of communist legacies resulting in structurally weak civil societies. A brief digression into the pre-communist experiences of Armenians can help to round out a fuller picture of who or what is 'civil' in Armenian civil society, and how.

As is the case for many young states, Armenia's civil society predates its statehood. A small nation in the backyard of three empires, Russian, Ottoman, and Persian, Armenian communities have long been divided between these players throughout their tumultuous history. Armenia has deep experience of community organization and self-governance both in the Ottoman and the Russian Empires (Der Matossian 2014; Göçek 2014). Communal self-organization has often been carried out despite totalitarian and oppressive political regimes of the dominant state. From the Armenian Constitutional Assembly in the Ottoman Empire of the nineteenth century to the large-scale political protests in 1965 in Soviet Armenia for the recognition of the Armenian Genocide (Suny 1993), civic organizing has been an integral part of Armenian political and social history. More recently, the mass demonstrations in support of the national self-determination initiatives in predominantly Armenian-populated Nagorny Karabakh in 1988 were among the first in the Soviet Union to challenge the Soviet order after the onset of Mikhail Gorbachev's perestroika, or restructuring, policy (Gessen 2017). Since its post-Soviet independence, mass protest, whether post-election or smaller-scale, issue-based peaceful demonstrations, have come to define Armenia's political culture (Ohanyan 2018; see also Chapter 2 in this volume).

In the post–Cold War period, Western democracy promotion programmes made Armenia, along with many other post-Soviet states, into a recipient of Western foreign aid, some of which was tied to civil society development.

Such programmes helped to create and expand the NGO sector, which some nevertheless argued to be ineffective in developing a genuinely liberal civil society and democratic transition (Ishkanian 2008). By the early 2000s, a new layer within civil society developed: grassroots civic initiatives evolved from the bottom-up, on such seemingly narrow and functional issues as environmental protection, labour and employment, and human rights (Ishkanian 2018; see also Chapter 2), which are sometimes described as more radical and confrontational towards the state, compared to the formal NGO sector. This nested nature of civil society in Armenia also strengthened horizontal links between NGOs and grassroots organizations, similarly to many Latin American countries, and unlike those in the Middle East. In contrast to the Middle East, the NGO sector in Armenia, while donor-driven by the West, as well as by diasporic networks from around the world, emerged as an important provider of social services, thereby reducing the state's leverage and space. As such, the NGO sector has played an important role in making the government irrelevant for large segments of society, thereby pressing civil society at large to find political solutions to seemingly intractable problems. Indeed, one report on civil society's role in the Velvet credits the links between the various segments of civil society in catalysing and scaling-up the originally small size and sporadic pattern of disobedience into a nationwide movement, producing authoritarian breakdown in the country (Andreasyan, Jamkochyan, Ishkanian, Manousyan and Manousyan 2018).

Another important factor is the role of transnational diasporic communities and their socioeconomic and political impact on their home states. Diasporic communities have shown their capacity to work as transnational advocacy networks: they have pressured for genocide recognition outside of the United States, but have also pressured the pre-Velvet Armenian government on various human rights issues. Slow but steady civil society mobilization found ways to connect with activists within Armenia's diaspora abroad. For instance, pressure from the diaspora on the government was present as it was debating the passage of a law on domestic violence, an issue that has been central for many local activists in the country. Diasporic communities also evolved as mechanisms of private giving, including remittances as well as private donations through established organizations. This kind of engagement from diasporic groups altered the political economy of state-society relationships, by making civil society relatively autonomous from the newly independent state. By making civic self-organization over the past two decades possible, diasporic engagement yielded a strategic political dividend contributing to the successful execution of the Velvet Revolution.

The analysis of the specific way in which Armenia's diaspora interacted with its stable competitive authoritarian system is crucial. In Levitsky's and

Way's (2010) linkage-leverage theory, post-Soviet states were described as less effective in producing and sustaining democratic transitions mostly because of the weakness in linkage with, and leverage from, the West, relative to East European countries. This framework discounts the powerful role that diasporic communities have played in Armenia in producing linkage and leverage with the West. Armenian diasporic communities have provided an important, albeit limited, economic linkage in the forms of trade and investment; technocratic linkage in building programmes training the country's elite in Western universities, in addition to EU-led educational programmes; and social linkage in terms of flows of tourists, which has also been an effective channel of information flows across borders. Future research needs to consider the size of these resources in order to produce answers on the extent to which diasporic communities shaped the Velvet Revolution, directly or indirectly (see Chapter 9). In short, the Armenian diaspora was a wild card omitted from much of the post-communist transition scholarship, which emphasized culture and geography as powerful factors hindering prospects of effective democratic transitions.

In contrast to the MENA region, then, civil society in Armenia enjoyed a certain degree of freedom from the state, partly as a result of the reappearance of Armenian statehood in the post-Soviet period. While government-organized 'NGOs' (or 'GONGOs') were deployed by the regime, with clear attempts to dominate civic space, civil society in Armenia emerged as organizationally layered and linked to various funding sources from Western donors to the transnational Armenian diaspora. Varied and diverse sources of funding added to the political autonomy of NGOs, enabling their linkages to the broader grassroots segments in society (Ohanyan 2009). Importantly, in contrast to the deeply entrenched and institutionalized authoritarianism in the MENA region, Armenia's form of authoritarianism was of the 'competitive' nature, in which relative media freedom and independent civic spaces regularly and often successfully challenged the government over the past decade (see Chapter 3).

The nested nature of civil society in Armenia was identified in a study by Paturyan and Gevorgyan (2014) where the authors established low levels of trust towards NGOs in Armenia and high levels of volunteerism, relative to neighbouring Georgia and Azerbaijan. Thus, if civil society during the Arab Spring was rather 'naked' in terms of its tools of political organization and mechanisms of contestation with the state, Armenia's democratic transition with its Latin flavour was rooted in networked and nested civil society structures (Ohanyan 2009). While in the Middle East, civil society organizations were either co-opted by the state or made marginal in their social service delivery by the large corporate apparatus of government, in Armenia the picture was different. Such varied levels and forms of civil society organization in the South Caucasus effectively re-engage with, and interrogate, the myth of post-communist civil society weakness, calling for greater attention to civic legacies and divergent historical pathways in each country. A regional, post-communist narrative needs to be supplemented with tailored and granular understandings of each national setting in the post-communist periphery. Theorizing from the peripheries and developing concepts and frameworks from the ground-up is overdue in comparative politics and international relations (Ohanyan 2018).

In sum, the mass mobilization in Armenia's Velvet Revolution represented the climax of a decades-long culture of peaceful protest in the country. Over the past twenty years, Armenia had experienced not only episodes of post-election and post-referendum mobilization, but also significant, myriad grassroots peaceful protest actions on such focused issues as pension reform, labour regulation and electricity tariffs. This discussion underscores the prevalence of the social bases of democratic transition, interacting with transnational actors in the Armenian case. A culture of civil disobedience was built on the decades-long work of activists focusing on human rights, environmentalism, women's rights and non-violence, explicitly non-political or minimally political causes. This pattern of progressive, cumulative mass mobilization preceding democratic transitions and generating splits within the ruling elite mirrors more closely the case of many Latin American transitions, in addition to the Philippines and South Korea (Stoner, Diamond, Girod and McFaul 2013), than the staccato post-Soviet colour revolutions.

Stateness for and against democracy

Institutional stateness is the second dimension of Armenia's democratic transition. It refers to the institutionalization and organizational durability of such state institutions as the parliament, the party system, the executive, administrative structures of governance at various levels, security apparatus and the military and so on. In explaining democratic transitions, Coleman and Lawson-Remer (2013) highlight how challenges of governance can undermine democratic transitions around the world. Examples include democratic reversals in Brazil, Serbia, Poland, Hungary, the Philippines, Russia and Georgia, to name a few. The weakness in state governance has fuelled democratic declines around the world, with corruption as a key cause mobilizing the political extremes on the right and the left. Importantly, the stateness variable is particularly essential when assessing the chances of democratic transition and consolidation in fractured regions, such as the South Caucasus (Ohanyan 2018). Social movements that break out in institutionally weaker states are more vulnerable to 'securitization' by outside forces. Such internal institutional weakness inside states adds to regional fragmentation, strengthening the chances for outside powers to undermine democratic transitions when they break out, and sabotage their consolidation when transitions succeed. Cases of democratic transition attempts during the Arab Spring and the Maidan are some cases in point, with the tragic events in Sudan in June 2019 being another.

Post-Soviet transitions lacked the advantage of institutionalized statehood, attempting democratization within the context of weak states. Russia is a case in point, where President Boris Yeltsin pushed ahead with economic restructuring riding on his political charisma instead of building the prerequisite institutions to support and legitimize this economic restructuring (Miller et al. 2012). Yet the basic institutional foundations of the state (its stateness), as a prerequisite of democratic transition to open up and to consolidate, are insufficiently researched in the context of the post-Soviet transitions. Indeed, Kraxberger (2007) recognizes the significance of a functioning state for effective democratic transitions, but also points out the lack of attention to it in the post-Soviet literature. Citing Bermeo (2003), he connects this oversight with a geographic bias towards European and Latin American cases of democratic transitions in the twentieth century, where democratic transitions unfolded under conditions of institutionalized statehood.

Levitsky and Way (2010) highlight the factor of stateness in their analysis of the importance of the incumbent's organizational power and the cohesion of state and governing party. They argue that hybrid regimes in post-communist Eurasia had varied capacities to thwart opposition movements, which, they maintain, explains the varied outcomes with democratic transitions in the region. Well-organized regimes and a dominant party apparatus are what enabled elites to dilute existing yet meagre democratic institutions, to co-opt opponents and to crack down on protests. They further argue that such organizational weakness at the state level explains the successful transfers of power during the colour revolutions in Georgia (2003) and Ukraine (2004), despite the organizational weaknesses within the opposition movement. They further highlight the Armenian case as featuring a cohesive and strong state coercive apparatus and incumbent ruling party, which successfully thwarted opposition movements and mass protests on numerous occasions.

Stateness matters for the democratic prospects of a country in three ways. First, the ruling regime can co-opt the institutions of statehood to consolidate its power. The Armenian case of stable competitive authoritarianism is an example, in which even the institutional changes within the legislature, while enhancing its organizational power, still legitimized the power of the executive, thereby contributing to the stability of the competitive authoritarian system in this case (Bonvecchi and Simison 2017). At the same time, by co-opting democratic institutions for regime survival, authoritarian regimes also end up legitimizing those same institutions. Co-optation may lead to legitimation by default as an unintended consequence, thereby enhancing institutional strength and durability over time. Operating within the political framework of democracy, and enhancing the institutional strength of the state unintentionally, ruling regimes end up aiding social movements when they do break out by providing them with the stability and predictability needed for the successful execution of such transitions.

The second dimension to the impact of stateness on a country's democratic prospects lies in the fact that institutionalized states, as was the case in Latin American transitions in 1980s, provide a predictable political framework and much-needed legitimacy for social forces. As such, the institutional stability of a state is a political resource for social forces that are mobilized for a democratic transition. Operating within the formal parameters of liberal statehood, albeit one captured by illiberal forces, a mass mobilization led by reformers fortunately does not have to face the burden of a double transitional bottleneck, so to speak: concurrently attempting to build the state while pushing for democratization. While creating the institutional foundations of the state to support their rule, authoritarian forces also make themselves vulnerable to challenge from society that can utilize these institutions to contest power, in addition to inviting intra-elite rivalries.

The interaction between the political institutions and civil society is a third dimension to stateness. Whether coercive or co-opting, the levels of stateness shape and influence the civil society fabric. It does so by shaping the political economy of democratic transitions when they emerge. The stability of political institutions (particularly the security forces) influence the strategies and contours of civil society mobilization tactics, when a democratic opening does present itself. The co-optation of civil society by the administratively large states in the MENA region is instructive, and indeed is a signature dimension in the rise of modern authoritarianism. States that are relatively effective in fulfilling their social functions and welfare provisions end up co-opting the social service delivery functions of civil society, thereby diluting the latter's political space in society.

In the Middle East, these dynamics have played out in the context of quite entrenched authoritarian regimes since independence. With many of them being oil-reliant rentier states, ruling regimes have enjoyed high levels of political autonomy from society. Oil-rich states in the Middle East have co-opted existing civil society organizations, and those without have exercised more direct forms of oppression and strategies to fragment small and sporadically emerging civic spaces. With longer experience of independent statehood, the regimes in the Arab world have developed sophisticated toolkits for demobilizing, depoliticizing and fragmenting existing civil society (Kamrava and Mora 1998). Resisting waves of economic liberalization, regimes have practiced various forms of state capitalism, which gave them the tools to create the corporative structures of civil society, and co-opt existing groups, ranging from cultural to business associations or tribal leadership structures.

As a result, the existing civil society organizations were wired vertically, connected to the state and resistant to global waves of mobilization encouraging transformation into political instruments capable of challenging the state. With large administrative states providing numerous social services, the role of civil society organizations in social service provision has been marginal, and the competition between civil society groups for the bigger share of the corporate pie at the state level extremely high (Kamrava and Mora 1998). This particular structural dimension of stateness and its subordination of civil society had direct strategic implications during the Arab Spring. The organizational weakness of civil society and its lack of deep and institutional capacities resulted in failure to capitalize on the political successes of mass-scale mobilization during the Arab Spring. The removal of sitting dictators proved much easier for social forces than producing a plan of action for the 'day after'. In Latin American democratic transitions that unfolded against military regimes, by contrast, economic crisis and deteriorating conditions in the global economy challenged the capacities of these regimes. They responded by abandoning their social functions and aggravated the income inequality in their countries. Lacking the resources to co-opt civil society, this economic crisis created space for civic organizing towards addressing the socioeconomic tasks in their respective countries.

Armenia's stateness indicator, and levels of its state cohesion and monopoly over the use of violence, are consistently marked highly by various ranking agencies and analysts. The Bertelsmann Transformation Index Survey defines 'stateness' in terms of the monopoly on the use of force, cohesive state identity, no interference of religious dogmas, and basic administration. While Armenia's ranking in terms of five groups of indicators has fluctuated over the years, the stateness indicator remained consistently high in the 2006–18 period. Similarly, the Fragile State Index, developed by the Fund for Peace, also places Armenia's level of fragility at much lower levels than those for Georgia or Ukraine, with their earlier experiences with democratic transitions. Specifically, for the period for 2006–18, Armenia's fragility index stayed relatively stable, ranging between sixty-nine and seventy-four, registering improvements (declines in the indicator) since 2009. For Ukraine, state fragility ranged between sixty-five and seventy-six. Georgia registered a range between seventy-four and ninety-one, registering a steady improvement (decline in the indicator) since 2009. For the same period, the security apparatus indicator for Armenia hovered between 4.5 and 5.2. For Georgia, the indicator ranged between 8.1 and 6.5; this weakness in the security apparatus is perhaps partly explained by its de facto loss of Abkhazia and South Ossetia. For Ukraine, the same indicator went from the low of 3.0 in 2006, peaking at 7.9 in 2015. These assessments of stateness are also supported in Levitsky and Way's study where Armenia is ranked as a stable competitive authoritarian regime, with a highly organized incumbent party and coercive apparatus of the state.

These findings support the rather obvious observation that Armenia's Velvet Revolution occurred against a backdrop of a certain level of state stability, with the Soviet collapse and the institutional challenges it entailed in the rearview mirror. Even if only nominally liberal, the Velvet developed within the political framework of statehood and benefited from the institutional stability of the administrative state. By contrast, the Rose and Orange revolutions had to grapple with much more systemic transformations and statebuilding. In this respect, the domestic political context within which Armenia's Velvet Revolution unfolded is again more reminiscent of Latin American democratic transitions where state institutions have been established, with most of the countries vacillating between authoritarianism and democracy throughout much of the twentieth century. The double bottleneck of simultaneously confronting an authoritarian regime and building state institutions was avoided by the democratic transitions in the region.

In Armenia, the condition of stateness has been significant both in terms of its coercive and co-opting dimensions. The strong coercive apparatus and the ruling party structure since Armenia's independence, while it thwarted opposition movements, also created the basic institutional foundations of the state. A key component of statehood is the ability of the government to maintain a monopoly over the use of violence. Building a strong coercive apparatus, regardless of the original incentives of the incumbent regime, produced strong institutional foundations of the state. While strong in its coercive apparatus, tragically demonstrated during the post-election protests in 2008, the co-opting mechanisms of the government with regard to civil society proved to be much weaker. Notwithstanding some support for GONGOs, the government lacked substantial means (or political foresight) to co-opt civil society organizations. Combined with Western donors and diasporic contributions, the capacities in civil society to organize for social issues has strengthened over the years, with clear political dividends for Armenia's democratic transition during the Velvet Revolution.

While largely produced through voter fraud and packed with members of the ruling RPA, the Armenian parliament also achieved significant institutional stability to become a second 'front-line' for the Velvet Revolution. The administrative structures of the state were functional enough to become sites of peaceful non-cooperation, which the protesters used to paralyse the state. From educational institutions to businesses (private and public) significant levels of institutional stability turned them into tools with which to attack the state and paralyse the regime.[2] Similar to Latin American transitions, the Armenian government was also stressed economically. With extensive corruption and governance ineptitude, civil society, some of which was diaspora-supported, emerged as a mechanism for social service delivery. Whether the Western-funded NGOs in the economic and social spheres, or diaspora-linked giving, the functions of social service delivery demarcated and crystallized institutional and political space for NGOs and civil society organizations. These organizations proved critical when the democratic breakthrough delivered by the Velvet materialized (Andreasyan et al. 2018).

The relative institutional stability provided by Armenia's 'stable competitive regime', in which the coercive apparatus and monopoly over violence are important indices, worked well for the Velvet Revolution. Pashinyan's strategy of working with as opposed to against state institutions utilized this opportunity quite effectively. Indeed, this was in sharp contrast to the colour revolutions in Ukraine (2004) and Georgia (2003), where the opposition movement was confronting a weak state. In the case of Georgia, Cheterian (2008) explains that Georgia's 'Rose Revolution' was a systemic effort to transform and modernize the state, rather than merely changing the elite structure. In this respect, the Rose Revolution was a genuine revolution, he explains, but also one that was confronting the challenge of statebuilding, in addition to democratization.

However, it is less clear whether this high level of stateness and ability to control the means of violence by the government is genuine (that is, reflecting the strong administrative capacities of the state), or politically subsidized by external actors. Some argue that Armenia's strong coercive apparatus has emerged as a result of the Nagorny Karabakh conflict with Azerbaijan, which empowered the Armenian military and added to its institutional strength in domestic politics (Grigoryan 2018). Another explanation for the stability of the state relates to the Russian factor. In contrast to the colour revolutions in Ukraine and Georgia, Armenia's Velvet Revolution unfolded within Russia's security orbit, not against it (see Chapter 7). In case of the Georgian and

Ukrainian colour revolutions, democratic aspirations were closely tied to geopolitical reorientation towards the West, which tinted the democratic credentials in both countries.

Conclusion: Theoretical and policy implications from Armenia's Velvet

This chapter has offered a two-dimensional model, focusing on the strategic interaction between popular agency manifested in patterns of mass mobilization and the levels of institutional maturity of the state, what I term stateness, to explain the Velvet Revolution in Armenia. This model seeks to correct the ahistorical and both culturally and geographically deterministic nature of the existing scholarship on post-Soviet transitions at large, and on Armenia in particular.

One implication of this argument is the questioning of whether either state- or society-focused approaches can explain transition outcomes *alone*. The combination of the two dimensions produces the following typology of possible cases of democratic transitions, which allows us to situate Armenia in a global context, while teasing out lessons from this case for the study of other cases around the world. While this typology allows the capture of the strategic interaction effect between the patterns of mass mobilization and levels of stateness, it can obscure the granular detail within the stateness variable. High levels of coercive apparatus may co-evolve with institutional collapse in other areas of state governance. 'Stateness' in this framework does include the coercive strength of states but also refers to the overall institutional development of the administrative state. Similarly, the lower right quadrant, while reflecting deep and long-term mass mobilization, can also include illiberal civil society actors, which can work to hijack the movement into a civil war, as was the case in Syria or Libya during the Arab Spring.

The argument presented here aligns with critiques of arguments claiming the weakness of civil society in Armenia as well as in the post-communist world in general (Foa and Ekiert 2016). Despite Armenia's vast experience with grassroots forms of public protest and civic organizing in politically unsettled contexts throughout the twentieth century, its nascent civil society in the aftermath of the Soviet collapse was reduced to its communist legacy by many analysts. Civil society in the post-communist world was consequently assessed in terms of the number of NGOs in a given country, most of which had emerged as a result of the West's democracy promotion strategies

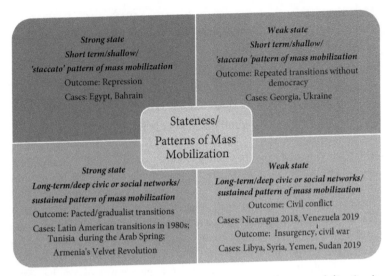

Figure 1.1 Strategic interactions between stateness and mass mobilization in explaining democratic transitions.

(Carothers 2009). The direct impact from the NGO-driven democracy promotion project has not been established, however, leading to criticism that civil society aid has contributed to unsustainable organizations and marginal impacts on civil society environments. Drawing from a study of twenty-seven post-communist countries and USAID aid programmes in each, for example, Spina and Raymond found no evidence that aid independently results in better civil rights environments (Spina and Raymond 2014).

The donor dependency of the NGO sector has also been criticized for eroding and weakening the administrative state in aid-recipient regions (Ohanyan 2008, 2009; Ishkanian 2008). While recognizing the limits of the aid-driven NGO sector and its impact on civil society, the current scholarship calls for new methods of measurement and data collection: capturing deeper forms of civil society engagement and indigenous mechanisms of public discourse is the main direction the advocates in this line of research call for. The recognition of varied historical trajectories and civic legacies in these states, variably shaping their current experiences in civil society development, is a fruitful research area moving forward, best realized with interdisciplinary research between the social sciences and humanities.

With regard to the stateness variable, future research in the Armenian context can benefit from focus on the specific dimensions of statehood with regard to conditioning its trajectory of authoritarianism over the past few decades, as well as the chances of sustained democratic consolidation. While the state's security forces have strengthened largely as a result of the Nagorny Karabakh conflict, its institutional capacities in delivering people-centred services and protecting the rule of law, independently of the government, remains questionable. Specifying additional dimensions of statehood, such as the extent of the welfare state, is also a fruitful area of research moving forward. Such a distinction is promising in explaining Armenia's democratic transition and chances of its consolidation, but also in offering predictive value in other cases of democratic transitions.

In addition, the impact of Armenia's specific type of authoritarianism on the contours of its civil society also is better captured by an interactive framework. Indeed, the separation between state and society has become increasingly challenging, particularly when considering the current state of Armenia's post-Velvet politics: 'authoritarian reserves' are deployed by the previous regime via supporting new 'un-civil' society groups (illiberal civil society organizations), as well as via working with the judiciary sector. Such forces have polarized the public space and incited violence. Although endowed with a relatively stable institutional foundation of statehood, the capacities of Armenia's institutions to protect the rule of law remain weak, and their ability to manage the still mobilized post-Velvet public space questionable.

Still, the Velvet Revolution reaffirmed much of the existing scholarship on authoritarian breakdown and democratic transitions. The importance of deep capacities in civil society and the value of indigenous actors are only some of the theoretical lessons learned from the Velvet. But the Velvet also raises new issues for scholars to consider. With a mass-scale political mobilization led by networked and nested structures of civil society, the Velvet Revolution has reinvigorated the debates on the thesis of weak civil society in the post-communist world. Who 'counts' and how as civil society, and by what criteria, are questions that need to be examined outside of the post-communist paradigm. Importantly, considering the polarized geopolitical context around the Velvet, its successful execution raises questions concerning lessons learned for democratic actors in managing their movements, and the role that external actors should play (or not play) in responding to such movements in an increasingly multipolar context where the neoliberal rules-based order is under stress.

Notes

1 In my writing, I use 'the Velvet' interchangeably with 'the Velvet Revolution' in order to highlight that this particular mode of political transition in Armenia has evolved in two tracks, in civil society and the institutions

of state. Importantly, this transition unfolded within the same political framework of a democratic state which the previous, competitive authoritarian, regime cosmetically pretended to uphold. While bubbling from below through social forces, it also unfolded with links to the formal institutions of power, primarily the parliament. As such, by developing within the institutional and legal contours of the state, this particular transition did not challenge the state. In this respect, and as effectively explained by Alexander Iskandaryan, it differs from more classic definitions of revolutions that were deliberately 'illegal' in challenging the state. Indeed, Iskandaryan provides the most exhaustive answer to this question, by clarifying that classic revolutions were 'viewed as a developmental leap, a way to break free of the previous policy' (Iskandaryan 2018: 466). I subscribe to Iskandaryan's argument that Armenia's democratic transition was not a revolution, defined in minimal terms, but rather a broad-based social movement.

2 Still, this should not obscure the fact that institutional strength remains a challenge for Armenian statehood, which is most visible in the case of the judiciary. Packed with loyalists of the previous regime, the judiciary has been used as an authoritarian reserve by the former regime, which has strengthened calls for transitional administration by the current government. The persistent weakness within the police in maintaining the rule of law post-Velvet also remains a challenge.

References

Andreasyan, Z., Jamkochyan, A., Ishkanian, A., Manousyan, A. and Manousyan, S. (2018) *From a Shrinking to a Post-Revolutionary Space: Reimagining the Role and the Relationships of the Armenian Civil Society* (in Armenian). Yerevan: Socioscope. Available at: http://socioscope.am/wp-content/uploads/2019/01/Socioscope-report_15.01_arm.pdf?fbclid=IwAR2PriEcWNL5ybOdk7W7dFFs9tBBBqTm-NMW23DcsBcwYrsxjqe4Ou-Aa9I (accessed 07 June 2019).

Angrist, M. (2013) Understanding the Success of Mass Civic Protest in Tunisia. *Middle East Journal*, 67 (4): 547–64.

Battaloglu, C. and Farasin, F. (2017) From Democratization to Securitization: Post-Arab Spring Political Order in the Middle East. *Digest of Middle East Studies*, 26 (2): 299–319.

Bermeo, N. (2003) What the Democratization Literature Says-or Doesn't Say-About Postwar Democratization. *Global Governance*, 9 (2): 159–77.

Bonvecchi, A. and Simison, E. (2017) Legislative Institutions and Performance in Authoritarian Regimes. *Comparative Politics*, 49 (4): 521–39.

Bribena, E. (2017) Civil Society and Nation Building in the Arab Spring: A focus on Libya. *Gender and Behavior*, 15 (2): 8981–91.

Broers, L. (2005) After the 'Revolution': Civil Society and the Challenges of Consolidating Democracy in Georgia. *Central Asian Survey*, 24 (3): 333–50.

Bunce, V. and Wolchik, S. (2018) Modes of Popular Mobilizations against Authoritarian Rulers: A Comparison of 1989, the Color Revolutions, and the MENA Uprisings. *Demokratizatsiya: The Journal of Post-Soviet Democratization*, 26 (2): 149–72.

Carothers, T. (2009) Democracy Assistance: Political vs. Developmental? *Journal of Democracy*, 20 (1): 5–19.

Cavatorta, F. (2019) The Middle East and North Africa. In: Haerpfer, C., Bernhagen, P., Inglehart. R. and Welzel, C., eds, *Democratization*. New York: Oxford University Press, 364–83.

Chenoweth, E. and Stephan, M. (2012) *Why Civil Resistance Works: The Strategic Logic of Nonviolent Conflict*. New York: Columbia University Press.

Cheterian, V. (2008) Georgia's Rose Revolution: Change or Repetition? Tension between State-Building and Modernization Projects. *Nationalities Papers*, 36 (4): 689–712.

Coleman, I. and Lawson-Remer, T. (2013) *Pathways to Freedom: Political and Economic Lessons from Democratic Transitions*. New York: Council on Foreign Relations Press.

Deane, S. (2013) *Transforming Tunisia: The Role of Civil Society in Tunisia's Transition*. London: International Alert. Available at: https://www.internat ional-alert.org/sites/default/files/publications/Tunisia2013EN.pdf (accessed 17 August 2019).

Der Matossian, B. (2014) *Shattered Dreams of Revolution: From Liberty to Violence in the Late Ottoman Empire*. Stanford: Stanford University Press.

Foa, R. and Ekiert, G. (2016) The Weakness of Postcommunist Civil Society Reassessed. *European Journal of Political Research*, 56 (2): 419–39.

Gessen, M. (2017) *The Future Is History: How Totalitarianism Reclaimed Russia*. New York: Riverhead Books.

Göçek, F. (2014) *Denial of Violence: Ottoman Past, Turkish Present, and Collective Violence Against the Armenians 1789–2009*. New York: Oxford University Press.

Grigas, A. (2016) *Beyond Crimea: The New Russian Empire*. New Haven and London: Yale University Press.

Grigoryan, A. (2018) The Karabakh Conflict and Armenia's Failed Transition. *Nationalities Papers: The Journal of Nationalism and Ethnicity*, 46 (5): 844–60.

Hale, H. E. (2012) Two Decades of Post-Soviet Regime Dynamics. *Demokratizatsiya*, 20 (2): 71–7.

Hale, H. E. (2015) *Patronal Politics: Eurasian Regime Dynamics in Comparative Perspective*. Cambridge: Cambridge University Press.

Hassan, A. H. (2011) Civil Society in Egypt Under the Mubarak Regime. *Afro Asian Journal of Social Sciences*, 2, No. 2.2 Quarter II. Available at: SSRN: https://ssrn.com/abstract=2346637 (accessed 24 September 2018).

Howard, M. (2003) *The Weakness of Civil Society in Post-communist Europe*. New York: Cambridge University Press.

Ishkanian, A. (2008) *Democracy Building and Civil Society in Post-Soviet Armenia*. London and New York: Routledge.

Ishkanian, A. (2018) Armenia's Unfinished Revolution. *Current History*, 117 (801): 271–76.

Jones, S. (2006) The Rose Revolution: A Revolution without the Revolutionaries? *Cambridge Review of International Affairs*, 19 (1): 33–48.

Kamrava, M. and Mora, F. (1998) Civil Society and Democratization in Comparative Perspective: Latin America and the Middle East. *Third World Quarterly*, 19 (5): 893–916.

Kraxberger, B. (2007) Failed States: Temporary Obstacles to Democratic Diffusion or Fundamental Holes in the World Political Map? *Third World Quarterly*, 28 (6): 1055–71.

Levitsky, S. and Way, L. (2005). International Linkage and Democratization. *Journal of Democracy*, 16 (3): 20–34.

Levitsky, S. and Way, L. (2010) *Competitive Authoritarianism: Hybrid Regimes After Cold War*. New York: Cambridge University Press.

Miller, L., Martini, J., Larrabee, S., Rabasa, A., Pezard, S., Taylor, J. and Mengistu, T. (2012) *Democratization in the Arab World: Prospects and Lessons from around the Globe*. Santa Monica: RAND Corporation.

Ohanyan, A. (2008) *NGOs, IGOs, and the Network Mechanisms of Post-Conflict Global Governance in Microfinance*. New York: Palgrave.

Ohanyan, A. (2009) Policy Wars for Peace: Network Model of NGO Behavior. *International Studies Review*, 11 (3): 475–501.

Ohanyan, A. (2018) Theory of Regional Fracture in International Relations: Beyond Russia. In: Ohanyan, A., ed., *Russia Abroad: Driving Regional Fracture in Post-Communist Eurasia and Beyond*. Washington DC: Georgetown University Press, 19–40.

Paturyan, Y. and Gevorgyan, V. (2014) Trust Towards NGOs and Volunteering in South Caucasus: Civil Society Moving Away from Post-Communism? *Journal of Southeast European and Black Sea Studies*, 14 (2): 239–62.

Payaslian, S. (2011) *The Political Economy of Human Rights in Armenia: Authoritarianism and Democracy in a Former Soviet Republic*. London: I.B. Tauris.

Pevehouse, J. (2002) Democracy from the Outside-In? International Organizations and Democratization. *International Organization*, 56 (3): 515–49.

Pio, C. (2013) Brazil. In: I. Coleman and T. Lawson-Remer, eds, *Pathways to Freedom: Political and Economic Lessons From Democratic Transitions*. New York: Council on Foreign Relations.

Snyder, E. (2018) US Democracy Aid and the Authoritarian State: Evidence from Egypt and Morocco. *International Studies Quarterly*, 63 (4): 795–808.

Spina, N. and Raymond, C. (2014) Civil Society Aid to Post-communist Countries. *Political Studies*, 62 (4): 878–94.

Stepan, A. and Linz, J. (2013) Democratization Theory and the 'Arab Spring'. *Journal of Democracy*, 24 (2): 15–30.

Stone, K., Diamond, L., Girod, D. and McFaul, M. (2013) Transitional Successes and Failures: The International-Domestic Nexus. In: K. Stoner and M. McFaul, eds, *Transitions to Democracy*. Baltimore: The Johns Hopkins University Press.

Suny, R. G. (1993) *Looking toward Ararat: Armenia in Modern History.* Bloomington: Indiana University Press.

2

Thirty years of protest

How Armenia's legacy of political and civic protests prepared the Velvet Revolution

Mikayel Zolyan

Ever tried. Ever failed. No matter.
Try again. Fail again. Fail better.

– Samuel Beckett

To many foreign observers, the Armenian 'Velvet Revolution' came as a surprise. To those unacquainted with the realities of Armenian politics, it seemed that the huge protests came out of nowhere to attract hundreds of thousands of people and engulf the whole country. To those familiar with Armenian realities, the fact of the protests themselves was not surprising, but what seemed unlikely was that these protests could ever succeed, since the numerous political and civic protest movements that had taken place in Armenia during preceding years had mostly ended in vain. Yet looking back at the political history of post-Soviet Armenia, it becomes obvious that the Velvet Revolution of 2018, or the 'Revolution of Love and Solidarity'[1] as some of its supporters preferred to call it, did not come out of nowhere. It was precisely the legacy of those 'failed' protests that had prepared the success of 2018. Mass protest and civic activism have been an important part of Armenia's political culture at least since the late 1980s. In this chapter, we analyse how this decades-long legacy of protests prepared the subsequent success of the Velvet Revolution.

Peaceful protest under the Soviet system: Protest mobilization in Armenia before 1991

One could argue that the roots of mass protest activity in modern Armenia go back at least to the 1960s. Prior to that time, Soviet Armenia hardly witnessed any mass protests, and if there was any political activism, it was extremely limited due to political repression that was dominant throughout the Stalinist period (Suny 1993: 113–61; Panossian 2006: 266–90). However, the relative liberalization of Nikita Khrushchev's era opened doors for a resurgence of political activism. In 1965 mass protests took place in Yerevan demanding the recognition of the events of 1915 as genocide, and to proclaim 24 April the official day of remembrance of the victims of the genocide. The protests took place on 24 April, as an officially sanctioned genocide remembrance ceremony was taking place in the Opera and Ballet State Theatre. Even though the protesters disrupted the official ceremony, the protest was largely peaceful, and it was not aimed directly against the Soviet regime. However, the fact that an unsanctioned mass rally took place in the mid-1960s was in itself quite remarkable. The Soviet government preferred to partially accommodate the demands of Armenians, even as it made clear that direct confrontation with the Soviet authorities would not be tolerated: arrests of 'extremist elements' followed these events. Moreover, the First Secretary of Armenian Communist Party Yakov Zarobyan, who was thought to be too 'soft' on the protesters, had to resign (on the 1965 protests, see Panossian 2006: 320–3; Suny 1993: 186; Dadrian 1977: 246–7; Conquest 1967: 101).

Throughout the 1960s and the 1970s, a vibrant 'dissident movement' scene emerged in Armenia (Panossian 2006: 323–7; Suny 1993: 185–91). The dissident movement can, with a certain degree of simplification, be divided into two currents, which can be called 'liberal' and 'national(ist)'. The nationalist current was more widespread, and included underground organizations such as the 'National Unity Party' (NUP), which was discovered by the Soviet authorities and some of its members became political prisoners (Kowalewski 1979). The emergence of the NUP was preceded by that of 'patriotic' organizations, some of which were discovered by the Soviet authorities even before 1965, such as the so-called 'seven patriots' who were put on trial in 1964 (Manukyan 2006: 89–90). When the Soviet system started to crumble some of the members of NUP, under the leadership of Ashot Navasardyan, later started the Republican Party of Armenia (RPA) (Panossian 2006: 326). It was precisely the RPA that later became a member of the government coalition in 1995 under Ter-Petrossian, subsequently came to constitute the core of the ruling political elite under Kocharian and Sargsyan, and was finally toppled by the 2018 revolution (by which time only a handful of original members remained). In 1977, in connection with terrorist acts in Moscow's metro system, several members of Armenia's nationalist underground were arrested and found guilty of terrorist acts, a verdict that remains a matter of controversy to this day (Panossian 2006: 326; Suny 1993: 187).

The 'liberal' current was represented mostly by members of the intelligentsia, who had connections with 'dissident' intellectuals from Russia and other Soviet republics. Among them were several intellectuals, such as Rafael Papayan, Edmon Avetyan and others, who were arrested and accused of 'anti-Soviet activities' (Ter-Abraamyan 2006). The 'liberal' and 'national' wing of the dissident movement cooperated in certain situations, as was the case when supporters of Paruyr Hayrikyan, who had split from the NUP, cooperated with the Armenian Branch of the Helsinki Group (Panossian 2006: 326). Most of these activities remained underground; yet in the late 1970s, there was a surge of protest activism in Armenia around the issue of the state language (Whitney 1978; Suny 1993: 188)

With the onset of Mikhail Gorbachev's perestroika ('restructuring') policy, new opportunities emerged for activism and protest. First, as in many other Soviet republics, activism focused on environmental concerns, which in the Soviet system were considered relatively safe, since such protests did not target Soviet authorities directly: environmentally focused rallies took place in Yerevan in October 1987 (Suny 1993: 196). However, the real game changer was the issue of Karabakh. On 20 February a rally for the unification of the Nagorno-Karabakh Autonomous Oblast' (region) with Armenia started simultaneously in Yerevan and Stepanakert. The Karabakh movement became the largest mass movement in Armenia's history, at least prior to the events of 2018.

What happened in Armenia in 1988, and the following years, became extremely important for the identity of post-Soviet Armenia as a state and society. In Armenian history textbooks, the chapters that deal with this period are usually simply entitled 'The Karabakh Movement' (Zolyan, Mkrtchyan and Hovhannisyan 2016: 20–6). This characterization shies away from giving a precise appraisal of what exactly the events of 1988–91 constituted in terms of a historical phenomenon, and more specifically whether the dramatic and profound changes that happened in Armenia constituted a revolution. In fact, the word 'revolution' was almost never used by the participants and observers of those events (Zolyan, Mkrtchyan and Hovhannisyan 2016: 63). Similarly, history textbooks of post-Soviet Armenia, even though they devote a significant amount of attention to the Karabakh movement, and the changes that it brought, refrain from using the term revolution, preferring to use terms like 'struggle for national liberation' (Zolyan, Mkrtchyan and Hovhannisyan 2016: 24)

Yet some, including both researchers and political figures, insist that what happened in Armenia between 1988 and 1991 constituted nothing less than a revolution. Thus, cultural anthropologist Harutyun Marutyan believed that the events of 1988–91 exhibited all the characteristics of a peaceful revolution, similar to the events in Central and Eastern Europe in 1989 (Marutyan 2018). A somewhat similar view, though without using the term 'revolution', was earlier expressed by one of the veterans of the 1988 movement, Vazgen Manukyan, independent Armenia's first prime minister, who compared the events of 1988 in Armenia to the Solidarity movement in Poland and complained that the Armenian government at the time was not doing enough to commemorate these events and to present their true significance to the outside world (Zolyan, Mkrtchyan and Hovhannisyan, 2016: 79–80). Ironically, I used the term 'Armenia's velvet revolution' in relation to the events of 1988–91 in one of my earlier articles, long before the events of 2018 that would come to be known by the same term (Zolyan 2011).

It is not the aim of this chapter to determine whether the events of 1988 should be considered a revolution or not, although it is possible to note the obvious similarities between the developments in Armenia in the late 1980s and the events that took place in some countries of Central and Eastern Europe in 1989. In both contexts one could witness a mass movement that mobilized a majority of the population and led to a peaceful change of government, in most cases through an election, and the dismantling of the communist system. Of course, there are also obvious differences, given the fact that Armenia at the time was a part of the Soviet Union, and the fact that the disagreements over the future of Nagorny Karabakh led to violence, and this violence eventually led to a full-blown military conflict. In any case, whether we consider the events of the late 1980s a revolution or not, it is hard to deny that these events represented a major upheaval, which included a mass protest mobilization that led to the unseating of the incumbent political elite and profound changes in the political system of the country. As such, the movement of 1988 became a blueprint for protest movements in post-Soviet Armenia.

Before protest became 'mainstream': Mobilizations after disputed elections in post-Soviet Armenia

The imagery and symbolism of 1988 was often evoked by leaders of post-Soviet Armenian protest movements. The unprecedented mobilization of that year became a yardstick against which the success of other protest movements in terms of popular mobilization was measured. However, the nature of these protests was significantly different from the nature of the Karabakh movement. Most major political protests in post-Soviet Armenia took place as a reaction to elections that were perceived as 'stolen'. As such, these protests could be described as attempted 'electoral' revolutions, attempts that were repeated in virtually every electoral cycle.

In fact, almost all presidential elections had been followed by major protests. This 'tradition' started with the disputed election of 1996, where the first democratically elected Armenian president Levon Ter-Petrossian faced his former ally Vazgen Manukyan, who in 1996 became a unified opposition candidate. If these protests had been successful, Armenia could have been credited as the first country in the post-socialist world to have a 'colour revolution' (Iskandaryan 2005). However, after the protesters supporting Vazgen Manukyan stormed the building of the National Assembly, they were dispersed by riot police, a state of emergency was declared in Yerevan and many opposition leaders were arrested or went into hiding (Astourian 2000; Human Rights Watch 1997). Although the protests were dispersed, this did not help President Ter-Petrossian to consolidate power. A formerly popular leader, who had been elected by a landslide in the previous election, he was now left at the mercy of the coercive agencies or security apparatus (*siloviki*, to use the Russian term). Eventually, Ter-Petrossian, deprived of democratic legitimacy, had to step down under pressure from a coalition of his former allies in February 1998 (Astourian 2000).

Since then, while the names of incumbents and contenders changed, the overall pattern remained the same (Zolyan 2010a). The incumbent, or the incumbent's anointed successor, faced an opposition consolidated around a common leader, usually a representative of the political elite, who had lost his position in power, but whose status as a former official lent him certain resources, whether political, financial or symbolic. Thus, the government camp was led by incumbent President Ter-Petrossian in 1996; Prime Minister and acting President Robert Kocharian in 1998; incumbent President Kocharian in 2003; Prime Minister and 'successor' Serzh Sargsyan in 2008; and incumbent President Serzh Sargsyan in 2013. As for the opposition, in 1996, the opposition front runner was Vazgen Manukyan, a former prime minister; in 1998, it was Armenia's former communist leader Karen Demirchian; in 2003 it was the latter's son Stepan Demirchian; in 2008 it was Ter-Petrossian, who had returned in the capacity of the opposition leader; and in 2013, when other prominent politicians refused to take part in the election, the opposition front runner and the protest leader was another former official, independent Armenia's former minister of foreign affairs Raffi Hovhannisian.

Thus, we have seen how different groups of political elites faced each other in the contest for power. Usually, one camp, which in terms of Armenian political discourse was usually referred to as 'the authorities' (or 'the power', in

Armenian *ishkhanut'yun*), was able to count on the administrative, financial and, most importantly, coercive resources of the state. The other camp, usually referred to as 'the opposition' (*ĕnddimut'yun*) was able to count on the support of the disgruntled population, or at least of its more rebellious part, as well as the support of civil society, which opposed the incumbent's non-democratic practices. In each case, the opposition could count on the wide support of a population that was tired of corruption, nepotism, government inefficiency and socioeconomic inequality. The government camp in turn usually played the 'national-patriotic card', emphasizing the need for stability, putting the accent on the need to provide security in conditions of the unresolved conflict in Nagorny Karabakh (Baghdasaryan 2013; Shubladze and Khundadze 2017). However, arguably, what was really instrumental for the victories of the government camp was the control over the administrative and coercive resources of the state, which was combined with control over the commanding heights of the country's economy. These resources allowed the government camp to engineer the necessary election results, in spite of the unpopularity of its leaders.

Of course, the electoral 'technologies' used in these cases were different, ranging from 'soft' ones, such as the use of administrative buildings and spaces for propaganda of a certain candidate, to more blatant ones, such as voter bribing and intimidation, up to and including 'hard' methods, such as stealing and stuffing ballots and violence against proxies and observers. There was also a certain evolution of these 'technologies', from obvious and blatant methods of electoral falsification that were widely used in the 1990s to more sophisticated and hard-to-detect methods of falsification that came to dominate the field in the 2010s (Gilbreath and Balasanyan 2017; OSCE/ ODIHR 1996, 1998, 1999, 2003, 2008, 2013).

It is outside of the scope of this chapter to determine to what degree each specific election was falsified. What matters for the purposes of this chapter is that falsifications took place in virtually every election, and in virtually every election many actors in the opposition and civil society refused to accept the election results as legitimate. Thus, these elections failed to perform one of the main functions that elections have in a democratic society, that of providing legitimacy to the government. Also, the elections in post-Soviet Armenia certainly failed to fulfil the other most important function of a democratic election, to produce the rotation of political elites. Throughout the whole post-Soviet history of Armenia, there was not a single occasion when elections led to a change of government. In fact, the only election in modern Armenian history, in which the opposition had been able to unseat an incumbent ruling party had taken place in 1990, when Armenia was still part of the USSR. Thus, it was obvious for the majority of Armenia's voters that they had little say in determining who would run the country.

At the same time, Armenian authoritarianism was never able to consolidate to a sufficient extent as to definitively dissolve the competitive opposition and remove any credible threat of government change. For most of the post-Soviet period, Armenia represented a hybrid regime, being categorized by Levitsky and Way as a competitive authoritarian regime and included in their well-known book on competitive authoritarianism (Levitsky and Way 2010). While parliamentary elections usually provided comfortable victory margins for the incumbent parties, presidential elections almost always contained an element of unpredictability. A vicious circle (from the point of view of the incumbent) existed: the existence of a relatively strong opposition meant that the incumbent's victory was not entirely guaranteed, in turn leading to more disgruntled voters joining the opposition camp, prompting the government to turn to either outright falsification or more sophisticated 'electoral technologies'. And when the official results of the elections, tainted by reports of fraud, failed to justify the expectations of opposition supporters, people took to the streets. Moreover, often the supporters of the leading opposition candidate were joined by supporters of other opposition candidates, who also complained of election fraud in a dynamic well-known from other cases of electoral revolutions (for example in 2004, former opposition candidate Artashes Geghamyan joined forces with the opposition front runner Stepan Demirchian, see Zolyan 2010a: 92–4).

However, in almost all cases after 1996, the incumbent government was able to consolidate its resources and wait out the protests, while the protest leaders were unable to sustain the dynamic of protest, and the protests usually withered away. Of course, there were certain variations in each specific case. In 2003, the incumbent was helped by a controversial Constitutional Court decision, which upheld the election results but suggested to hold a referendum of confidence in the president. Not surprisingly, the referendum was never held, and the protest demanding the enactment of the referendum was violently dispersed by riot police on 12 April 2004 (Zolyan 2010: 94).

The exception to this rule was 2008, when the protest dynamic was apparently so strong that it could be stopped only by a major violent crackdown. At the time the opposition consolidated around former president Ter-Petrossian, who, despite the controversies surrounding him since the 1990s, was able to attract a significant following due to his promises to 'clean out the Augean stables', in other words to get rid of the corruption in the state system. Arguably, what made the protest of 2008 so dangerous for the government camp was the fact that Ter-Petrossian also commanded the loyalty of a large part of the political elite that had emerged in Armenia as a result of the transformations of late 1980s and early 1990s. The protests of 2008 were growing larger day by day, so the strategy of 'waiting out' would not work for the government camp, and a violent crackdown ensued resulting in ten deaths, the bloodiest episode of protest crackdown in Armenia's post-Soviet history (Human Rights Watch 2009).

One could argue that over time, post-election protests had become an element of the political culture or even of the political system of post-Soviet Armenia. Though time after time they failed to attain their main goal, that is, to change the top leadership of the country, they led to a certain balancing of the political system. Also, they determined the composition of the opposition sector of Armenia's political spectrum, as those opposition leaders who failed to support such protests or displayed their inability to lead them lost their standing in the eyes of the pro-opposition part of the society. The protests, even when they were not successful, could also boost the political capital of certain leaders. Thus, the 2008 events helped to reanimate Ter-Petrossian as a pro-democracy leader and the figurehead of the Armenian opposition for several years, in spite of the damage done to his democratic credentials by the dispersal of protests at his own re-election as president in 1996.

Even though the incumbents ultimately prevailed in all these crises, the very fact of post-election protests presented a major dilemma for Armenia's authoritarian leaders. These protests not only presented a danger, but even when they were unsuccessful, they undermined the legitimacy of the government, made it vulnerable to external criticism and pressure, and limited their ability to exercise control over society. Arguably, the constitutional reform of 2015, apart from ensuring the political longevity of Serzh Sargsyan, was also supposed to deal with the issue of post-election protests. The experience of Armenian elections suggests that it was relatively easy for the incumbent parties to win in parliamentary elections. Explaining this requires separate empirical research, but we can speculate with some basis that this difference is due to the fact that in parliamentary elections, the voters were offered to vote not on the personality of the incumbent or their chosen successor, who was often personally hated and blamed for all the negative phenomena in the country, but for someone much more acceptable, such as a local mayor or a local businessman who, obviously, was also a member of the ruling party. Thus, ensuring a majority for the incumbent through a parliamentary election proved to be a much easier task than doing the same at the presidential election. After the constitutional reform took place and the first parliamentary election was held in April 2017, Serzh Sargsyan indeed pointed out that this was the first election in years that was not followed by protests (Zolyan 2017)

Though post-election protests always failed to produce the result that its participants were hoping for, that is, a change of government, ultimately they contributed significantly to the events of 2018. First of all, these protests were a major factor that prevented Armenia from becoming a full-fledged autocracy, and created incentives for the government to turn from more blatant falsifications to more nuanced strategies. Thus, arguably, repeated mass mobilization and the prospect of its recurrence was one of the factors that prevented Sargsyan from simply removing the limit on presidential terms, as has been the case in many similar situations in other countries, and led him to opt for the more risky path of transition to a parliamentary republic. Protests also served as a breeding ground for Armenia's political activists. Many of the activists of the 2018 Velvet Revolution became involved in opposition activism through participation in post-election protests. Nikol Pashinyan, who became the leader of the 2018 revolution, was a close ally of Ter-Petrossian in 2008, playing a key role at the protest rallies. The post-election protests created networks of activism that enabled mass mobilization in 2018. And, last but not least, the post-election protests helped to normalize the very act of protesting, making contentious politics a major part of political culture in Armenia, distinguishing it from many other post-Soviet states.

Small but efficient: Civic activism and protest in pre-revolutionary Armenia

The post-election protests were not the only 'source' of political or civic activism in Armenia prior to the 2018 revolution. There was another current that may have been less notable to outside observers but played a major role in the processes leading to the revolution. Throughout the post-Soviet period, there was a significant number of various movements – big and small – which focused on specific issues or as Armenian activists would often call them 'struggles', which are widely referred to as 'civic initiatives' (on these, see Ishkanian 2008, 2015; Zolyan 2010b; Gevorgyan and Bagiyan 2015; Paturyan and Gevorgyan 2016).

Certain initiatives of this kind existed in Armenia in the 1990s and the early 2000s. These included for example, several waves of student-led protests against the abolition of deferral of military service for university students. One of these groups, 'For Development of Science' united activists who later became prominent in the protests of 2008 and 2018, and after that became members of the post-revolutionary government and parliament (Lragir.am 2017). Another civic initiative of this kind was formed after the events of

12 April 2004, when the police cracked down on opposition protests and numerous opposition activists found themselves in jail. In the wake of these events a group of civil activists, mostly young people and students, with some participation from local NGOs, demanded an end to the persecution of opposition activists, though no overtly political demands were put forward (Ishkhanyan and Babajanyan 2004). Later, some of these activists formed a group called *Sksel a* (in translation: 'it has started'), which did not have a clear political agenda, but voiced opposition to the existing political system through non-political actions, such as celebration of folklore holidays, performances and rock concerts (Panorama 2017).

However, the 'Golden Age' of such initiatives started after 2008, helped by several factors. First, the post-election protests of 2008, which had a high degree of youth participation, led to an emerging interest among youth towards political and civic agendas. Second, the post-2008 political set-up, in which the government was facing strong opposition from supporters of Ter-Petrossian, made the government more responsive to the demands of various civic groups, especially if these demands were not openly political. Finally, and probably most importantly, the spread of relatively cheap and high-speed internet, particularly of social networks such as Facebook, provided tools for mobilization and the articulation of demands, which previous civic initiatives and movements had severely lacked (Zolyan 2010b; Gevorgyan and Bagiyan 2015).

While these civic initiatives and movements were quite diverse there were certain traits that united them. First, the majority of activists were of a young age, either students or young professionals. This also meant that these groups widely used internet and social networks. It also helped to ensure that many of the civic movements were quite innovative and creative in their protesting activities. The actions of civic activists were often reminiscent of a carnival or an art performance, contrary to the grimmer and more predictable rallies often held by purely political protesters.

Most of these movements and initiatives emerged in response to specific policies or steps taken by the authorities. While initiatives were addressed explicitly at these policies rather at government per se, it was nevertheless the government that was the receiver of their demands. Unlike the participants of post-election protests, civic activists usually did not demand resignation of the incumbent, bringing instead rather more specific demands, some of which could be satisfied by the government without creating an existential danger for the regime. Consequently, in most cases, in spite of being critical of the government, they advocated negotiations and dialogue with the government and expected the government to meet their demands. This was connected to the second unifying characteristic of most of these movements.

Most civic activists declared their activism to be non-political, or at least non-partisan, and were at great pains to distance themselves from political parties, including those in the opposition camp. At the same time, they also were at pains to distinguish themselves from the more traditional NGOs usually associated with Western donors and grants, and which have been widely demonized by government propaganda in the former Soviet Union (Ishkanian 2015; Paturyan and Gevorgyan 2016).

This distancing from a political agenda was both a strength and a weakness of the civic movements. On the one hand, they were more likely to succeed, compared to post-election protests. While all post-election protests in post-Soviet Armenia failed to achieve their major goal, that is, to overturn the election results, many of the civic initiatives were successful in achieving their specific aims. Thus, at different times, activists were able to prevent the demolition of an open-air cinema theatre in central Yerevan, to block the building of boutique shops on the territory of a park, to prevent a change in the law on education in order to allow foreign language schools in Armenia or even to force the government to modify its proposed pension reform (Zolyan 2010b; Paturyan and Gevorgyan 2016).

At the same time, insistence on the non-political and/or non-partisan nature of civic activism was also a limitation, which prevented cooperation with political forces and made it easier for the government to deal with and work around civic initiatives. While many of the civic activists involved in these initiatives hoped to weaken or even dismantle the ruling regime, in fact, their activities did little damage to the overall system. Thus, the Mashtots Park Movement, while it created a significant problem for the government entailing a confrontation in central Yerevan lasting for months, eventually failed to prevent the government from scoring an important election victory in the 2012 parliamentary election. The *Dem em* movement, which struggled against the pension reform, also helped to bring down Tigran Sargsyan's cabinet in 2014. However, the cabinet's dissolution was also connected to the balance between political forces at the time, and ultimately the replacement of Tigran Sargsyan with Hovik Abrahamyan only made the regime stronger in the mid-term perspective (Paturyan and Gevorgyan 2016: 44–5).

However, while the civic movements described in this section were unable to dismantle or even weaken the authoritarian regime in Armenia, they were instrumental in preparing the revolution in other ways. Thus, they helped to foster a thriving culture of creative, innovative, mostly youth-based civic protest and activism in Armenia, which made the Velvet Revolution possible. Many of the activists who were among the initiators of 2018 protests were socialized into protest activism through civic movements such as the ones described earlier. Second, these initiatives helped to preserve a sufficiently wide space for freedom, in spite of the existence of an authoritarian regime. The constant protests by various civic groups, which were normally peaceful, colourful and creative, and, in most cases, were not directly articulating anti-government agenda, helped to normalize protest, contentious politics and civic activity in the eyes of Armenian society. Unlike the post-election protests, which normally produced little result or even ended with a violent crackdown, civic movements of this kind were not put down violently, and often succeeded in achieving their goals, prompting more similar protests and mobilizing more and more young people into civic activism.

The dichotomy of civic/political protest dominated Armenia's protest scene throughout most of the 2000s and 2010s. However, by mid-2010s, this trend started to change, as the two currents of protest activism merged, leading to the emergence of new forms of protests, which in terms of their goals and aims were clearly political, but not necessarily partisan.

Writing on the wall: 'Electric Yerevan' and *Sasna Tsrer*

Two major cases of protest preceded the Velvet Revolution: the so-called 'Electric Yerevan' in June 2015 and the events related to the *Sasna Tsrer* group in July 2016 (on Electric Yerevan see Derluguian and Andreasyan 2015; Paturyan and Gevorgyan 2016: 48–52; on *Sasna Tsrer* see Ishkanian 2016; Markedonov 2016; de Waal 2016; Zolyan 2016; Fomin and Silaev 2018). In both these cases, the protests did not achieve significant results and, in the short-term perspective, even seemed to consolidate the regime. Thus, months after Electric Yerevan, in December 2015, the government was able to successfully pass the referendum on the constitutional transition to a parliamentary republic, paving the way for Serzh Sargsyan to preserve power after the end of his presidential term, even if, as subsequent events showed, only for one week. The *Sasna Tsrer* episode shook Armenia to the core, and was probably one of the reasons why Hovik Abrahamyan's government resigned, but the Republican Party's confident victory in the 2017 parliamentary election seemed to show that the regime had re-emerged even more strong and stable after these events (Zolyan 2017). Yet today, in hindsight, it seems that both Electric Yerevan and *Sasna Tsrer*, albeit unsuccessful and controversial (especially the latter), paved the way for the Velvet Revolution, although in more complicated ways than may appear on the surface.

Both the Electric Yerevan and *Sasna Tsrer* episodes were difficult to categorize, at least in terms familiar from Armenian and, more generally, post-Soviet realities. Electric Yerevan was a mass protest, led not by a political party or a group, but by young activists, with goals that seemed apolitical, yet that suggested obvious political consequences. Its declared aim was to protest against rising electricity prices, caused by mismanagement at the Armenian Electric Networks company, at the time a subsidiary of the Russian conglomeration, United Electric Networks. Yet many of the participants and those observing Electric Yerevan read more into the protests. For some, the protest was about rejecting government policies, or the political system altogether, while for others, mostly in the international media covering the events, it was about combating Russian influence. The latter perception was commonly repeated both in Russian and Western media, leading to comparison with the Ukrainian 'Maidan' events of 2014. These comparisons were rejected by the majority of protest participants, leading to emergence of the slogan 'This is not Maidan, this is Marshal Baghramyan' (referring to the fact that the protest was taking place on Yerevan's Marshal Baghramyan Avenue), which arguably was designed specifically to deflect comparisons with the Ukrainian events (Derluguian and Andreasyan 2015; Paturyan and Gevorgyan 2016).

Contrary to the political protests of the previous years, Electric Yerevan was distinguished by a festive atmosphere, which later came to be repeated in the Velvet Revolution. This atmosphere was due to the large presence of young people, many of them previously uninterested in politics. As one participant put it, in Electric Yerevan 'the hipsters from the bars of P'arpetsi Street [the nightlife district in Yerevan] met with the veterans of political protests' (author's personal communication). The tactic behind Electric Yerevan was to seal off Baghramyan Avenue, the street where the presidential palace and parliament are located, which is also one of the main transport arteries of Yerevan. When the protests spilled over to the adjacent France Square, sealing off two other major avenues of central Yerevan, the protest threatened to create chaos in the entire Armenian capital. Ultimately this tactic did not work, as the government succeeded in convincing a part of the activists to move to Freedom Square, where they did not cause any problems for traffic. However, Electric Yerevan showed that sealing off streets could be an efficient tool, and it is no coincidence that many of the activists who started 'closing streets' in April 2018, were also active participants of Electric Yerevan. Using trash collectors to seal off the streets was another 'trademark move' of the 2018 revolution that was first introduced during the Electric Yerevan protest (author's personal observation).

Arguably, Electric Yerevan's main weakness was the lack of clear political leadership and, consequently, of a clear political programme. The movement's leaders, mostly young men, were newcomers to politics, who lacked the experience and the symbolic capital to lead the movement effectively, while professional politicians stayed out of the movement. As a result, in the absence of clearly defined political texts produced by the protesters, the government was able to dominate the media agenda, spinning the movement in such a way as to permit the situation to be kept under control. The lack of unity and clear mechanisms of decision-making among the activists also meant that it was relatively easy for the government side to split the movement by making limited concessions. While many activists called for the continuation of the protests and the advancing of political demands, up to and including the dismissal of the government, others did not agree. A split followed in the movement, with the pro-government media supporting the 'moderate' wing among the activists. 'The moderates' moved their protest to the Freedom Square, where the protest could not affect the movement of city transport, and as such presented little danger to the authorities. Finally, when there were few people left on Baghramyan Avenue, the police cleared the street and opened it for traffic, signifying the end of Electric Yerevan (Paturyan and Gevorgyan 2016: 48–9).

The other major protest action that preceded the Velvet Revolution, the *Sasna Tsrer* episode, was very different from Electric Yerevan, but it also evades clear categorization. Government figures and pro-government media used the terms 'terrorists' and 'terror attacks' to describe *Sasna Tsrer* and their actions; however, when the members of the group were arrested, no charges of terrorism were applied. *Sasna Tsrer* supporters called the events 'an armed uprising'. To make matters more complicated, apart from the violent action undertaken by the *Sasna Tsrer*, using weapons, there were also peaceful – or at least unarmed – demonstrations by citizens. To complicate things even more, not all participants of these rallies identified as *Sasna Tsrer* supporters, with some even openly rejecting violence as a political strategy.

Whatever the qualifications, the facts are the following. In the early hours of 17 July, an armed group, which included opposition activists and veterans of the Nagorny Karabakh conflict, seized the headquarters of an elite police regiment in the Erebuni district of Yerevan. During the attack on the police building, there was an exchange of fire in which one senior police officer was killed and several policemen were taken hostages (who were freed later). The group called itself *Sasna Tsrer* (meaning 'the daredevils of Sassoun', although it can also be translated as 'the madmen of Sassoun'), after an Armenian epic tale that tells the story of heroes who defy common sense by challenging and overcoming enemies far superior in strength. On the morning of the attack, the group spread its manifesto through social networks, demanding the resignation of President Serzh Sargsyan and calling for the people of Armenia to take to the streets and to start an uprising against the regime. They also demanded the release of Zhirayr Sefilyan, a well-known opposition figure and Karabakh war veteran, who had been arrested a few months earlier. The members of the group also said they resisted any possible concessions in the issue of Nagorny Karabakh, talk of which became common in Armenia in the aftermath of the so-called four-day war in April 2016 (de Waal 2016; Fomin and Silaev 2018).

As news of the action spread, the government started rounding up activists, in order to prevent possible rallies in support of *Sasna Tsrer*. However, rallies, albeit not large in scale, started in Yerevan from 18 July. Most of these rallies centred on the Erebuni district of Yerevan, where the police station seized by the group was located. Clashes also took place in the district of Sari Tagh, and as a result of these clashes, the police, which had used stun grenades, were accused of police brutality and the use of excessive force. Dozens of activists had been rounded up. The rallies continued until the members of *Sasna Tsrer*, isolated in the police compound, agreed to surrender to the authorities, thus ending the siege and crisis.

Thus, in spite of some initial nervousness and chaotic responses, the government was ultimately able to contain this crisis as well. However, the *Sasna Tsrer* episode was a serious warning to Serzh Sargsyan's government, as it showed the real extent of its unpopularity in Armenian society. Many Armenians were ready to support the violent actions of a fringe political group, as long as they were aimed against the incumbent government. Moreover, many Armenians, among them public figures, either publicly supported the *Sasna Tsrer*, or, even when they rejected their violent methods, blamed the government for creating such a desperate situation that encouraged people to take violent action (Fomin and Silaev 2018).

Overall, in hindsight Electric Yerevan and *Sasna Tsrer* today seem to be the 'writing on the wall' that the Armenian government had ignored. Both these events, though in very different ways, played their part in preparing the Velvet Revolution. On the one hand, Electric Yerevan showed the potential for a youth-based, innovative and peaceful protest. However, it also showed that the lack of political leadership was detrimental for protests, leading many activists to question the 'apolitical/non-partisan' narrative that had dominated Armenian civic activism for several years. Arguably, it was this lesson of Electric Yerevan that helped Armenian activists of various stripes to put aside their ideological differences and concerns about 'politicization' and 'partisanship' and consolidate around Pashinyan and his Civil Contract party during the April 2018 events. Another important lesson learned from Electric Yerevan was that focusing on a foreign policy agenda, particularly on issues such as combating Russian influence, was a recipe for failure, as it could both divide the protesters and invite a negative reaction from Moscow, which in turn would strengthen the position of the incumbent. Hence, the strong insistence of Pashinyan, and other spokespersons of the 2018 movement, that the Velvet Revolution was completely free of any foreign political agenda or context.

The *Sasna Tsrer* incident, on the other hand, showed the degree to which Serzh Sargsyan's government had lost support among the Armenian society. Even when faced with an unprovoked violent attack against government forces, the government failed to receive public support. It became obvious that the desperation of a part of Armenian citizens with the state of affairs in the country was so deep that they did not necessarily even reject violent methods of political struggle, including those that the government itself considered 'terrorism'. On the other hand, it also showed to opposition and civic activists that violent actions were in themselves a road to nowhere, as the violence gave the government the justification to use force and prevented the more moderate part of opposition and civil society from supporting the 'uprising'. These lessons were not lost on the revolutionaries of 2018, who made every effort to emphasize that the protests were peaceful, and called on their supporters to refrain not only from using violence first but also even from responding to violence with violence.

Epilogue: From Freedom Square to Republic Square

The Velvet Revolution of 2018 did not come out of nowhere. In fact, Armenia's political and civic activists had acted almost exactly according to the Silicon Valley management mantra 'fail often, fail early'. Protests and activism had been a major part of post-Soviet Armenia's political culture, and by 2018, Armenia's protest tradition had acquired decades of experience that the 'Velvet revolutionaries' could draw upon. It had also created a symbolic and political space for protest activity, which is often non-existent in most autocracies. Thus, 2018's revolutionaries could draw upon Armenia's rich tradition of protest and activism, going back at least to the Karabakh movement of 1988, or even further into the past. However, probably, one of the keys to the success of the movement in 2018 was also the fact that many things were done differently, as compared to the previous protest movements. Analysing the similarities and differences between the revolution of 2018 and previous protest movements could be a topic for a separate chapter, if not a book on its own. Therefore, we shall limit ourselves to one example: the choice of Republic Square as the venue for the main rallies in 2018, as it also helps to capture the evolution of protest movements in Armenia.

Throughout the post-Soviet period, Freedom Square (formerly the Theatre Square) was the symbolic centre of protest movements, a status it inherited from 1988, since the first Karabakh movement rallies took place there. Since then, most large protest movements in Armenia had viewed Freedom Square as their main gathering point. This was especially true of the 2008 movement, which, being led by Karabakh movement veterans Levon Ter-Petrossian and his team, sought to symbolically re-create the atmosphere of 1988 by selecting this venue. However, the 1 March 2008 crackdown, which became probably the most traumatic episode in the history of protest in Armenia, also started from Freedom Square, adding a dark side to its symbolism (Petrosyan 2018). In any case, for three decades, it was Freedom Square that served as the symbolic centre of protests and rallies in Yerevan. In Yerevan's symbolic geography, Freedom Square was 'the people's square', while Republic Square symbolized power and statehood. The symbolic significance of Freedom Square started to break down with the Electric Yerevan and *Sasna Tsrer* events. Electric Yerevan focused on Baghramyan Avenue and the adjacent France Square, and in fact it began to unravel precisely at the moment that the protests moved to Freedom Square. In 2016, there was virtually no attempt to 'reclaim' Freedom Square, as most rallies took place close in the vicinity of the police station captured by *Sasna Tsrer* (Zolyan 2016).

Interestingly, in 2018, some of the initial rallies also took place on Freedom Square, Baghramyan Avenue and France Square (Petrosyan 2018). However, the tactics of spreading the protest, through sealing off roads in all possible locations, changed the logic of protests, creating a new decentralized model of protests. And then came the decision to hold evening rallies at the Republic Square. In fact, at the time, many supporters were hesitant about the decision to hold the rally on the Republic Square: some thought that the square was too big and that the rallies would seem too small, which would hurt the protests (Petrosyan 2018). However, ultimately, holding rallies at the Republic Square proved a major success. It also showed that 'this time' everything was different. Moreover, moving the protests to Republic Square became a symbol of the people's victory, symbolizing the reclaiming of the state by the people: 'the people' took 'the state' – from which they had been alienated for so long – under their control.

Thus, metaphorically speaking, in three decades the protest movement in Armenia has gone down a road of less than a mile, from Freedom Square to Republic Square. Yet behind this seemingly small distance there are dozens of big and small marches, rallies, sit-ins, street performances, one-person-protests, hunger strikes and more. Almost every imaginable form of individual and collective protest had been tried in post-Soviet Armenia in the years preceding the revolution of 2018. In fact, looking back at this history today, it seems almost inevitable that, sooner or later, these years of experience were destined to produce a major shift in Armenian society.

Note

1   This second term for the events of April 2018 is also popular, and Nikol Pashinyan has himself used it, for example in his meeting with US national security adviser John Bolton in October 2018. See 'Nikol Pashinyan, John Bolton discuss issues on Armenian-American relations agenda', press release, 25 October 2018, http://www.primeminister.am/en/press-release/item/2018/10/25/Nikol-Pashinyan-John-Bolton/ (accessed 1 June 2019).

References

Astourian, S. (2000) *From Ter-Petrosian to Kocharian: Leadership Change in Armenia*. Berkeley: University of California.

Baghdasaryan, G. (2013) 'Working the Enemy's Mill' – Putting the Brake on Internal Development in Nagorny Karabakh: A Media Study of the Image of the Enemy. In: J. Javakhishvili, L. Kvarchelia, eds, *Myths and Conflict in the South Caucasus, Volume 2: Instrumentalisation of Conflict in Political Discourse*. London: International Alert, 92–108.

Conquest, R. (1967) *Soviet Nationalities Policy in Practice*. London: Bodley Head.

Dadrian, V. (1977) Nationalism in Soviet Armenia – A Case Study of Ethnocentrism. In: Simmonds, G., ed., *Nationalism in the USSR and Eastern Europe*. Detroit: University of Detroit Press, 202–57.

Derluguian, G. and Andreasyan, Zh. (2015) Fuel Protests in Armenia. *New Left Review*, 95 (September–October): 29–48.

Fomin, I. and Silaev, N. (2018) Armyanskiy Natsionalizm Protiv Armyanskogo Gosudarstva: Raskoly i Koalitsii v Diskurse o Sasna Tsrer. *Polis. Political Studies*, 3: 78–92.

Gevorgyan, V. and Bagiyan, A. (2015) Online versus Offline Activism: The Case of Armenia. *Caucasus Research Resource Centers (CRRC) Methodological Conference on Transformations in the South Caucasus and its Neighborhood*. Available at: https://tcpa.aua.am/files/2016/08/Online-vs-Offline-Activism-in-Armenia.pdf (accessed 17 May 2019).

Gilbreath, D. and Balasanyan, S. (2017) Elections and Election Fraud in Georgia and Armenia. *Caucasus Survey*, 5 (3): 238–58.

Human Rights Watch. (1997) *Human Rights Watch World Report 1997 – Armenia*. New York: Human Rights Watch.

Human Rights Watch. (2009) *Democracy on Rocky Ground: Armenia's Disputed 2008 Presidential Election, Post-election Violence, and the One-Sided Pursuit of Justice*. New York: Human Rights Watch.

Ishkanian, A. (2008) *Democracy Building and Civil Society in Post-Soviet Armenia*. London: Routledge.

Ishkanian, A. (2015) Self-determined Citizens? A New Wave of Civic Activism in Armenia. *Open Democracy*, 16 June. Available at: https://www.opendemo cracy.net/en/selfdetermined-citizens-new-wave-of-civic-activism-in-arm enia/ (accessed 17 May 2019).

Ishkanian, A. (2016) From Civil Disobedience to Armed Violence: Political Developments in Armenia. *Open Democracy*, 19 July. Available at: https:// www.opendemocracy.net/en/odr/from-civil-disobedience-to-armed-viole nce-political-developments-in-armen/ (accessed 17 May 2019).

Ishkhanyan, V. and Babajanyan A. (2004) *Hasvhehardar: Halatsanq ev Dimadrut'yun. [Reprisal: Persecution and Resistance]*. Yerevan: Center for Free Speech.

Iskandaryan, A. (2005) Fenomen Tsvetnykh Revolyutsiy kak Yadro Politicheskogo Diskursa v Stranakh Yuzhnogo Kavkaza. In: Iskandaryan A. ed., *Caucasus Media Institute, Caucasus-2004: Yearbook of the Caucasus Media Institute*. Yerevan: Caucasus Media Institute, 6–16.

Kowalevski, D. (1979) The Armenian National Unity Party: Context and Program. *Armenian Review*, 31 (4): 362–70.

Levitsky, S. and Way, L. (2010) *Competitive Authoritarianism: Hybrid Regimes After the Cold War*. Cambridge: Cambridge University Press.

Lragir.am. (2017) 'Hanun Gitut'yan Zargats'man 2004' Nakhadzernogh Khmbi Andamneri Haytararut'yunĕ. *Lragir.am*, 8 November. https://www.lragir. am/2017/11/08/164322/ (accessed 8 April 2020).

Manukyan, S. (2006) Vozniknovenie Natsionalisticheskogo Diskursa i Podpol'nogo Dvizheniya v Armenii v Nachale 1960-ykh godov. In: Gerasimova, E. and Lezhava, N., eds, *Yuzhny Kavkaz: Territorii, Istorii, Lyudi*. Tbilisi: Heinrich Boell Stiftung, 81–92.

Markedonov, S. (2016) Armenia's Changing Culture of Protest. *Carnegie.ru*, 27 July. Available at: https://carnegie.ru/commentary/64185 (accessed 17 May 2019).

Marutyan, H. (2018) Karabakh Movement or What was Happening in Armenia 30 Years Ago. *EVN Report*, 25 February. https://www.evnreport.com/politics/ the-karabakh-movement-or-what-was-happening-in-soviet-armenia-30- years-ago (accessed 17 May 2019).

OSCE/ODIHR (Organization for Security and Co-operation in Europe/ Office for Democratic Institutions and Human Rights). (1996) Election Observation Mission Armenia Presidential Election. Final Report, 24 September. Warsaw: OSCE/ODIHR.

OSCE/ODIHR. (1998) Election Observation Mission Armenia Presidential Election, 16 March and 30 March. Final Report, 9 April. Warsaw: OSCE/ ODIHR.

OSCE/ODIHR. (1999) Election Observation Mission Armenia, Parliamentary Elections, 30 May 1999. Final Report, 30 July 1999. Warsaw: OSCE/ODIHR.

OSCE/ODIHR. (2003) Election Observation Mission Armenia Presidential Election, 19 February and March 5. Final Report, 28 April. Warsaw: OSCE/ODIHR.

OSCE/ODIHR. (2008) Election Observation Mission Armenia Presidential Election, 19 February. Final Report, 30 May. Warsaw: OSCE/ODIHR.

OSCE/ODIHR. (2013) Election Observation Mission Armenia Presidential Election, 18 February. Final Report, 8 May. Warsaw: OSCE/ODIHR.

Panorama. (2017) Transparency International and Sksel a Youth Movement Organize Election Fair in Komitas Park. *Panorama.am*, 5 May. Available at: https://www.panorama.am/en/news/2007/05/05/transparency/1407650 (accessed 17 May 2019).

Panossian, R. (2006) *The Armenians: From Kings and Priests to Merchants and Commissars*. New York: Columbia University Press.

Paturyan, Y. J. and Gevorgyan, V. (2016) *Civic Activism as a Novel Component of Civil Society*. Yerevan: Turpanjian Center for Policy Analysis American University of Armenia.

Petrosyan, S. (2018) Rodennots'n u Hanrapetut'yan Hraparakĕ. *Evnmag.com*, 18 September. https://evnmag.com/%D5%BC%D5%B8%D5%B8%D5%A4%D5%A5%D5%B6%D5%B6%D5%B8%D6%81%D5%B6-%D5%B8%D6%82-%D5%B0%D5%A1%D5%B6%D6%80%D5%A1%D5%BA%D5%A5%D5%BF%D5%B8%D6%82%D5%A9%D5%B5%D5%A1%D5%B6-%D5%B0%D6%80%D5%A1%D5%BA%D5%A1%D6%80%D5%A1%D5%AF%D5%A8-1023df06a8db (accessed 17 May 2019).

Silaev, N. and Fomin, I. (2018) My Step Aside from Sasna Tsrer: The Dynamics of Protest Coalitions in Armenia, 2016 and 2018. *Demokratizatsiya: The Journal of Post-Soviet Democratization*, 26 (4): 483–507.

Shubladze, R. and Khundadze, Ts. (2017) Balancing the Three Pillars of Stability in Armenia and Georgia. *Caucasus Survey*, 5 (3): 301–22.

Suny, R. G. (1993) *Looking Toward Ararat: Armenia in Modern History*. Bloomington: Indiana University Press.

Ter-Abraamyan, H. (2006) Yerevanskaya Gorodskaya Sreda i Inakomyslie. In: Gerasimova, E. and Lezhava, N., eds, *Yuzhny Kavkaz: Territorii, Istorii, Lyudi*. Tbilisi: Heinrich Boell Stiftung, 13–37.

de Waal, T. (2016) Armenia's Crisis and the Legacy of Victory. *Open Democracy*, 3 August. Available at: https://www.opendemocracy.net/en/odr/armenia-s-crisis-and-legacy-of-victory/ (accessed 17 May 2019).

Whitney, C. (1978) Georgian and Armenian Pride Lead to Conflicts with Moscow. *The New York Times*, 26 June. https://www.nytimes.com/1978/06/26/archives/georgian-and-armenian-pride-lead-to-conflicts-with-moscow-georgian.html

Zolyan, M. (2010a) Armenia. In: Ó Beacháin, D. and Polese, A., eds, *The Colour Revolutions in the Former Soviet Republics: Successes and Failures*. London and New York: Routledge, 83–100.

Zolyan, M. (2010b) Armenia's Facebook Generation: Social Networks and Civic Activism in Armenia. *Newsletter of the Institute of Slavic, Eastern European and Eurasian Studies,* University of California, Berkeley, Fall 2010.

Zolyan, M. (2011) Armenia's 'Velvet Revolution': Successes and Failures. In: Jobelius, M., ed., *South Caucasus: 20 Years of Independence*. Washington DC: Friedrich Ebert Stiftung, 41–59.

Zolyan, M. (2016) The Standoff in Yerevan. *Open Democracy*, 20 July. Available at: https://www.opendemocracy.net/en/odr/standoff-in-yerevan/ (accessed 17 May 2019).

Zolyan, M. (2017) To Be or Not to Be Prime-Minister? Serzh Sargsyan's Dilemma and What it Means for Armenia's Politics. *EVN Report*, 8 August. https://www.evnreport.com/politics/to-be-or-not-to-be-prime-minister (accessed 17 May 2019).

Zolyan, M., Mkrtchyan, S. and Hovhannisyan, H. (2016) *A New Beginning: State-Building and Representation of the Events of 1988–1991 in the Political Discourse of Republic of Armenia*. Yerevan: Regional Studies Center.

3

How Serzh Sargsyan and the Republican Party of Armenia lost control of a competitive authoritarian system

Laurence Broers

Introduction

On 23 April 2018, Agence France Presse reported Serzh Sargsyan's resignation under the headline 'Armenia's "soft" authoritarian' (AFP 2018). This headline flagged not only the peaceful manner of his departure but also Sargsyan's image over the preceding decade as Armenia's president. Compared to many of his post-Soviet peers, Sargsyan had a reputation as a 'consensual' politician. He regularly consulted experts and activists from civil society, and unusually for an autocrat, looked upon ridicule with equanimity. For years he had tolerated parody comparing him to the Soviet children's cartoon character Cheburashka, accounting for the strange spectacle of demonstrators burning and stamping on Cheburashka toys in the streets of Yerevan during the 'Velvet Revolution'. And with his political survival at stake, Sargsyan neither shut down the internet nor used force to disperse protesters. More Eduard Shevardnadze than Joseph Stalin, Sargsyan appears destined to go down in history as a mild autocrat who, at the brink, opted for statesmanship. Yet as scholars of authoritarianism remind us, authoritarian leaders are distinct from the regimes they lead. The aura of softness surrounding Serzh Sargsyan belies the prominence of coercion in Armenia's post-Soviet history.

Since independence Armenia has been repeatedly convulsed by episodes of political violence. Some of this violence has been insurgent terror directed against the state. Most notoriously, in October 1999, assassins broke into the National Assembly building and murdered several key figures of the national leadership, including Prime Minister Vazgen Sargsyan and Parliamentary Speaker Karen Demirchian. More recently, a fringe oppositional group, *Sasna Tsrer*, seized a police station in a Yerevan suburb in July 2016, leading to the deaths of two policemen and a sympathizer bringing the insurgents supplies (see Chapter 2). State violence directed against dissent has been no less prominent. In 1996, security forces broke up crowds protesting the results of presidential elections awarding a narrow victory to Levon Ter-Petrossian. More than a decade later, on 1 March 2008, police violently scattered Ter-Petrossian's supporters, now in opposition, protesting Serzh Sargsyan's narrow victory in presidential elections. In events still considered an open wound in Armenia today, eight demonstrators and two servicemen were killed, and as many as 150 or more were injured.[1] Thus, if Sargsyan left office with a reputation for softness intact, we must concede that the edges of contentious politics in post-Soviet Armenia have at times been very hard indeed.

Juxtaposed with the Velvet Revolution's peaceful outcome in April 2018, this history raises important questions. A first question concerns the prevalence of political competition in Armenia. Even if the country's trajectory since independence has often been parsed as a 'failed transition', this is not for want of contested politics. Why has Armenia featured such vigorous contestation? A second question is how this contentious history can be reconciled with authoritarian endurance. In other words, why did Armenia's initially promising transition never happen, despite a seemingly pluralistic and competitive domestic arena? And finally, one of the most critical questions posed by the Velvet Revolution is why was coercion as a response to mass mobilization possible in 2008 but not a decade later? How and why did Serzh Sargsyan and the ruling Republican Party of Armenia (RPA) lose control over the system they had created? This chapter seeks answers to these questions from the perspective of the regime that existed in Armenia until 2018, and the decline of its authoritarian power. The chapter aims first to explain the sources of competitive politics in post-Soviet Armenia, before turning to explanations of why these did not lead to democratic transition and how authoritarian rule was sustained. Finally, the chapter turns to the outcomes of the Velvet Revolution to explain why a regime that had appeared stable collapsed so quickly and unexpectedly in April 2018.

The sources of competitive politics in Armenia

Armenians wryly observe that theirs is a nation of kings, in which every individual is opinionated enough to be leader. Another joke has it that from two Armenians, you'll get three political parties. These stereotypes allude to a significant political reality: what might be termed the disputatiousness of Armenian political culture and the highly competitive nature of the country's post-Soviet politics. This reality owes not to innate cultural traits, of course, but to the impacts of three significant structural factors, namely, a vibrant nationalist tradition, a fractured political elite and a political economy scarce in resource rents.

The historically conditioned potential for nationalism, rooted in pre-communist traditions of literacy and schooling in the national culture, to express opposition to Soviet rule is a significant determinant of post-Soviet regime trajectories (Way and Casey 2018). The Armenian awakening (*zartonk*), beginning in the eighteenth century, contributed significantly to the modernization of Armenian culture and its transformation into a national identity. By 1926, nearly 40 per cent of the population of Soviet Armenia was literate (Kaiser 1994: 130), a relatively high figure contributing to the potential for anti-Soviet, non-communist elites to later form (and, under certain conditions, attempt a transition to democracy). From the 1960s, there was a vivid dissident culture in Soviet Armenia, combining popular sentiment focused on the memory of genocide (commemorated annually from 1965), anti-Soviet sentiment and an ideology of territorial restoration focused on claims to lands in Turkey and elsewhere in Soviet Transcaucasia. By the 1980s, this culture had essentially displaced communist ideology in Armenia, which had become a 'game' at which Soviet Armenian officials were adept (Panossian 2006: 380). However, while endowed with a national culture fiercely distinct from Soviet ideology, due to the historical fragmentation of spaces and people identified as Armenian, Armenian political culture was itself extremely fractured: among Western and Eastern Armenian linguistic and cultural traditions, dual Catholicosates of the Armenian Church at Echmiadzin in Armenia and Antelias in Lebanon, myriad diaspora communities, plural (and rival) political parties in the diaspora, territorialized Armenian communities in Georgia and Azerbaijan, and the disputed primacy of revolutionary or evolutionary approaches to achieving Armenian goals. These fractures were not resolved by sovereignty in 1991. As Gerard Libaridian observed in 2004, the 'absence of consensus underlies Armenian politics today' (Libaridian 2004: 9).

A second critical variable in post-Soviet regime trajectories is the legacy of the 1985–91 perestroika era for elite unity. The cohesiveness or fracture of political elites can be understood in terms of Bruce Bueno de Mesquita and his co-authors' 'selectorate theory' (Bueno de Mesquita et al. 2002). According to their theory, in non-democratic contexts the selectorate (*s*) comprises the set of people who have an institutional say in the choice of leader, while the winning coalition (*w*) is the minimum number of individuals needed to retain power. Winning coalitions are small in authoritarian states, consisting essentially of the autocrat and his inner circle, but selectorates can vary according to variables such as elite unity and economic resources. Where the selectorate is large, winning coalition members are more likely to be loyal, as they can easily be replaced. Yet where the selectorate is small, the possibility of landing in a new winning coalition is higher, and defection is more likely. Bueno de Mesquita and his co-authors frame this as the 'loyalty norm', arrived at by the ratio of the winning coalition to the selectorate (*w/s*). Eric McGlinchey used these insights to argue that perestroika-era legacies for ruling parties were a key factor mediating the size and stability of selectorates in Central Asia, and the kind of authoritarianism that resulted (McGlinchey 2011). While Uzbekistan and Kazakhstan preserved unified executive-oriented ruling parties, Kyrgyzstan did not, contributing to a competitive – if not democratic – politics of elite fracture in that republic.

These insights frame the competitiveness of post-Soviet Armenian politics as a result of the small and fragmented selectorate inherited from the perestroika era. In the late 1980s, the Armenian Communist Party (ArmCP) was discredited by its inability to deliver in the two paramount policy theatres of the day – unification with Nagorny Karabakh and relief following the devastating earthquake in north-west Armenia on 7 December 1988. In its place, the Karabakh Committee, subsequently institutionalized as the Pan-Armenian National Movement (PANM), appeared as a second or shadow government. The Karabakh movement initially expressed loyalty to the Soviet centre for as long as Armenians believed Moscow would meet its demands. When it rapidly transpired that this would not be the case, the Karabakh issue became a powerful engine of anti-Soviet Armenian nationalism. As anti-Soviet sentiment took off, the ArmCP crumbled rapidly as a political force. Even though it won over half of the seats in May 1990 elections to the Supreme Soviet (parliament), only 25 of its 136 deputies were able to form a faction (Iskandaryan, Mikaelian and Minasyan 2016: 43). The party ran into serious personnel problems, being unable to recruit and supply personnel for senior positions (Iskandaryan, Mikaelian and Minasyan 2016: 44); between 1988 and 1991, the ArmCP Central Committee ran through four first secretaries, and the party did not even nominate a candidate in Armenia's first presidential election in October 1991 (Iskandaryan, Mikaelian and Minasyan 2016: 46). Armenia was one of the first Soviet republics to feature a non-communist government, as the PANM became the dominant force and Levon Ter-Petrossian Armenia's first post-Soviet president, winning 83 per cent of the vote in October 1991. The legacy of this era was that unlike in Soviet successor states where communist elites simply adopted a symbolic nationalism and carried on, post-Soviet Armenian presidents did not inherit a large executive-oriented political party; instead they needed to continually construct winning coalitions from within a fragmented political elite.

Elite fracture combined with a third structural factor conditioning political competition: Armenia's economic resource profile. While the structure of the Soviet economy diminished the self-sufficiency of all of the Union's constituent republics, Armenia was the least self-sufficient. Industrialized rather than agrarian, its economy was oriented to complex industrial production dependent on import and export flows synchronized with units elsewhere in the Soviet Union that rapidly ceased to exist in the early 1990s. Similarly, while all Soviet successor states experienced severe economic decline with the collapse of the command economy, Armenia's was especially severe – compounded by escalation to full-scale war in 1992 and Azerbaijan's long-term blockade of previously crucial communications routes. Armenia's GDP dropped by 56 per cent in 1990–3, and half a million jobs – accounting for one third of all those employed – disappeared (Iskandaryan, Mikaelian and Minasyan 2016: 49). In this environment informality flourished. Armenian specificities – opportunities to plunder earthquake aid and prolonged violent conflict – compounded wider post-Soviet trends. Thus, while Armenia had been a leader in the early independence period in terms of land privatization, the introduction of a national currency and the stabilization of monetary policy, the war with Azerbaijan empowered commodity-based cartels, which became the basis for enduring patron-client networks. Armenia consequently emerged from the two-year war with Azerbaijan as a strong coercive state, but a weak developmental one. Without significant natural resources, it was less a rentier than a kleptocratic economy that emerged, with flourishing informality and low extractive capacity shored up by Russian asset-for-debt acquisitions, diasporan investment and remittances.[2]

Armenia's post-independence trajectory consequently reflects the impacts of a contested national tradition, competition within the elite and scarce resources in repeatedly narrow presidential wins and the transience of ruling parties. In 1996, Ter-Petrossian was re-elected with 51.7 per cent of the vote, over Vazgen Manukyan's 41.3 per cent. His successor, Robert Kocharian, never won a first-round vote, attracting only 39 per cent in 1998 and 49.5 per cent in 2003. In 2008, Serzh Sargsyan won with 52.8 per cent, which rose to 58 per cent when he was re-elected in 2013. These percentages, augmented by fraud, indicate the reality of electoral competition. Super-majority wins on the back of large and well-financed selectorates, of the kind seen in Azerbaijan or Kazakhstan, were beyond the realm of possibility for Armenian presidents. The PANM served as a catch-all coalition unifying the independence movement for as long as the Soviet Union existed, but fragmented soon after to yield the principal opposition party, Vazgen Manukyan's National Democratic Party, in addition to a host of smaller parties. According to European Commission data, by the mid-1990s, no political party commanded more than 28.8 per cent of voter support; in a 1997 poll, no less than 43.3 per cent indicated that they 'would never vote for' the PANM – a remarkably high percentage for what was supposedly a ruling party (Iskandaryan, Mikaelian and Minasyan 2016: 76–7). After Ter-Petrossian's resignation in 1998, the PANM was also exiled, to return in 2012 only after a major re-brand.

Armenia therefore featured a fragmented arena that was potentially conducive to political pluralism, and by implication democracy. Yet despite multiple determinants of political pluralism, Armenia remained doggedly resistant to a full democratic transition. While many elections were fiercely contested and oppositional forces frequently mounted effective electoral campaigns, none of Armenia's elections over its first twenty-six years of independence were free of controversy. Two parliamentary elections, in 1998 and 2007, attracted faint approbation from the international monitoring missions fielded by the Organization for Security and Co-operation in Europe (OSCE). The overall trend, however, was towards the monetization of votes by an impoverished electorate (Gilbreath and Balasanyan 2017). For fourteen years between 2004 and 2018, Armenia flatlined at a score of 4.5–5 on Freedom House's scale from 1 ('free') to 7 ('not free'), situating the country at the harder end of an intermediate 'partly free' category (Freedom House 2018).

This conjunction of competitive politics and authoritarian endurance account for Armenia's membership of the 'competitive authoritarian' set of post–Cold War regimes (Levitsky and Way 2010). In their seminal study, Steven Levitsky and Lucan Way identified competitive authoritarian regimes as an emergent regime type responding to the decline of authoritarian patronage after the end of the Cold War. These regimes adopted the formal institutions of democracy, such as multiparty elections and democratic constitutions, but deployed a wide range of informal and authoritarian practices to ensure that the performance of competitive politics did not spill over into a real transfer of power. Competition in such regimes, then, is free (up to a point), but not fair. As Levitsky and Way note, competitive authoritarian regimes may transition to democracy, consolidate into fully fledged authoritarian regimes or experience repeated power transitions without democratizing. Armenia, however, did not fit easily into these patterns. In the two decades following 1998, it neither democratized nor consolidated into a fully authoritarian state, nor did it experience power transitions – a colour revolution – from one elite faction to another. Given its contentious politics, the fractured nature of its elite and the lack of cohesive patronage, how should authoritarian endurance in Armenia be interpreted?

Authoritarian endurance in Armenia: legitimation, repression and co-optation

In a 2017 study, Rati Shubladze and Tsisana Khundadze argued that authoritarian endurance in Armenia could be explained in terms of Johannes Gerschewski's model of the 'three pillars of stability' (Gerschewski 2013). Briefly put, Gerschewski's model argues that authoritarian regimes operate through the balancing of three core pillars of policy: their efforts to legitimate their rule, to repress or coerce dissent, and to co-opt potential rivals. Under Presidents Kocharian and Sargsyan, Shubladze and Khundadze argued that the Armenian case 'demonstrates a successful stabilization of [these] three pillars' (2017: 316). In this section, I build on these authors' insights and link them to the preceding analysis.

Legitimation

The question of legitimacy for Armenia's first post-Soviet elites was embedded within the movement for unification with Nagorny Karabakh, subsequent military victory over Azerbaijan and the national security concerns that proceeded from it (Ghaplanyan 2018). Presidents Ter-Petrossian, Kocharian and Sargsyan all came to power on the basis of a political narrative focused on Karabakh, even if the emphasis varied. Ter-Petrossian sought to rein in ethno-nationalism with an emphasis on statehood as a framework within which to solve Armenian problems. Under Kocharian and Sargsyan, however, identity and Armenian exceptionalism came to dominate the narrative (Ghaplanyan 2018). As regime commitments to democratization and reform proved illusory, the capacities to provide national security and sustain Armenian war gains increasingly framed the narrative about legitimacy. This owed, on the one hand, to the high degree of trust in the military in the wake of victory, and on the other hand, to the foregrounding of national security by the prospect of a deeply asymmetric rivalry with oil-rich Azerbaijan. A 2007 poll indicated a trust rating of 85 per cent in the army, with the church coming second at 77 per cent (IRI et al. 2007: 54). This declined over the following decade (see further), but nevertheless continued to exceed trust in the executive at a rate of 3:1 or more (Caucasus Barometer 2018). Under Presidents Kocharian and Sargsyan, the Armenian government, unlike in Georgia, did not seek to win legitimacy through social programmes, but relied instead on strategies of repression and co-optation (Shubladze and Khundadze 2017: 307).

Repression

Multiple forms of low-intensity repression were deployed under Presidents Ter-Petrossian, Kocharian and Sargsyan, including the outlawing of specific parties, the targeting of funders of opposition and pressure on oppositional media outlets. Without the restriction of explicit aspirations to join a Euro-Atlantic axis, however, regimes in Armenia enjoyed leeway to exercise more direct coercion. This was deployed to deal with recurring popular mobilization. Although Armenia had the smallest population of any of the states examined in their wide-ranging study, Levitsky and Way note (2010: 213) that the opposition was more mobilized in absolute terms than any other case, except Ukraine in 2004. Direct coercion, the capacity for which was an important legacy of the Karabakh war, was repeatedly used to meet this challenge. Paramilitary groups had been a prominent feature of the domestic political scene in Armenia since 1989–90. These were later reined in to form the Armenian armed forces that waged and won the Karabakh war. A crucial legacy to the post-Soviet Armenian state was a large and cohesive security force, cemented by this common experience and possessed of the 'stomach' to use force against a civilian population. In 1996, Vazgen Manukyan's supporters were violently dispersed by security forces with water cannon and teargas, resulting in fifty-nine injuries (Navasardian 1996). In April 2004 demonstrations against President Robert Kocharian were violently dispersed on Yerevan's Baghramian Avenue (Mediamax 2004). The 1 March 2008 post-electoral violence superseded these earlier incidents in lethality (on these events see Shirinyan 2011). Thus, naked coercion at moments of contentious politics was needed repeatedly in Armenia in order to substitute for more genuine political hegemony.

Co-optation

The periodic use of coercion to repress dissent is politically very costly. Combined with the small and fragmented political elite bequeathed to post-Soviet Armenia by the perestroika era, this made co-optation a particularly important pillar of authoritarian survival. As we have seen, Presidents Ter-Petrossian, Kocharian and Sargsyan all confronted the problem of forming a winning coalition from within the narrow confines of a fractured political elite. Moreover, rather than membership of a large, well-financed and loyal selectorate, anyone with sufficient economic resources could acquire membership of it, defined as 'those who have the positions ... to aspire to make and break leaders' (Bueno de Mesquita et al. 2002: 561). This created the opening for different kinds of political group to gain entry to the selectorate.

These groups leveraged different sources of material and symbolic capital to gain access to the selectorate, and were often enabled to do so by incumbent presidents unable to sustain winning coalitions without them (see Table 3.1).

In the early 1990s, the first such newcomers were the 'early entrepreneurs', those who leveraged know-how and Soviet black-market connections to gain access to the privatization process. Khachatur 'Grzo' Sukiasyan is the exemplar of this group, who worked in the Ministry of Industry in 1992–4 and later supported Ter-Petrossian's return to politics in 2008.[3] A second and much more important group was the 'veterans', those who took control of key commodities and economic sectors under conditions of blockade and war in 1989–94 and those who fought the war, often at the head of their own paramilitary formations. The relatively protracted nature of violent conflict compared to other post-Soviet theatres (except Chechnya) and the fact of military victory mediated the prominence of this group. The quintessential figure here is Vazgen Sargsyan, the founder of the powerful Yerkrapah veterans' association, who served as Armenia's minister of defence and then prime minister. In the aftermath of the Karabakh war, the 'veterans' enjoyed enormous symbolic capital and were able to impose themselves on President Ter-Petrossian, as he faced a serious challenge from his former colleague Vazgen Manukyan in the 1996 presidential election. Ter-Petrossian's alignment with Yerkrapah was hardly voluntary, and as events transpired, ended with his own removal and prolonged exile from power. The 'veterans' encroachment on the selectorate was cut short by the assassinations of Vazgen Sargsyan and several of his allies in the National Assembly in October 1999. President Robert Kocharian, a native of Karabakh without a power base in Armenia, subsequently built his own winning coalition by bringing in a number of big business operators. Coming to be known by the generic term 'oligarchs', these figures were defined by loyalty to 'veteran' patrons or to Kocharian and Serzh Sargsyan (then serving as minister of defence). Some 'oligarchs' entered parliament, bringing with them a specific quantity of votes, and some formed their own political parties serving the function of 'loyal opposition'. The archetypal figure here is Gagik 'Dodi Gago' Tsarukyan, a businessman with wide holdings who later formed the Prosperous Armenia party.

Co-opting newcomers to the selectorate provided presidents with additional resources with which to construct their winning coalitions. But this also came at a significant risk. One risk was take over. This is in effect what happened to President Ter-Petrossian, who was forced to resign by an alliance between Kocharian, then his prime minister, and the 'veterans'. A longer-term, systemic cost was de-legitimation, and hence de-stabilization of the pillar of legitimacy. As noted earlier, all of Armenia's presidents drew

Table 3.1 Expanding Winning Coalitions in Post-Soviet Armenia

Group	Sources of Wealth/ Influence	Examples
The 'early entrepreneurs' (early 1990s)	Proximity to privatization; commodity cartels working around blockade; Soviet black-market connections	Khachatur 'Grzo' Sukiasyan (SIL Holdings) Vano Siradeghian (Minister of Internal Affairs, 1992–6) Nikolay Barsegh
The 'veterans' (1994–9)	Control over wartime provisioning and supply; symbolic legitimacy of winning military victory	Vazgen Sargsyan (founder of Yerkrapah veterans' union; later served as minister of defence and prime minister; assassinated 1999) Manvel Grigoryan (leader of Yerkrapah, deputy minister of defence)
The 'oligarchs' (2000s)	Fealty to 'veteran' patrons; state-granted monopolies; entry into parliament; political party formation	Gagik 'Dodi Gago' Tsarukyan (Armenian Olympic Committee; business interests in Multi-group holding; leader of Prosperous Armenia party) Gurgen Arsenyan (metal, timber; founded United Labour Party) Ruben 'Nemetz Rubo' Hayrapetyan (head of Armenian Football Federation; business interests include tobacco, hotels and textiles)
The 'cronies'	Kinship ties to the president	Telman and Petros Ter-Petrossian Aleksandr 'Sashik' Sargsyan Mikayel 'Mishik' Minasyan

Source: Author's interview with Richard Giragosian, Director, Regional Studies Center, Yerevan, 8 May 2015.

NB: This table is arbitrary in the sense that some individuals have participated in more than one group.

upon the overarching narrative of the Karabakh war and national security, whether as a political revolutionary in the case of Levon Ter-Petrossian, or as wartime civil leaders in Nagorny Karabakh in the cases of Robert Kocharian and Serzh Sargsyan. Over time, however, the link between this narrative and those co-opted into the winning coalition became increasingly tenuous. 'Veterans' whose claim to have defended the nation was at least implicitly recognized by the populace were displaced by 'oligarchs', who could make no such claim. In many cases, 'veterans' simply became 'oligarchs'. Figures such as Yerkrapah chair Manvel Grigorian converted symbolic capital into material wealth, secluding rampant profiteering behind ritualized rhetoric evoking the transcendental and ever-present threat of 'the Turk'.[4] Neither were Armenian presidents willing or able to prevent encroachment on their winning coalitions by 'cronies', who leveraged kinship links to gain access to the elite (see Table 1). Legitimacy was the weakest of the three pillars of authoritarian stability in Armenia, as the lack of it came to define not only the leadership but also the political system as a whole. Systemic de-legitimation in turn spurred popular mobilization by the electorate seeking to reclaim politics from these patrimonial expansions of the winning coalition. This generated a succession of political crises necessitating, as we have seen, the use of naked coercion.

Coercion provided short-term 'resolutions' to these crises, but they only amplified the deeper problem of systemic de-legitimation against which crowds were mobilizing in the first place. From the 2000s, the RPA was developed as a vehicle for avoiding such crises and expanding a loyal selectorate. The RPA grew out of a paramilitary group formed in 1990 during the Karabakh conflict (Iskandaryan, Mikaelian and Minasyan 2016: 56). The party was initially rooted in nationalist and quasi-Aryan ideas encapsulated by the term *tseghakron*, associated with Garegin Nzhdeh and the early twentieth-century Armenian partisan tradition.[5] The party became part of Ter-Petrossian's ruling coalition in 1995, and was briefly led by Vazgen Sargsyan before his assassination. With its associations of opposition to Levon Ter-Petrossian and legitimacy rooted in the Karabakh war, the RPA was later co-opted by Kocharian as an institutional solution to the absence of a strong executive-oriented party. The party became the key gateway to political mobility, as RPA membership became increasingly synonymous with political office through Kocharian and Sargsyan's presidencies (AREG 2014: 33). Under Sargsyan the RPA mainstreamed, in Armenian political scientist Alexander Iskandaryan's words, as 'a trade union of public officials and affiliated businesses offering career trajectories to ambitious young people without too many scruples' (Iskandaryan 2018: 469). As 'a machine with no ideological adhesive, purely a coalition of convenience',[6] the RPA was a project in stabilizing and institutionalizing a larger selectorate that would ease the persistent problem of constructing sufficient winning coalitions.

As Shubladze and Khundadze argued in 2017, after the rocky start to Sargsyan's presidency, by the latter half of the 2010s, his regime appeared to have found an effective balance among the three pillars of authoritarian stability. This was evident in Armenia's low profile in the democratic transition literature. The most commonly posed question about the country's regime politics was why transition had failed and Armenia appeared in the 'colour revolution' literature only as a counterfactual (Zolyan 2010). Tropes of citizen apathy, securitization and hopelessness dominated the discourse about the state of democracy in the country, inside and out.

The Velvet Revolution as legitimation failure, coercive decline and co-optation success

How do the aforementioned perspectives help us to understand the outcomes of April 2018? In this last section, I argue that from the perspective of regime power, the Velvet Revolution can be understood as a terminal destabilization of the three pillars of authoritarian stability. Simply stated, a series of events saw the haemorrhaging of Sargsyan's already sparse legitimacy, while also diminishing the regime's ability to use coercion to repress popular dissent. On the other hand, the regime's co-optation strategy appeared to have been sufficiently effective as to generate within the regime conceit, complacency and grave under-estimation of societal discontent. In this situation, it only took a few tactical errors on Sargsyan's part, duly committed, and a determined counterforce, provided by Nikol Pashinyan, to lead to a 'revolutionary' situation.

Legitimation failure

While a legitimacy deficit had become the norm for all leaders of post-Soviet Armenia, Sargsyan began his presidency with nothing less than a full-blown legitimacy crisis following the 1 March 2008 violence that accompanied his election as president. Successive foreign policy demarches, notably the demise of the attempted opening with Turkey and Armenia's volte face on membership of the Eurasian Economic Union (EAEU), further corroded Sargsyan's standing. National security nevertheless continued to stand in for other forms of legitimacy. This was possible due to the deteriorating state of security surrounding the Line of Contact with Azerbaijan, as escalating ceasefire violations and skirmishes generated a climate of insecurity peaking in 2014–16. But if Sargsyan was still able to draw upon the deep reservoir of symbolic legitimacy associated with those who fought the Karabakh war, there was a catch. He was thought of, in Richard Giragosian's memorable formulation, as the 'last of the Mohicans' (Mamyan 2013), that is, the last of a militarist elite that had come to power because of the conflict of the early 1990s. The 'last of the Mohicans' moniker captures both the tacit recognition that Sargsyan could still claim some legitimacy as a 'Mohican' who had defended the nation and, crucially, the expectation that he would soon be replaced by a different kind of leader.

In 2016–18, Sargsyan's tenuous claim to legitimacy unravelled through the collapse of the 'last of the Mohicans' premise. First, the 'four-day war' with Azerbaijan in April 2016 shattered the Mohican myth. To be sure, the Armenian deterrent against a wider war appeared to hold and little of strategic importance changed as a result. Yet the four-day war jolted Armenian society out of a well-worn confidence in its own military superiority, and accentuated the ambivalence of alliance with Russia – Azerbaijan's primary arms supplier. More than 90 Armenian servicemen died, in addition to a small number of civilians, and the prospect of Azerbaijani recapture of territories occupied in 1992–4 became more than an abstract threat. The regime's responses to the four-day war compounded public shock and disappointment. The firing of a small number of high-ranking military officials was insufficient to quell wider concerns, as the four-day war instigated a public debate about the role and influence of the army in Armenian society. Media coverage of issues such as the army's participation in elections, party membership within the army and corruption related to military expenditures increased.[7] Yet this trend towards a re-calibration of the relationship between army and society was deflected into a new direction by the 'Nation-Army' (*Azg-Banak*) doctrine propagated by new Minister of Defence Vigen Sargsyan from late 2016 (Pambukhchyan 2018). Although nebulous on detail, the concept posited at the very least a renewed equality between army and society; at worst, it posited a renewed subordination of society to army. In the context of a recent failure by the army to protect the nation, it was widely perceived as 'a re-enactment of the regime's entitlement to legitimacy'[8] and was roundly criticized by liberal forces in Armenian society (Titizian 2018).

Against this backdrop, Sargsyan's manoeuvres to prolong RPA and his own personal rule cast a growing cloud of doubt as to when – or indeed whether – he would leave the political stage. Armenia's transition to a parliamentary system could be sold as an approximation with the practices of Euro-Atlantic partners, and a kind of compensation for Armenia's abandonment of its association agreement with the European Union (EU) in favour of EAEU membership in 2013. It came with specific measures, justified by security concerns, to ensure a stable parliamentary majority (Galyan 2015). Few observers, inside or outside of Armenia, assumed that this majority would be constituted by any force other than the RPA. That left the question of who would become the country's prime minister and leader under the new parliamentary system from April 2018. Uncertainty surrounded this issue until late 2017, as Sargsyan appears to have toyed with different ideas under a wide variety of different pressures. Alternative succession figures in the form of Prime Minister Karen Karapetyan and Minister of Defence Vigen Sargsyan were plausibly discussed. Yet it appears that a combination of concerns about security after the four-day war and the cumulative impact of poor briefing on the mood in the country led Sargsyan on 11 April 2018 to renege on his earlier promise not to pursue nomination as prime minister. This came less than two weeks after another major blunder when Sargsyan had applied to privatize – and been granted ownership over – the formal presidential residence.[9] Adding insult to injury, the symbolism could not have been more obvious or ill-judged. Physically and figuratively, the state was being privatized by a narrow clique still resting on military laurels dating back to the 1990s that were simply no longer recognized by an exasperated populace.

Two significant vulnerabilities accompanied the transition from President to Prime Minister Serzh Sargsyan. The first was the window between his resignation as president on 9 April and his inauguration as prime minister on 17 April. Between these dates, the authoritarian trap would open briefly before resealing again. It was an opportune moment of tactical vulnerability in which to initiate a series of protest actions, diligently converted by Nikol Pashinyan and his followers. The second vulnerability was that under the new parliamentary system, 'you could topple the head of government without toppling the head of state'.[10] With the widely known former prime minister and diplomat Armen Sarkissian elected Armenian president under the new constitution in January 2018, ousting the prime minister appeared 'less subversive of security and the state'.[11] As had previously been the case, coercive capacity could potentially have compensated for legitimation failure and short-term vulnerabilities. But for a variety of reasons, in the decade between 2008 and 2018, the Armenian regime's ability to use coercion had undergone a dramatic decline.

Coercive decline

As Nikol Pashinyan and his associates mobilized during the 9–17 April window, they were aware that 'weapons had been repeatedly used [to quell protest] in the past; there was complete carte blanche for any regime in

Armenia to do this.'[12] Yet despite this past record, and the high stakes in terms of regime survival, coercion was not deemed a legitimate or realistic response. There are many ways to contextualize the Velvet Revolution's non-violent outcome: the opposition's strategic learning gained over a decade of protest, the non-violent tactics of protesters, Serzh Sargsyan's personality, and the digital deterrent of social media and an instant global audience, including Armenian communities across the world. All these are relevant to understanding the turn of events in Yerevan in April 2018. Here, I focus on coercive decline, meaning in particular decline in the *will* – as opposed to the capacity – to use coercion.

The key motivations of the military in any state are to maintain cohesion, to uphold prestige by being seen as an effective defender of the nation, and to secure economic interests for both the army as an institution and the individuals within it (Bellin 2012). Shooting civilians is of course extremely costly and can damage all of the military's core interests in cohesion, discipline, prestige and legitimacy. These costs may be mitigated, however, under some circumstances. If protesting crowds can be legitimately broken down into smaller identity categories, or plausibly depicted as small groups of troublemakers who are using violence, shooting on them may be easier to justify. These costs may also be mitigated if the military is still organized along patrimonial lines. If the military has no corporate identity of its own and is personally invested in the survival of a particular regime, it may be willing to kill for it. However, any reformed military with a distinct corporate identity will be more likely to see for itself a future separate from the regime, and will consider very carefully the costs for that future of fulfilling orders to shoot on civilians. Under these conditions, military leadership may be willing to give an authoritarian-turned-liability what David Sorensen has termed the 'velvet shove'.[13]

In 2018, neither of these mitigating factors was present, as they were, arguably, in 2008. While the crowd in 2008 had been substantial, numbering up to 40,000, it was associated predominantly with Levon Ter-Petrossian and supporters of the opposition. While many eyewitnesses of the protests from 19 February to 1 March 2008 attest to its peaceful tactics, stone-throwing, Molotov cocktails and some looting were also reported at the time (International Crisis Group 2008: 3). The crowd in 2018 was significantly larger and broader in composition: 'This crowd was a metonym for the nation and there was shock at the size of it. It was a crowd defined by kindness and discipline: people followed orders ... not a single shop window was broken'.[14] Timing also reinforced the homology of crowd, nation and non-violence. Swelling protests on the 17–22 April period anticipated the annual popular procession to the Tsitsernakaberd genocide memorial on 24 April. This was simply not a crowd that could be parsed or fragmented into categories such as 'opposition' or 'hooligans'.

Concurrently, patrimonial loyalties no longer offered a counter-logic for the use of violence, due to a significant degree of modernization within the Armenian armed forces and law enforcement agencies since the 2000s. In a 2005 report, researchers for the United Kingdom–based organization Saferworld concluded that the 'ten years since the ceasefire in Nagorno Karabakh have not seen major changes to the Armed Forces or the Ministry of Defence' (Avagyan and Hiscock 2005: 25). They observed that under conditions where no real reforms of the security sector had taken place, the 'only civilians that have any control over the Armed Forces are the President, the Defence Minister, and a small circle around them' (Avagyan and Hiscock 2005: 26). There appeared to be neither resources nor motivation to enact civilian control and professionalization of the armed forces, two central tenets of security sector reform. Serzh Sargsyan's replacement of Vano Siradeghian as Minister of Internal Affairs in 1996 alleviated but did not end that ministry's notoriety for corruption. A June 2002 Law on the Police downgraded the ministry to an adjunct body of the government, a move that many observers in Armenia saw as the personalization of President Kocharian's control over the police, 'no longer answerable to anyone but him' (Avagyan and Hiscock 2005: 27). In 2008, Kocharian also still enjoyed the personal loyalty of a variety of paramilitary and informal 'praetorian' units associated with his wider network.

Under President Sarsgyan, this context evolved significantly. His presidency coincided with the onset of a regional arms race, a gradual escalation in the degree and type of ceasefire violations along the Line of Contact with Azerbaijan, and a growing public understanding on the necessity and urgency of security sector reform. Sargsyan prioritized partnership with NATO through mechanisms such as the Euro-Atlantic Partnership Council, the Partnership for Peace (PfP) programme and the PfP Planning and Review Process, as one means to achieve this goal (Novikova and Sargsyan 2013: 11). The issue of the first Strategic Defence Review in 2011 indicated that security sector reform was receiving serious policy interest. The degree of progress should not be overestimated, yet in some areas it was tangible. One such area was Armenia's participation in peacekeeping operations under NATO's auspices in Kosovo, focused on establishing an Armenian Peacekeeping Battalion with complete interoperability with NATO forces (Novikova and Sargsyan 2013: 12). While the scope of professionalization overall remains limited due to the need to maintain a large army, this brigade was 'considered as a basis for the Armenian professional army', a vanguard for the stated policy aim of professionalizing the Armenian army (Novikova and Sargsyan 2013). It would be representatives of this battalion who gave Serzh Sargsyan the 'velvet shove' by marching with protesters in Yerevan on 22 April. Although Sargsyan was himself a member of the broader patrimonial network associated with those who came to power in 1998 and a former minister of defence of Armenia, as president, he had overseen the appointment of new types of professionalized military cadres: '[Minister of Defence] Seyran Ohanian and [Deputy Minister of Defence] David Tonoyan were not loyalists, and events proved that.'[15] Having invested in the professionalization of the military, Sargsyan – unlike Kocharian – was afraid of issuing an order that would not be followed.

Another significant factor is the army's own anger and frustration at being blamed for the violence on 1 March 2008.[16] Those events – never properly investigated – inaugurated a relative decline in public trust in the army, compounded by revelations of non-combat related deaths in 2011, and in the middle of the decade by a slew of scandals concerning corruption and political influence within the army. The same concerns dominated public perceptions of the army in the aftermath of the 2016 four-day war. An army that had ostensibly failed to defend the nation in April 2016, and which two years later fired on a peaceful crowd that in its scale and diversity embodied that same nation, would quite simply have been an army with no future. The coincidental conjunction of the protests with a sacred date in the national calendar only made the use of force a symbolically even more costly option.

Co-optation success

The possibility of a large-scale security operation to quell the April 2018 protests nevertheless still assumes that Sargsyan and his regime were capable of accurately perceiving the threat to their power. That perception did not materialize in time, however, due to the apparent effectiveness of the regime's co-optation strategy. Co-optation, as I have argued earlier, is structurally determined in the Armenian context by a fractured political elite and narrow winning coalitions. Ostensibly 'opposition' parties such as the Armenian Revolutionary Federation-Dashnaktsutyun (ARF-D) and the 'Land of Law' (Orinats Yerkir) were co-opted by being brought into Kocharian's and Sargsyan's winning coalitions. New actors appearing in the selectorate on account of their wealth, such as Gagik Tsarukyan, were also co-opted in the form of 'constructive' opposition.

Under Serzh Sargsyan's presidency, co-optation evolved to engage not only emerging powerful individuals and groups, but also ideas and discourses. This was in turn a product of authoritarian adaptation to a diversified media environment. Irina Ghaplanyan observes that Sargsyan's presidency differed from those of his predecessors in 'the intensity and sophistication with which his narrative was produced' due to his son-in-law Mikayel Minasyan's 'tighter and wider grip on television media to the employment of online media and social networks by an increasingly technocratic and young team aimed at popularizing Sargsyan and his policies' (Ghaplanyan 2018: 112–13). This apparatus was brought to bear in various co-optation projects.

First, Sargsyan actively pursued a number of foreign policies, such as rapprochement with Turkey and association with the EU, that neutralized the scope for Western criticism of authoritarianism in Armenia.[17] While also serving local goals, especially in the case of the EU association agreement, these moves in effect 'co-opted' important Euro-Atlantic interlocutors. Association with the EU was cut short by Russian intervention in 2013, yet Sargsyan then turned to constitutional reform to a parliamentary system as alternative route to the appearance of Western-friendly reform. Of course, the parliamentary transition was also rooted in domestic logic, but it served to co-opt voices likely to be critical of continued incumbency by any other means.

The centenary of the Armenian Genocide in 2015 offered another opportunity. Some of the most successful discourses of authoritarian power are those that produce and reflect social attitudes and opinions, in effect co-opting core popular beliefs (see Lewis, Heathershaw and Megoran 2018). The 2015 commemoration, with its associated ceremonies, publicity campaign and positioning of Armenia in the role of global watchdog on genocide, offered opportunities for the Armenian government to co-opt a deeply felt schema of identity politics into its brand. The canonization of one-and-a-half million victims by the Armenian Apostolic Church was a symbolic act affirming a rare moment of consensus between regime and society (France 24 2015).

Genocide commemoration also offered an opportunity for the subtle co-optation of more contrarian views. On 23 April 2015, Los Angeles–based diasporan Armenian rock band System of a Down (SOAD) played a concert on Yerevan's Republic Square. In the light of SOAD singer Serj Tankian's previous exchanges of sarcastic open letters on the state of Armenian politics with President Sargsyan (Panorama.am 2013), the concert had an obvious political subtext. Tankian did nothing to hide this on stage, where he called openly for the introduction of a genuine egalitarian and civic politics in the country. The rain-swept concert, attended by youths bearing the Armenian tricolour and posters emblazoned with rebellious slogans (one declared: 'Fuck System, Save Nature'), crystallized a moment of national elation and unity. I wrote in my notes afterwards:

For a moment at least, all the contradictions between an angry hard rock band of diasporans raised in Los Angeles and a weary post-Soviet republic dissolved. It was a night that the youngsters on the square will remember for the rest of their lives, a night when all the endless fractures and contradictions of being Armenian today were eclipsed. As all the best rock music is, this was rock as political activism, and anyone who had doubted the appropriateness of a rock concert on the eve of a genocide centenary saw their doubts similarly dissolve in the deluge. As if someone had really wanted to rain on the Armenian party, the driving rain that had only intensified as the concert went on, suddenly ceased shortly after SOAD left the stage. They did so after the various band members had hugged each other, and after a group hug that seemed to sum up SOAD's message: 'We have shit to deal with. But we've got this nation and we've got this republic. Let's get to work.'

Permitting what they knew would be an oppositional political celebration on Republic Square, which unlike Yerevan's Freedom Square was not a site previously associated with dissent (see Chapter 2), was in some ways a bold move by the Armenian authorities. It appeared to co-opt SOAD's dissident message, projecting a subliminal message about the openness of dissent in Sargsyan's Armenia, and consequently the reasonableness and acceptability of his regime. At the time the SOAD concert came off as a triumph for all concerned. But the fact that in April 2018 Republic Square served as the stage for a Velvet Revolution enacting the very same ideals that Tankian had evoked three years earlier indicated that it had been 'a huge strategic mistake to open up this space for this kind of presence among the population'.[18]

Perceiving this mistake was still in the future, however. Although its co-optation of *civil* society was rather limited, the regime's co-optation of *political* society appeared, on the basis of the April 2017 parliamentary elections, to be considerably more solid. These were the first elections to take place after the 2015 referendum on the transition to a parliamentary system, and the resulting parliament would play a key role in the transition scheduled for 2018. The election delivered the best possible regime result, with the RPA winning a 'modest' 49.2 per cent of the vote, with co-opted coalition partners Prosperous Armenia and the ARF-D winning 27.4 per cent and 6.6 per cent, respectively.[19] Therefore, despite the multiple setbacks that Sargsyan's presidency had encountered, the election delivered a parliament overwhelmingly in the palm of the incumbent. Moreover, this was achieved with neither clear condemnation by the OSCE election-monitoring mission nor popular protest. The OSCE election-monitoring report attests to the sophistication of election management in Sargsyan's Armenia, noting that the election 'was well administered and fundamental freedoms were generally respected'. Although some irregularities are noted, the report highlights a more diffuse and empirically elusive 'lack of public confidence and trust in the elections' (OSCE/ODIHR 2017: 1).

The election appeared to attest to several significant outcomes. The first was the implosion of the traditional opposition in the form of the Armenian National Congress (ANC), which received a mere 1.7 per cent. The ANC ran on a platform advocating, inter alia, compromise with Azerbaijan, which in the aftermath of the April war was a strategy akin to electoral suicide. Second was the rise of a new and seemingly less consequential opposition, the *Yelk'* ('Way Out') alliance, which received 7.8 per cent. Subsequent events would prove otherwise, but it is important to note that before 2018, Nikol Pashinyan was seen as a youngish firebrand rather than a serious politician, running a party, Civil Contract, that to all intents and purposes resembled a NGO more than a national party. Pashinyan did not enjoy wide confidence in the population or international community, and he was not regarded as a formidable figure on the Armenian political stage in the same way as Ter-Petrossian.[20] Third, and most importantly, the April 2017 parliamentary election appeared to attest to a new, long-sought after Armenian variant of hegemony by co-opting the populace itself. Civic activist and veteran electoral precinct chair Isabella Sargsyan captures the general climate of co-optation: 'These were the worst elections I had seen in 20 years of working in electoral precincts because there was no resistance … . And this was central Yerevan. [The incumbent regime] just distributed cash, and everyone sold out.'[21] This was, in other words, a 'civilized authoritarianism' that no longer needed to rely on truncheons and tear gas.

With the benefit of hindsight, we can now see that the April 2017 election in reality had two other crucial outcomes. The first was to generate a collective sense of shame that the election had indeed been sold by the populace to the regime. One year later, suppressed popular shame burst onto the streets of Yerevan in quest of redemption. (Election posters for the post-revolutionary December 2018 election capitalized on this emotion, depicting children enjoining voters not to 'sell my future'.) The second was that alongside public complicity, the election manufactured regime complacency. Sargsyan entered the final lap of his proposed transition lulled into a false sense of security, inaccurately briefed by his aides and vulnerable to surprise. In the words of Alexander Iskandaryan: 'As late as 20 April no one understood that a mass security operation might be necessary – and by 22 April everyone understood that such an operation was simply out of the question.'[22]

Conclusion

This chapter has sought to provide explanations for both the intense competitiveness in Armenian politics and the authoritarian endurance of its regime. I have explained competitiveness in Armenian politics in terms of historical legacies and structural factors resulting in a fractured political elite, a small selectorate and a continual struggle to build winning coalitions. Authoritarian rule was eventually stabilized through a balancing of the three pillars of legitimacy, repression and co-optation. Over time, however, these pillars became unbalanced as Serzh Sargsyan's regime increasingly neglected legitimacy, unwittingly oversaw a decline in the will to use coercion and focused disproportionately on co-optation. In hindsight, we can see that by 2018, the façade of stability in fact concealed advanced authoritarian decline.

The perspectives discussed in this chapter have a number of implications. The first is a refinement of our understanding of the regime type in post-Soviet Armenia, up to and including 2008, as not only a competitive authoritarian regime but also a *coercive* competitive authoritarian regime. This authoritarian outcome was mediated by the perestroika legacy of a small and fragmented elite, combined with low resources but high coercive power inherited from the Karabakh war. This can be contrasted with outcomes in Azerbaijan and Georgia (see Table 3.2). In Azerbaijan, Mikhail Gorbachev's large-scale intervention in January 1990 allowed the Azerbaijani communist party to be maintained. Although briefly ejected from power in 1992–3, the Azerbaijani communist elite returned to power and maintained the integrity of a large selectorate in the form of the New Azerbaijan Party, later bolstered by petrodollar flows. These conditions have mediated a higher loyalty norm than in Armenia and lavish public spending, resulting in a more hegemonic variant of authoritarianism (LaPorte 2013). In Georgia, the 9 April 1989 intervention by Soviet interior ministry troops failed to rescue Georgia's communist party, and the radical nationalist opposition captured power. With neither substantial resources nor high coercive power, however, Georgia exhibited a more competitive and less coercive variant of authoritarianism, characterized by Christofer Berglund (2014) as somewhere between dominant power politics, 'feckless pluralism' and democracy.

Second, this chapter highlights the importance of endogenous factors and path-dependent contingency in the outcomes of the Velvet Revolution. Its arguments substantiate the implicit claim to local, rather than geopolitical, causalities asserted by the term 'Velvet Revolution'. By the same token, this argument should not be taken to suggest that the Velvet Revolution was in any way pre-determined. Even if – as this and other chapters in this volume suggest – the Velvet Revolution or something like it was a strategic inevitability, given the base conditions in Armenia's political economy, in April 2018, it came as a devastating tactical surprise. Most of my interviewees in February 2019 concurred that had any other candidate apart from Serzh Sargsyan been nominated as prime minister, there would have been no comparable groundswell of protest. Even then, just two weeks before

Table 3.2 Variables Mediating Regime Politics in the South Caucasus[a]

	Perestroika Period	Economic Resources	Coercive Capacity	Authoritarian Outcome
Armenia	Limited intervention, Party collapse	Low	High	Coercive/competitive authoritarianism
Azerbaijan	Large-scale intervention, Party maintained	High	Medium	Hegemonic authoritarianism
Georgia	Failed intervention, Party collapse	Low	Low	Competitive authoritarianism/ 'feckless pluralism'

[a] Adapted from McGlinchey (2011: 46, Table 1.4).

Sargsyan's resignation, there was no notion among the small protests that what would transpire was actually possible. As late as 20 April, there appear to have been differences of opinion among Pashinyan and his associates on the appropriate strategy, as well as mental preparation for imminent legal prosecution – or worse.

Finally, the arguments presented in this chapter suggest that political competition will continue to be intense in Armenia. Defection, fragmentation and the struggle to sustain winning coalitions will continue to be salient features of the Armenian political scene. The continued presence in the Armenian parliament of 'velvet survivor' Gagik Tsarukyan indicates that there is still considerable room for informal alliances and doing politics 'the old way'. What remains to be seen is whether winning coalitions will democratize to sustainably include the electorate, taking Armenia on the path to dominant power politics and feckless pluralism, or whether authoritarian practices will be revived down the road to reconstitute a competitive authoritarian regime.

Acknowledgements

I am grateful to Armen Grigoryan, Stephen F. Jones and Anna Ohanyan for comments and advice in writing this chapter. All errors of fact or judgement remain mine alone.

Notes

1 The numbers of those injured in March 2008 is still uncertain, as many of those injured may not have sought forensic reports for fear of further persecution. During parliamentary hearings on the draft law on compensation, parliamentarian Lena Nazaryan cited the figure of 63 persons suffering severe or mid-level injuries, while Minister of Justice Artak Zeynalyan presented a list of 187 persons killed and injured, a number not yet finalized (Harutyunyan 2019).
2 Author's interview with Richard Giragosian, Director, Regional Studies Center, Yerevan, 8 May 2015.
3 In a throwback to the Soviet underworld, many of the big players in Armenia's informal politics have been known by a shortened nickname, the use of which reflects a simultaneous familiarity and contempt.
4 In a 2016 interview, Manvel Grigorian attributed all negative developments in post-Soviet Armenia from blockade and economic isolation to the 1999 parliamentary assassinations to 'the Turks'. Author's interview with Manvel

Grigorian, Chairman of the Board of Yerkrapah, Yerevan, 8 June 2016. Two years later Grigorian was publicly disgraced when police raids of his properties after the Velvet Revolution discovered hoards of clothing, food, medicine and other items donated to the army and population in Nagorny Karabakh in April 2016.

5 Author's interview with Richard Giragosian, Director, Regional Studies Center, Yerevan, 14 February 2019.

6 Author's interview with Alexander Iskandaryan, Director, Caucasus Institute, Yerevan, 6 February 2019.

7 Author's interview with Vahe Grigoryan, independent lawyer, Yerevan, 11 February 2019.

8 Author's conversation, foreign diplomat, Yerevan, February 2019.

9 Sargsyan subsequently demurred on 19 April in a virtue-signalling exercise that came too late (Armenpress 2018).

10 Author's interview with Babken Der-Grigorian, Acting Minister of the Diaspora, Yerevan, 19 February 2019.

11 Ibid.

12 Interview with Vahe Grigoryan.

13 Intervention by David Sorensen, Workshop on Regional Implications of Political Change in Tunisia and Egypt, Washington, D.C., 28 February 2011, cited in Bellin (2012: 134, endnote 33).

14 Author's interview with Anahit Shirinyan, independent analyst, Yerevan, 14 February 2019.

15 Interview with Giragosian, 14 February 2019.

16 Interview with Vahe Grigoryan.

17 Author's interview with Vladimir Karapetyan, Press Secretary to the Prime Minister, Yerevan, 20 February 2019.

18 Author's interview with Gevorg Ter-Gabrielyan, Director, Eurasia Partnership Foundation, Yerevan, 18 February 2019.

19 These results translated into 55.2 per cent of seats being allocated to the RPA, 29.5 per cent to Prosperous Armenia, 8.6 per cent to *Yelk'* and 6.7 per cent to the ARF-D.

20 Author's interviews, Yerevan, February 2019.

21 Author's interview with Isabella Sargsyan, civic activist, Yerevan, 18 February 2019.

22 Interview with Iskandaryan.

References

AFP (Agence France Presse). (2018) Serzh Sarkisian, Armenia's 'soft' Authoritarian. *AFP (Agence France Presse)*, 23 April. https://www.indoprem ier.com/ipotnews/newsDetail.php?jdl=Serzh_Sarkisian__Armenia_s__s

oft__authoritarian&news_id=1372792&group_news=ALLNEWS&news_d
ate=&taging_subtype=TURKEY&name=&search=y_general&q=TURKEY,%
20&halaman=1 (accessed 27 November 2019).

AREG (Scientific Youth Cultural Association). (2014) *The Political Elite of Post-
independence Armenia: Characteristics and Patterns of Formation.* Yerevan:
Edit Print.

Armenpress. (2018) Serzh Sargsyan Refuses the Ownership Right of the Private
House Granted to Him by Cabinet Decision – Aysor.am. *Armenpress.*
Available at: https://armenpress.am/eng/news/930605.html (accessed 15
April 2019).

Avagyan, G. and Hiscock, D. (2005) *Security Sector Reform in Armenia.* London:
Saferworld.

Bellin, E. (2012) Reconsidering the Robustness of Authoritarianism in the
Middle East: Lessons from the Arab Spring. *Comparative Politics*, 44 (2):
127–49.

Berglund, C. (2014) Georgia between Dominant-power Politics, Feckless
Pluralism and Democracy. *Demokratizatsiya*, 22 (3): 445–70.

Bueno de Mesquita, B., Morrow, J. D., Siverson R. M. and Smith, A. (2002)
Political Institutions, Policy Choice and the Survival of Leaders. *British
Journal of Political Science*, 32: 559–90.

Caucasus Barometer. (2018) Caucasus Barometer Time Series Dataset for
Armenia. Variable: Trust Towards Army. Available at: https://caucasusbaro
meter.org/en/cb-am/TRUARMY/ (accessed 15 April 2019).

France 24. (2015) Armenian church makes saints of 1.5 million genocide
victims. *France 24*, 23 April. Available at: https://www.france24.com/en/20
150423-armenia-church-turkey-canonization-sainthood-genocide-victims
(accessed 15 April 2019).

Freedom House. (2018) Armenia Profile. Available at: https://freedomhouse
.org/report/freedom-world/2018/armenia (accessed 15 April 2018).

Galyan, A. (2015) Gearing towards Consensualism or Unrestrained
Majoritarianism? Constitutional Reform in Armenia and its Comparative
Implications. *Constitutionnet*, 23 October. http://www.constitutionnet.org/
news/gearing-towards-consensualism-or-unrestrained-majoritarianism-co
nstitutional-reform-armenia (accessed 5 July 2018).

Gerschewski, J. (2013) The Three Pillars of Stability: Legitimation, Repression,
and Co-optation in Autocratic Regimes. *Democratization*, 20 (1): 13–38.

Ghaplanyan, I. (2018) *Post-Soviet Armenia: The New National Elite and the
New National Narrative.* London and New York: Routledge.

Gilbreath, D. and Balasanyan, S. (2017) Elections and Election Fraud in
Georgia and Armenia. *Caucasus Survey*, 5 (3): 238–58.

Harutyunyan, S. (2019) Marti 1-2-i iradardzut'yunneri hetevankʹov
p'vokhhatutsʹum statsʹvogh tuzhatsneri tʹivy 63-itsʹ kavelana. *1in.am*, 24
April. Available at: https://www.1in.am/2547543.html (accessed 3 June
2019).

IRI (International Republican Institute), Baltic Surveys Ltd/The Gallup
    Organization and the Armenian Sociological Association. (2007) *Armenia
    National Voter Study*. Available at: http://www.asa.sci.am/downloads/IRI
    /2007%20March%20Armenia-poll.pdf (accessed 15 April 2019).
Iskandaryan, A. (2018) The Velvet Revolution in Armenia: How to Lose Power
    in Two Weeks. *Demokratizatsiya: The Journal of Post-Soviet Democratization*,
    26 (4): 465–82.
Iskandaryan, A., Mikaelian, H. and Minasyan, S. (2016) *War, Business and
    Politics. Informal Networks and Formal Institutions in Armenia*. Yerevan:
    Caucasus Institute.
International Crisis Group. (2008) *Armenia: Picking up the Pieces*. Europe
    Briefing No. 48. Available at: https://www.crisisgroup.org/europe-central-as
    ia/caucasus/armenia/armenia-picking-pieces (accessed 15 April 2019).
Kaiser, R. (1994) *The Geography of Nationalism in Russia and the USSR*.
    Princeton: Princeton University Press.
LaPorte, J. (2013) Hidden in Plain Sight: Political Opposition and Hegemonic
    Authoritarianism in Azerbaijan. *Post-Soviet Affairs*, 31 (4): 339–66.
Levitsky, S. and Way, L. A. (2010) *Competitive Authoritarianism: Hybrid Regimes
    After the Cold War*. Cambridge: Cambridge University Press.
Lewis, D., Heathershaw, J. and Megoran, N. (2018) 'Illiberal Peace?'
    Authoritarian Approaches to Conflict Management. *Cooperation and
    Conflict*. DOI:10.1177/0010836718765902
Libaridian, G. J. (2004) *Modern Armenia: People, Nation, State*. New Brunswick
    and London: Transaction Publishers.
Mamyan, M. (2013) Richard Giragosian: 'President Sargsyan is the Last of the
    Mohicans'. *Hetq*, 23 October. Available at: https://hetq.am/en/article/30207
    (accessed 15 April 2019).
McGlinchey, E. (2011) *Chaos, Violence, Dynasty: Politics and Islam in Central
    Asia*. Pittsburgh: Pittsburgh University Press.
Mediamax. (2004) The 'Soap Bubble Revolution'. *Mediamax*, 8–14 April,
    republished 11 April 2019. Available at: https://www.mediamax.am/en/new
    s/5-10-15/33063/ (accessed 15 April 2019).
Navasardian, B. (1996) Bitter Victory in Yerevan. *WarReport*, 46: 18–19.
Novikova, G. and Sargsyan, S. (2013) Armenia. In: Centre for European and
    North Atlantic Affairs, ed., *Armenia and Security Sector Reforms: Challenges
    and Opportunities*. Bratislava: Centre for European and North Atlantic
    Affairs, 1–16. Available at: http://www.cenaa.org/data/databaza/Chapter-1-
    Armenia-Novikova-Sargsyan.pdf (accessed 10 June 2019).
OSCE/ODIHR (Office for Democratic Institutions and Human Rights). (2017)
    Republic of Armenia Parliamentary Elections 2 April 2017 OSCE/ODIHR
    Election Observation Mission Final Report. Available at: https://www.osc
    e.org/odihr/328226?download=true (accessed 15 April 2019).
Pambukhchyan, A. (2018) The 'Nation-Army' Concept: The Story of Failed
    National-Militaristic Propaganda in Armenia. *Foreign Policy Centre*, 18 July.

Available at: https://fpc.org.uk/the-nation-army-concept-the-story-of-fail
ed-national-militaristic-propaganda-in-armenia/ (accessed 10 June 2019).

Panorama.am (2013) Serzh Sargsyan Replies to Open Letter of Serj Tankian.
Panorama.am, 26 February. Available at: https://www.panorama.am/en/new
s/2013/02/26/sargsyan-tankyan/575544 (accessed 15 April 2019).

Panossian, R. (2006) *The Armenians. From Kings and Priests to Merchants and
Commissars*. London: Hurst & Co.

Shirinyan, A. (2011) *Armenia's Lost Spring: Challenging the Democracy*.
Documentary Film. Yerevan: n.p.

Shubladze, R. and Khundadze, T. (2017) Balancing the Three Pillars of Stability
in Armenia and Georgia. *Caucasus Survey*, 5 (3): 301–22.

Titizian, M. (2018) Is This What You Wanted? *EVN Report*, 3 April. https://ww
w.evnreport.com/raw-unfiltered/is-this-what-you-wanted (accessed 12 July
2018).

Way, L. A. and Casey, A. (2018) The Structural Sources of Postcommunist
Regime Trajectories. *Post-Soviet Affairs*, 34 (5): 317–32.

Zolyan, M. (2010) Armenia. In: Ó Beacháin, D. and Polese, A., eds, *The Colour
Revolutions in the Former Soviet Republics: Successes and Failures*. New York
and London: Routledge, 83–100.

Armenian civil society

Growing pains, honing skills and possible pitfalls

Yevgenya Jenny Paturyan

Introduction

In April 2018, peaceful mass mobilization of the Armenian public around opposition politician Nikol Pashinyan caught many observers and analysts by surprise. Before the dramatic protests, now widely referred to as the 'Velvet Revolution', most researchers described the Armenian public as rather apathetic and depoliticized (Hakobyan et al. 2010; Iskandaryan 2015; Mkrtichyan, Vermishyan and Balasanyan 2016). Armenian civil society was characterized as gradually developing but still largely detached from the broader public. Few people were involved in civil society organizations or informal groups. One could hardly speak of social movements in Armenia.

The largest cases of mobilization seen in Armenia before the April 2018 uprising were campaigns that attracted a few thousand people. One could mention the *Dem Em* ('I am against') protest against a pension reform in 2014 that attracted around 10,000 people at its peak, the 'Electric Yerevan' protest against an electricity price hike in 2015 (10,000–20,000 people) and demonstrations in support of peaceful resolution of the *Sasna Tsrer* ('Daredevils of Sassoun') incident, when a group of gunmen took a police station hostage in Yerevan in 2016 (see Chapter 2). News sources reported that 'thousands' joined those demonstrations. While these instances of mobilization made an important contribution to Armenia's political and civic life, none of them came close to the Karabakh movement beginning in 1988, which galvanized hundreds of thousands (some estimate the largest demonstrations reached half a million people) over extended periods of time.

For many Armenians, the demonstrations of 1988–9 remained an archetype of what a 'real' nationwide mobilization should look and feel like.

The April 2018 protests also started small. However, they grew bigger every day and spread beyond the capital, consistently displaying remarkable levels of self-organization and unwavering commitment to non-violence. In political science terms, Armenia witnessed a clear case of an 'upward scale shift', defined by Tilly and Tarrow (2015: 125) as 'coordination of collective action at a higher level (whether regional, national or even international) than its initiation'.[1] This chapter asks whether the strength of the mobilization, its self-organization and its peaceful nature can be attributed to Armenian civil society, at least to some extent? To address this question, the chapter looks at the recent history of Armenian civil society, the skills and strategies it has developed over the last three decades, differentiating between the formal (NGO sector) and the informal (activist campaigns) domains of Armenian civil society. It then looks at the contribution of Armenian civil society to the two weeks of mobilization in April 2018. The chapter concludes with a tentative discussion of potential pitfalls civil society faces in 'post-revolutionary' Armenia.

A few conceptual clarifications are in order. Civil society is a notoriously vague concept that can mean different things to different people. Its popularity among scholars, policy-makers, donors, activists, politicians and so on leads to it being used (and misused) in myriad ways, adding to the confusion. For the sake of clarity, a brief definition of the concept is in order.

One of the most prominent theoreticians of civil society, Michael Edwards, notes that there are three interrelated approaches to understanding civil society as forms, norms and spaces (Edwards 2011, 2013). When thinking of forms, scholars usually define civil society as a multitude of voluntary organizations and groups that operate outside of the market and the state domain and pursue goals beyond the individual self-interest of its members (Diamond 1999; Salamon, Sokolowski and List 2003; Anheier 2004). When discussing norms, authors in this field describe civil society as a society that is 'civil', that is, non-violent, tolerant, active, self-organized, public-spirited and so on. The emphasis is on qualities of good citizenship, rather than on forms of organizing or activities performed through collective action (Hall 2000; Trentmann 2000; Kopecký and Mudde 2003). This approach highlights the fact that civil society is inherently a normative concept. The understanding of civil society as a space emphasizes the fact that there is a sphere between the market, the government and private life where citizens join forces to discuss societal problems and elaborate possible solutions. This approach is inspired by the works of Habermas (1991, 1996).

This chapter looks at civil society as forms: formal and informal entities that operate mostly outside of the market and state domains. People engage in those entities voluntarily to pursue goals beyond their self-interest (Diamond 1999; Edwards 2013). Collective action within the realm of civil society can take many shapes: structured or informal, traditional or new, indigenous or inspired by foreign models. Edwards (2013) compares a civil society of a given country to an ecosystem, where diversity of organizational forms is a sign of health and robustness. According to this perspective, civil society should be diverse, for the sake of its own survival. But capturing the entire diversity of the ecosystem of Armenian civil society in a research project is a formidable task. To make it tangible, this chapter focuses on the two most common forms of Armenian civil society in action: NGOs (non-governmental organizations) and the so-called civic initiatives – activist campaigns that have become a common feature of Armenian civil life, as described further.

Having clarified some of the conceptual hurdles around the term 'civil society', and identified its most prominent Armenian manifestations, the chapter turns to a brief history of the development of Armenian civil society.

Armenian civil society: Three decades of development

Although the focus of this chapter is on recent history, it is important to note that Armenian civil society was not born around the time of the collapse of the Soviet Union. It existed in some form under the Soviet rule and the years (probably centuries) preceding it. Mass mobilization both for political and humanitarian purposes happened from time to time. The contribution of volunteers to the Battle of Sardarapat[2] and the building of the First Armenian Republic in 1918, the humanitarian role of civil society in the aftermath of the 1915 Genocide and the underground nationalist organizations of Soviet Armenia – and a large spontaneous demonstration in 1965[3] – are some of the manifestations of Armenian civil society. Numerous community organizations of the Armenian diaspora (see for example Libaridian 1999, Chapter 5) would also fall under the definition of civil society.

This chapter, however, focuses on Armenian civil society of the late 1980s to the present day, starting from the Karabakh movement and humanitarian relief both for refugees arriving from Azerbaijan and for the people who lost their homes and relatives during the devastating Spitak earthquake of 1988. The last thirty years of Armenian civil society development can be roughly divided into three stages (Ishkanian 2008; Hakobyan et al. 2010; Abrahamian and Shagoyan 2011; Ishkanian et al. 2013). We might be witnessing the fourth stage now, but it is too early to say. The dates are approximate; it is hard to say exactly when each stage started except for the Karabakh movement. The three plus one stages are:

I. The Karabakh movement and humanitarian aid (1988–91)
II. 'NGO-ization' of Armenian civil society (1992–2006)
III. Re-emergence of activism (2007–18)
IV. Post-revolution? (2018–?)

Stage I: The Karabakh movement and humanitarian aid (1988–91)

When the Soviet Union loosened its tight grip on self-organization in civic and political domains in the mid-1980s, Armenian civil society received a new impetus. Similar to other Soviet republics, environmental movements started to appear (Dawson 1995; Carmin and Fagan 2010; Hakobyan and Tadevosyan 2010; Ishkanian et al. 2013; Kankanyan 2015). In terms of formal entities, many organizations (sports, arts, professional, etc.) were already in place, but those were closely affiliated with and financially supported by the state. Encouraged by Mikhail Gorbachev's policies of perestroika ('restructuring') and glasnost ('openness'), a few new organizations were established to promote the human rights agenda.

In 1988, mass demonstrations in support of the unification of Nagorny Karabakh with Armenia started.[4] The Karabakh movement dominated the early phase of post-communist Armenian civil society development, with its positive (mobilization, solidarity, collective action, networks and skills) and negative (disappointment, disillusionment, cynicism and fatigue) implications. But there was another, perhaps as powerful though less spectacular, force that mobilized Armenians at the time: humanitarian assistance. Refugees and survivors of ethnic pogroms started arriving from Azerbaijan in 1988. Then, on 7 December of that year, an earthquake of devastating magnitude laid waste to Armenia's second largest city and erased a few other settlements from the face of the earth. Hours later, volunteers were rushing in to help. It took people several days to realize that better organizational structures were needed. Some of those were being formed on the spot, using existing institutions and organizations. For example, members of a mountaineering club formed a self-sufficient rescue team that cooperated with foreign Red Cross rescuers working in the earthquake zone; workers from a factory formed teams and worked in shifts, using factory buses to get back and forth; and people lined up to donate blood and/or money, volunteered at the airport to unload arriving humanitarian aid, visited hospitals and so on. The Armenian diaspora also contributed significantly.

These two cases of mass mobilization in 1988 were very different. The Karabakh movement was on the boundary between political and civil society; the earthquake response had little to do with politics. The first was a textbook example of a movement; the second included both formal and informal entities. So already at this stage of Armenian civil society development, we witnessed an impressive level of activity and diversity of organizational forms. But these two 'faces' of Armenian civil society in the late 1980s and the early 1990s have something in common with each other, and with the April 2018 protests: rapid mass mobilization and self-organization, both using existing institutions and creating new structures. Thus, surprising as the 2018 mobilization was, it was neither unique nor unprecedented.

Stage II: NGO-ization of Armenian civil society (1992–2006)

Perhaps intense mobilization over an extended period of time comes with a cost. The turbulent and energetic early 1990s were followed by demobilization and cynicism, which stemmed from two factors: economic and political.

The economic situation in the newly established Republic of Armenia was grim. A new market economy had to be introduced on the outdated and underperforming ruins of Soviet institutions. Corruption was among the few informal institutions that survived the transition and thrived in the new environment. As if jumpstarting the inert Soviet economy was not challenging enough, Armenia had to cope with the consequences of the earthquake and an economic blockade imposed by Azerbaijan. In particular, the country was starved of energy resources. Armenians refer to these times as the 'cold and dark years': no electricity, no gas, no heating in houses and widespread poverty.

In stark contrast to the majority of the population struggling to make ends meet, the former leaders of the Karabakh movement[5] emerged as victorious political elites and seemed to thrive. They ran businesses or governmental affairs (sometimes both) from well-furnished, heated offices; drove expensive cars accompanied by entourages of bodyguards; and built private houses resembling small castles. Some benefited from the war effort; many benefited from mismanaged large-scale privatization. Many Armenians who genuinely supported the Karabakh movement in the late 1980s felt betrayed and bitterly disappointed by the mid-1990s. The echoes of this disappointment reverberated over decades. Until the Velvet Revolution, one could often hear the opinion that social movements are not worth participating in because they were ultimately attempts to grab power by cunning and ambitious political entrepreneurs.

In these difficult conditions, Armenia was trying to consolidate its democracy – or at least that was the official ideology. Within the framework of democratic assistance, foreign aid to NGOs started pouring in. Together with the money came the organizational requirements of what a 'proper' NGO should look like. While people withdrew from activist and social movement varieties of civil society, the NGO sector proliferated. First hundreds and then thousands of NGOs mushroomed, crowding out other forms of civil society organization (Ishkanian 2008). Initially, the newly founded NGOs focused on the service sector. Starting from the beginning of the twenty-first century, NGOs shifted their focus from service to advocacy, again under the influence of funding agencies and their priorities (Blue and Ghazaryan 2004).

This 'NGO-ization' of Armenian civil society had both positive and negative outcomes. A rather professional, well-developed NGO sector promoted a human rights agenda, served as a watchdog, a source of expertise, an alternative information channel and a platform for democratic discourse. NGOs monitored elections and shed light on electoral fraud. They published reports documenting the misuse of public resources, environmental degradation, human rights abuses and so on. They lobbied for or against legislative proposals. They partnered with international organizations or with government institutions to implement development projects. They provided services to beneficiaries. In other words, they did the things typically expected of NGOs, to various degrees of success.

The negative aspects of 'NGO-ization' had to do with the feeble connection between the NGOs and the broader public. The NGO sector is perceived at best as having its own agenda or at worst as serving some foreign agenda. This creates fertile ground for conspiracy theories about NGOs being the 'corrupting tool of the West' that tries to undermine the Armenian culture, family, identity, or some other vaguely defined 'Armenian values'. However, Armenian civil society would not remain 'NGO-ized' forever. The diversity of the ecosystem of Armenian civil society was gradually restored. As living conditions improved, people started regaining interest in public affairs. Also, a younger post-Soviet generation was beginning to enter the public sphere.

Stage III: Re-emergence of civic activism (2007–18)

Starting around 2007, although the date is somewhat arbitrary, a new form of civil society becomes visible in Armenia (Ishkanian et al. 2013). This is usually timed to the appearance of the 'Save Teghut Civic Initiative' – a group of environmental activists who tried to prevent the construction of a mine in a pristine forest in the north of Armenia. The term 'civic initiative' became popular to describe this new form of activism. It is a self-denomination used by activists who join forces to pursue a specific goal: stop a mining project, save a public park, prevent a historic building from being demolished, protest against a new policy and so on. Such groups usually remain rather informal and coordinate their activities through social media. There is also networking between groups: activists join various initiatives, transferring acquired skills and lessons learned from previous successes or failures. A series of interviews we conducted with activists in 2015–16 indicated that many activists knew each other and joined each others' campaigns out of solidarity.[6] Past successes inspired new campaigns, while past failures were critically reflected upon. Activists were clearly accumulating knowledge and building networks.

Over the decade following 2007, civic initiatives grew from being new to being commonplace. They became the default mode of struggle for many young people. Horizontal structures, spontaneity, flexibility, narrow focus and relatively rapid outcomes (positive or negative results) characterize civic initiatives and show how these are different from the more formal entities of civil society, such as NGOs. Perhaps the biggest difference is in the use of finances. NGOs can hardly operate without grants. Civic initiatives refuse foreign funding and rely on resources their members can mobilize (Ishkanian et al. 2013). One such valuable resource is social media. Its rapid spread in Armenia greatly contributed to the visibility of civic initiatives and to the ability of activists to network, reach out and learn from each other's experiences. Facebook is simultaneously the main organizational platform, the recruitment network and the information dissemination channel for activists engaged in civic initiatives.

It is interesting to note that while activists called their campaigns 'initiatives', in interviews and discussions with researchers, many agreed that the words 'initiative', 'campaign' or 'movement' did not exactly represent what was happening in Armenia at the time of our fieldwork in 2015–16. The words that the activists thought best described the ongoing cases were 'struggle' or 'battle' (in Armenian: պայքար, *paykar*). The activists were also worried about the terms 'activism' and 'activist' (the English words are used in Armenia without translation), as these terms seemed to have acquired a negative connotation. Some activists believed this was a result of black PR by the Republican Party of Armenia (RPA) government. Regardless of the source, however, there is a striking similarity to the earlier stage. First, NGOs were perceived as 'foreign', and hence potentially harmful to some putative 'Armenian interests'. Now activists were also being depicted as 'foreign' to an extent, replicating a common post-Soviet pattern whereby independent civic activity is 'securitized' as a threat to core national interests posed by interfering 'outside actors'.

Stage IV: A new 'post-revolutionary' stage?

If the Velvet Revolution results in genuine democratization, Armenian civil society will find itself in a new context. Democracies are more conducive to civil society (Keane 1988; Linz and Stepan 1996; Diamond 1999; Warren 2001; Anheier, Katz and Lam 2008; Salamon, Sokolowski and Haddock 2017), meaning that Armenian civil society will yet again have to adapt. It will have to change some of its tactics and repertoires of action, revisit some of its goals and step up to new challenges. If Armenia's new government fails to live up to democratic standards, civil society will have to cope with some serious disappointments. In either case, it is likely we are at the beginning of a new stage of Armenian civil society development, but it is hard to say what this stage will look like. In either of the two scenarios (democratic development or stagnation/setback), civil society will need to be wary of a few predictable pitfalls, elaborated in more detail towards the end of the chapter.

The role of civil society in the Velvet Revolution

Did civil society help the successful mobilization and peaceful resolution of the standoff in April 2018? It is hard to give a definitive answer or to prove anything empirically. Many factors contributed to the change of government in 2018, of which civil society was one. It is hard to isolate its impact from a web of interdependent processes and random occurrences. But some things can be suggested with confidence. It is highly plausible that Armenian civil society strengthened the protest movement in a number of ways. It provided ideas, knowledge and skills acquired during previous episodes of contention. Previous success stories also inspired a new generation of activists. Both formal and informal entities of Armenian civil society disseminated information and served as communication channels and mobilization networks. The unfolding events were broadcast live by several independent online media news sources, myriad Facebook livestreams and other social media platforms, greatly increasing the visibility of the protests and providing information. Civil society provided experienced leaders and numerous 'foot soldiers' that swelled the ranks of the protesters. Two weeks of protest in spring 2018 that resulted in the change of government were strengthened by knowledge and skills honed by Armenian civil society in the preceding decades. The uprising was enriched by civil society's human and social capital.

Nikol Pashinyan's political movement started out as a civic initiative: 'My Step' (Իմ քայլը, *Im k'aylĕ*) mirrored previous civic initiatives and was referred to as such. Another civic initiative, 'Reject Serzh' (մերժիր Սերժին, *merzhir Serzhin*), was organized by activists initially not affiliated with Pashinyan. At some point, the two groups joined forces, and the two names ('Make a step, reject Serzh' – Քայլ արա, մերժիր Սերժին, *K'ayl ara, merzhir Serzhin*) became the main chant that echoed through the streets. Activists brought their knowledge of peaceful resistance to the protests. The steadfast commitment to non-violence and the resulting self-discipline was impressive. As an observer, I witnessed a number of cases when protesters prevented someone within the crowd from acts that could be interpreted as provocations. Of course, Nikol Pashinyan repeatedly emphasized non-violence in his speeches and through his actions. But it takes dedication and self-discipline to uphold non-violence across numerous mass protest locations over a two-week period. This requires a critical mass of people who have internalized peaceful resistance principles and are able to prevent others from rash or feckless behaviour. Civil society clearly contributed to that critical mass. During our prior discussions with activists, many related stories of how by engaging in various campaigns, they learned to remain peaceful despite pressure in the years preceding the 2018 uprising.

Civic activists also contributed to the tactics of network resistance and self-organization. While Pashinyan was leading crowds through streets, numerous other spots of resistance materialized temporarily and dispersed, just to reappear shortly after at a new location. A group of thirty to forty people would block a crossroad for a while; the police would arrive to find most of them gone and blocking another crossroad a few blocks away. Fluid, mischievous and humorous: the activism was omnipresent and constituted a major headache for the authorities, yet it was never malicious enough to justify a harsh response. How does one legitimize a crackdown on teenagers playing football in the street? On middle-aged men barbequing *khoravats* (Armenian kebab) in the city square? On IT specialists 'working' with their laptops on their laps, their chairs neatly lined up to block a street? It was a festival of resistance, whose positive, celebratory mood was reminiscent of the Electric Yerevan civic campaign against an electricity price rise in 2015 (see Chapter 2).

The positive framing of campaigns was not what Nikol Pashinyan was previously known for. After walking from Gyumri to Yerevan, he held his first meeting in the Opera Square on Friday, 13 April. I went to observe it.

It was the usual grim Armenian political protest with around 500 people: mostly middle-aged men dressed in dark clothes, with gloomy and solemn expressions.[7] Pashinyan was (yet again) talking about a fascist regime and the oppressed Armenian people. The protesters spent the weekend encamped near the Opera Square, blocking a major crossroad. I visited twice. There were about thirty to fifty people loitering around. One could see some young faces, but the whole affair seemed irrelevant. *Civilnet*, a major independent online news outlet that was covering the protests, published a series of interviews with participants. Some of the more telling headlines were 'The police are ignoring us', 'I am unhappy with public indifference' and 'This is not how you do a revolution'.[8] Interviewees stressed that they were there because they believed in the cause of the protest, but they did not necessarily believe in the political leaders of the protest. One interviewee said she had not seen a single policeman and that made her even more suspicious.

On Monday, 16 April, Pashinyan changed both his narrative and his tactics. Instead of 'fascist regime' and 'oppressed Armenian citizens', the words we repeatedly heard were 'revolution of love and harmony' and 'proud Armenian citizens'. Instead of pitching tents in a public space, he marched around the city, particularly passing by high schools, colleges and universities. Leaders of previous activist movements marched by his side. Was this a coincidence? Or did Pashinyan's new allies suggest new tactics and a change in rhetoric? Either way, the change of style produced immediate results. Young people started joining. The energy of the movement grew every day, and the tone for the subsequent protest campaign was set; it was unmistakably the tone of peaceful, festive resistance rather than a grim political standoff. The overall atmosphere of celebration and the narrow focus on Serzh Sargsyan's individual resignation (another similarity to activist campaigns that had focused on simple single issues) made it relatively easy for many people – such as those not in principle opposed to the ruling RPA – to join.

In addition to specific ideas, knowledge and skills, civil society influenced the April 2018 uprising in a more general way: by providing inspiration. In particular, the 'glorious past' of the Karabakh movement was an inspiration for young people. In February 2018, a series of events were organized to mark the thirtieth anniversary of the movement. The black-and-white pictures of huge crowds in the streets, of thousands of fists raised in solidarity, evoked nostalgia in some and admiration in others. Many of my students at the American University of Armenia in Yerevan asked me about the Karabakh movement. More than once I heard them say 'I wish something like this would happen in our times.' In April, those very same students went out into the streets and made it happen.

Civil society after 2018: Potential pitfalls

Currently, Armenia is at a critical juncture, similar to the early 1990s. The country has a real chance to consolidate democracy, yet the risk of retrenchment and stagnation is just as real. Either way, civil society will have to adapt to the fast-changing context in which it is now operating. Its cordial post-revolutionary relationship with the government was, of course, good news in general, but it had pitfalls as well. The overall situation in the country also provided both opportunities and challenges for further civil society development. I will first discuss the pitfalls related to civil society–government relations and then address broader issues of the country context.

One concern is a sudden 'depletion' of civil society. Some of its best cadres took positions with the government, resulting in a civil society brain drain, particularly in the fields of human rights, democratic reforms and development. The most passionate and educated advocates of certain values, who joined civil society because that was the only sphere through which they could promote those values, now had a chance to address burning problems at the state level (or at least they believed they had that chance). The government is open; it is actively recruiting because it is short on experts and specialists. Many people left their NGO positions or their activist engagements to join Nikol Pashinyan's government. A similar scenario is said to have happened in Georgia after the Rose Revolution in 2003, where civil society lost a substantial amount of its human and social capital (Broers 2005). It is possible that Armenia is going through a similar scenario now. Put simply, less human and social capital makes civil society less effective.

Related to the first concern, the second potential problem is civil society's weakened ability to criticize the government. It is weakened not only because civil society lost some of its best intellectual potential but also because many positions in the new government are held by their former colleagues. Ethically and psychologically it is harder to scrutinize and criticize your former leaders, co-workers or fellow activists. Yet a civil society that stops performing its watchdog and public sphere functions is a weaker civil society. Because Armenia is at a critical juncture, we need a vigorous debate about the future course of action now more than ever. The fact that the government had a strong majority in the parliament after the December 2018 parliamentary election meant that scrutiny of government actions from various angles and by various actors assumed extreme importance. Someone needs to keep a critical eye on what the government is doing. Civil society is a natural ally of the political opposition: if it is too friendly with the government, the oversight function suffers.

Another possible negative outcome of many civil society cadres moving into government is a potential radicalization of the remaining civil society entities. Those who are left (who choose to stay, or who are not offered any positions with the government) are the 'fighters' rather than the collaborators. These tend to be people who have an aversion to the complications of politics, the need to compromise and to navigate various demands. According to the argument made earlier, one might think this is not a problem. Those who want to work with the government take up government offices, while those who do not remain in civil society and continue being the government's critics. But criticism needs to be constructive and fair. If civil society has few good policy specialists left, and those who are left tend to be of the more radical type, the criticism coming from civil society might come through as too harsh and unhelpful. The government then tends to respond either defensively or dismissively.

This leads me to a few concluding remarks about the overall atmosphere in the country as of this writing in March–April 2019, particularly those aspects that are unhelpful for civil society and any society in general. Radicalization peaked during the parliamentary election campaign in November–December 2018. The 'black and white' rhetoric was initiated by Pashinyan's government and was taken up by the RPA in an unsuccessful bid to secure votes. Polarization of the society deepened. Shortly before the elections, a colleague of mine remarked that she felt less free to express her opinion as compared to the 'pre-revolution' Armenia. Of course, no one was being persecuted for their views: what she meant was social pressure. By saying the 'wrong' thing about either Pashinyan's camp *or* his opponents, one risked unleashing a wave of indignation from friends, colleagues or strangers; things could turn particularly nasty on social media. Armenia's widespread newly found passion for politics is admirable, but blank dismissals of 'the other camp' as crooks and liars who have either 'brought Armenia to the brink of disaster' or who will 'lead Armenia to a disaster' is unhealthy. It is particularly unhealthy for civil society, which is supposed to be a sphere of diversity, not an arena for pitched battles between 'black' and 'white' camps.

Another attribute of post-revolutionary Armenia is hyper-mobilization. Protest is the default mode for struggle whenever someone disagrees with government actions. In the months after the Velvet Revolution, there was hardly a week without some protest, blocking off streets or a strike. It is good that people have found their voice and a sense of agency. However, one cannot help wondering: Is this sustainable? Is this efficient? What happens to the diversity of repertoires of action? If civil society is an ecosystem of various species, then the true strength of civil society is its richness, diversity, flexibility and adaptability to changing conditions. I am all in favour of protest as a quintessential democratic 'people power' mechanism, but activism should not be reduced to disjointed, short-lived protests here and there in reaction to almost any step the government takes or fails to take. There has to be a larger purpose and a better reason than simply saying 'we do not like this government decision.'

A last danger is the repetition of the Karabakh movement scenario: powerful mobilization fuelled by great expectations leading to monumental achievements (independence and victory in a war), but also leading to bitter disappointments in a derailed democratic project. Currently, most Armenians are excited and optimistic, and many people expect too much from the new government. Disappointments are inevitable. But it is a question of the degree of disappointments and who they will affect most. If Pashinyan's government fails to deliver on its core promises of genuine democratization, human rights, the rule of law and anti-corruption, most of his best and brightest supporters are in for a big disappointment.[9] Will they take to the streets again or turn to the polling stations to right wrongs once again? Will they see this as a temporary setback, but still on the right path? Or will they dismiss democracy as a 'myth' and all leaders as 'liars who just want power', in ways similar to what happened in the mid-1990s? The latter would be a tragic scenario. We can hardly afford another lapse into cynicism, another generation lost to activism and another twenty years of stagnation in our public life. The stakes are very high.

Conclusion

The Armenian Velvet Revolution of April–May 2018 was a big surprise for many. But it was not the first time in recent Armenian history that such a rapid and large mobilization happened. A more careful look at the *longue durée* of Armenian history and deeper roots of civic self-organization helps explain some of the April 2018 mobilization. Many questions, however, remain unanswered. Perhaps a Putnam-style historic excursus into the medieval roots of Armenian civic communalism can shed some light on the question that continues to intrigue us today. How is it that from time to time seemingly apathetic Armenians mobilize en masse? Is Armenian civil society in fact stronger than it looks?

The argument made in this chapter is that civil society contributed skills and networks to the 2018 uprising, strengthening its peaceful, festive element and hence made it harder for the government to retaliate. Civil society also provided inspiration: previous successful cases of mobilization served as reference points, particularly for the younger generation of activists eager to test their mettle for a worthy cause. The parallels of the April 2018 events with the Karabakh movement are striking. Both had a political issue at their core that led to a change of government, although, initially, the Karabakh movement did not have a goal of challenging the Soviet regime.[10] Both started rather unexpectedly and grew rapidly. Both had support from environmental movements. At the peak of mobilization, both were cross-cutting and truly national: including people from all walks of life, across generations, all over Armenia and in the diaspora. Both were peaceful: the Karabakh movement less so, but given the scale, the intensity and the lack of experience with peaceful protests at the time, there was remarkably little violence. Both had their leaders arrested, which did not harm the movement and only increased the leaders' popularity. Both had their leaders almost idolized at some point. Thirty years later, the Karabakh movement probably inspired many young people in 2018. Hopefully the Velvet Revolution will not lead to the disappointment that many people involved in the Karabakh movement later experienced. This will largely depend on the government's ability to deliver on its promises of democratization and the rule of law. It is up to the active segments of Armenian society, including civil society, to hold the government to this task.

Notes

1   Tilly and Tarrow define upward scale shift as 'one of the most significant processes in contentious politics. It moves contention beyond its local origins, touches on the interests and values of new actors, involves a shift of venue to sites where contention may be more or less successful, and can threaten other actors or entire regimes' (Tilly and Tarrow 2015: 125).

2   In May 1918, Armenian troops, strengthened by thousands of volunteers, stopped the advancement of the Turkish army forty kilometres west of the capital Yerevan. The victory at Sardarapat is often described as pivotal in securing the survival of the Armenian nation (Hovannisian 1967; Balakian 2003).

3   Thousands of people took to the streets to demand the recognition of 1915 Armenian Genocide. People were chanting 'lands' (հողեր, *hogher*) (Karlsson 2007).

4   An autonomous region located in Soviet Azerbaijan, with a population featuring an overwhelmingly ethnic Armenian majority and a troubled history of belonging to various colonial powers.

5 It is important to note that most of the leaders of the Karabakh movement in Armenia were from the Republic of Armenia (not from Karabakh). Some of the new Karabakh elite moved to Armenia at a later stage. This passage refers to people who rose to prominence from within Armenia.

6 We conducted interviews within the scope of a research project on activist campaigns in Armenia and the relationships between activists and NGOs. The project focused on five cases of activism in Armenia from 2007 to 2015, and employed a range of methods (see Paturyan and Gevorgyan 2016 for a detailed description of the research project).

7 In Armenia, until recently, there seemed to be a disconnect between 'political' and 'non-political' protests and demonstrations. A typical political protest/demonstration would be organized by a political party and/or a political opposition leader(s) to express dissatisfaction with the ruling government in general (rather than criticism of a specific policy/issue/decision). Such protests would usually attract men in their late thirties and above, interested in politics and disgruntled with the government. In a stark contrast to demonstrations initiated by political parties, activists would organize protests against specific issues (an electricity price rise, the preservation of a public park and so on) and would frame those protests as 'non-political'. To emphasize the difference, activists would shun political parties and would not allow politicians to deliver speeches at demonstrations. Protests like Electric Yerevan attracted a very different crowd: people from all walks of life, including many young people. Demonstration participants were not necessarily interested in politics, neither were they opposed to the government in general. They could be ambivalent towards the government or even pro-governmental but opposed to the specific policy/decision the activists were protesting against. The atmosphere at such gatherings was usually a great deal more positive and less confrontational. On this distinction see too Mikayel Zolyan's discussion in Chapter 2.

8 Some of these interviews, and the rather forlorn backdrop to the protests at this time, can be seen at https://www.youtube.com/watch?v=aiRa8ZlW-bc&t=37s and https://www.youtube.com/watch?v=-aUbhsDcvNc&t=16s (accessed 19 April 2019).

9 By 'best and brightest', I do not mean educated people, professionals, or people committed to Western democratic ideas, or any such thing. I mean people from all walks of life who marched, blocked streets and literally put their bodies on the line, motivated by an inner moral compass, a sense of justice and human dignity.

10 One could argue that the 'My Step' and 'Reject Serzh' initiatives that merged at the outset of the 2018 protests initially had a narrow goal of ousting one specific person: President-turned-Prime Minister Serzh Sargsyan. Although Nikol Pashinyan spoke of the 'revolution of love and peace' early in the movement, the focus of the protests was on Serzh Sargsyan. When he did

resign, the celebrations in the streets resembled those in European countries after winning a football world cup. The idea of removing the Republican Party of Armenia from power came two days later. Pashinyan's popularity at the time was unprecedented; he was to become a prime minister and complete the transition of power from the Republican Party to the newly emerged revolutionary elite.

References

Abrahamian, L. and Shagoyan, G. (2011) From Carnival Civil Society Toward a Real Civil Society: Democracy Trends in Post-Soviet Armenia. *Anthropology and Archeology of Eurasia*, 50 (3): 11–50.

Anheier, H. K. (2004) *Civil Society: Measurement, Evaluation, Policy*. Sterling: Earthscan Publications.

Anheier, H. K., Katz, H. and Lam, M. (2008) Diffusion Models and Global Civil Society. In: Albrow, M., Anheier, H., Glasius, M., Price, M. E. and Kaldor, M., eds, *Global Civil Society 2007/8*. London: Sage Publications, 245–57.

Balakian, P. (2003) *The Burning Tigris: The Armenian Genocide and America's Response*. New York: HarperCollins.

Blue, R. N. and Ghazaryan, Y. G. (2004) *Armenia NGO Sector Assessment: A Comparative Study*. Yerevan: World Learning for International Development.

Broers, L. (2005) After the 'Revolution': Civil Society and the Challenges of Consolidating Democracy in Georgia. *Central Asian Survey*, 24 (3): 333–50.

Carmin, J. and Fagan, A. (2010) Environmental Mobilisation and Organisations in Post-Socialist Europe and the Former Soviet Union. *Environmental Politics*, 19 (5): 689–707.

Dawson, J. I. (1995) Anti-Nuclear Activism in the USSR and its Successor States: A Surrogate for Nationalism? *Environmental Politics*, 4 (3): 441–66.

Diamond, L. (1999) *Developing Democracy: Toward Consolidation*. Baltimore and London: The Johns Hopkins University Press.

Edwards, M. (2011) Introduction: Civil Society and the Geometry of Human Relations. In: Edwards, M., ed., *The Oxford Handbook of Civil Society*. Oxford: Oxford University Press, 3–14.

Edwards, M. (2013) *Civil Society*. Cambridge: Polity Press.

Habermas, J. (1991) *The Structural Transformation of the Public Sphere: An Inquiry Into a Category of Bourgeois Society*. Cambridge: MIT Press.

Habermas, J. (1996) *Between Facts and Norms – Contributions to a Discourse Theory of Law and Democracy*. Cambridge and London: The MIT Press.

Hakobyan, L. and Tadevosyan, M. (2010) *Impact of Environmental Organizations on Policy Change in Armenia*. Case Study. Yerevan: Counterpart International. Available at: http://program.counterpart.org/

Armenia/wp-content/uploads/2011/02/CSI-Case-Study-5.pdf (accessed 24 May 2011).

Hakobyan, L., Tadevosyan, M., Sardar, A. and Stepanyan, A. (2010) *Armenian Civil Society: From Transition to Consolidation*. Analytical Country Report. Yerevan: Counterpart International. Available at: http://program.counterpart.org/Armenia/?page_id=48 (accessed 24 May 2011).

Hall, J. A. (2000) Reflections on the Making of Civil Society. In: Trentmann, F., ed., *Paradoxes of Civil Society. New Perspectives on Modern German and British History*. New York and Oxford: Berghahn Books, 47–57.

Hovannisian, R. G. (1967) *Armenia on the Road to Independence, 1918*. Berkeley: University of California Press.

Ishkanian, A. (2008) *Democracy Building and Civil Society in Post-Soviet Armenia*. London and New York: Routledge.

Ishkanian, A., Gyulkhandanyan, E., Manusyan, S. and Manusyan, A. (2013) *Civil Society, Development and Environmental Activism in Armenia*. London: The London School of Economics and Political Science (LSE). Available at: http://eprints.lse.ac.uk/54755/ (accessed 27 March 2014).

Iskandaryan, A. (2015) Armenia: Stagnation at Its Utmost. *Caucasus Analytical Digest*, 76: 2–4.

Kankanyan, N. (2015) Environmental Activism in Armenia. Master's Thesis. Yerevan: American University of Armenia.

Karlsson, K. (2007) Memory of Mass Murder: The Genocide in Armenian and Non-Armenian Historical Consciousness. In: Mithander, C., Sundholm, J. and Troy, M. H., eds, *Collective Traumas: Memories of War and Conflict in 20th-Century Europe*. Brussels: P.I.E. Peter Lang (38), 13–46.

Keane, J. (1988) *Democracy and Civil Society*. London: Verso.

Kopecký, P. and Mudde, C. (2003) *Uncivil Society? Contentious Politics in Post-communist Europe*. London and New York: Routledge.

Libaridian, G. J. (1999) *The Challenge of Statehood: Armenian Political Thinking Since Independence*. Watertown: Blue Crane Books.

Linz, J. J. and Stepan, A. (1996) *Problems of Democratic Transition and Consolidation. Southern Europe, South America, and Post-Communist Europe*. Baltimore and London: Johns Hopkins University Press.

Mkrtichyan, A., Vermishyan, H. and Balasanyan, S. (2016) *Independence Generation. Youth Study 2016 - Armenia*. Yerevan: Friedrich-Ebert-Stiftung. Available at: http://www.fes-caucasus.org/news-list/e/independence-generation-youth-study-2016-armenia/ (accessed 28 August 2017).

Paturyan, Y. and Gevorgyan, V. (2016) *Civic Activism as a Novel Component of Armenian Civil Society*. Yerevan: Turpanjian Center for Policy Analysis. Available at: http://tcpa.aua.am/files/2012/07/English-3.pdf (accessed 28 August 2017).

Salamon, L. M., Sokolowski, W. S. and List, R. (2003) Global Civil Society: An Overview - The Johns Hopkins Comparative Nonprofit Sector Project. Available at: http://www.jhu.edu/cnp/research/index.html (accessed 28 August 2017).

Salamon, L. M., Sokolowski, S. W. and Haddock, M. A. (2017) *Explaining Civil Society Development: A Social Origins Approach*. Baltimore and London: Johns Hopkins University Press.

Tilly, C. and Tarrow, S. (2015) *Contentious Politics*. 2nd edn. New York: Oxford University Press.

Trentmann, F. (2000) Introduction: Paradoxes of Civil Society. In: Trentmann, F., ed., *Paradoxes of Civil Society: New Perspectives on Modern German and British History*. New York and Oxford: Berghahn Books, 3–47.

Warren, M. E. (2001) *Democracy and Association*. Princeton and Oxford: Princeton University Press.

5

Donning the Velvet

Non-violent resistance in the 2018 Armenian Revolution

Jonathan Pinckney[1]

Introduction

On 17 April 2018, the Armenian parliament elected long-time former president Serzh Sargsyan as Armenia's prime minister. Protests against his election had been small and sparsely attended. A lack of faith in Sargsyan's political alternative and remembrance of a violent crackdown on protesters ten years previously when Sargsyan first came into office held the opposition in check. The prime minister seemed well placed to continue his tight grip on Armenian politics indefinitely. Yet less than a week later, Sargsyan was gone. A mere two weeks after that, a majority of Sargsyan's own party members voted opposition leader Nikol Pashinyan, thrust into the office on the wave of a 'Velvet Revolution', into power as his replacement.

In this chapter, I draw upon one of the revolution's most distinctive features – non-violent resistance as its primary tactical repertoire – to help explain its trajectory and long-term prospects.[2] Non-violent revolutions are almost always unexpected, even shocking (Kuran 1991). Even those who end up leading them rarely anticipate their trajectories. Yet by tracing the common threads from Republic Square in Yerevan through the Euromaidan in Kiev to Wenceslas Square in Prague and the fall of the Berlin Wall, a growing literature on non-violent resistance can give insight into the causes and consequences of these transformative events. What can we learn about Armenia's Velvet Revolution from the growing literature on non-violent resistance? I examine two topics: the factors that helped the revolution succeed and what we may expect in the future.

I summarize the factors that led to success using Ackerman and DuVall's (2006) three 'engines' of non-violent resistance. The first engine is unity, bringing together diverse organizations and social groups around a shared agenda. The second is strategic planning, the careful sequencing of tactics to achieve maximum political leverage. The third is non-violent discipline, the strict avoidance of violence even in the face of violent government repression. I argue that all three played important roles in the events of 2018 and help us understand the revolutionary outcome.

I am also cautiously optimistic about the long-term impact of the Velvet Revolution. Political transitions initiated by non-violent resistance tend to lead to more democratic outcomes than the alternatives (Chenoweth and Stephan 2011; Celestino and Gleditsch 2013; Bethke and Pinckney 2019), and mobilization of society towards building new political institutions during transitions – a major focus of the Pashinyan administration – is a key force pushing in this democratic direction (Pinckney 2018). Challenges certainly remain for the new regime. Yet there are encouraging signs that the Velvet Revolution is likely to initiate significant democratic progress.

The remainder of the chapter proceeds as follows. First, I introduce the concept of non-violent resistance and situate the Armenian Velvet Revolution in the tradition of twentieth- and early twenty-first-century resistance movements. Next, I illustrate the role of the three strategic factors of unity, strategic planning and non-violent discipline in helping the Velvet Revolution succeed. Then I reflect on the likely next stages in the Armenian transition and conclude with some reflections on its challenges.

Non-violent resistance

Non-violent resistance is 'a technique of socio-political action for applying power in a conflict without the use of violence' (Sharp 1999: 567). Thus, it is action that takes place outside traditional avenues of political power but that does not rely on physical violence or the threat of physical violence for its coercive force. Non-violent resistance seeks to achieve leverage over opponents by organizing a systematic withdrawal of cooperation from a system of power, particularly through undermining the loyalty of the central social groups and institutions that maintain a regime's power. These are often referred to as a regime's 'pillars of support' (Helvey 2004; Schock 2005). If this withdrawal of cooperation can be wide and coordinated enough, then even the most robust political regime will have difficulty maintaining itself (Chenoweth and Stephan 2011). This organized withdrawal of consent can take many different forms, and uses many different tactics, depending on the context. Foundational non-violent resistance scholar Gene Sharp (1973) identified 198 distinct non-violent resistance tactics, and his list is far from exhaustive. Typical tactics include public demonstrations, strikes and boycotts. The intention of such tactics is in part, but not exclusively, communicative. Non-violent resistance does not just communicate opposition to a regime or policy; it actively seeks to disrupt the continued operations of that regime or policy.

Non-violent resistance has no necessary connection to an ideological aversion to violence, and to engage in non-violent resistance does not imply that one is a pacifist (Schock 2003). Most major non-violent resistance movements of the last century have been led by people who adopted non-violent tactics primarily for instrumental rather than ideological reasons (Ackerman and Kruegler 1994). Even ostensible pacifists have typically approached violence in a more nuanced way, acknowledging some appropriate uses. Mahatma Gandhi, for instance, participated in the British army during the First World War, and advocated for independent India to have a strong military. The key feature in defining whether one is engaged in non-violent resistance is not what one believes but what one does.[3]

Non-violent resistance campaigns[4] have been a common feature of global politics in recent decades. More than a hundred major non-violent resistance movements seeking regime change, secession or an end to military occupation have occurred since 1945 (Chenoweth and Lewis 2013). Countless more movements of non-violent resistance for less extreme goals regularly take place around the world.[5] Non-violent resistance movements have pushed for democratization (Bratton and Van de Walle 1997; Brancati 2016), for greater ethnic autonomy and self-determination (Bartkowski 2013; Cunningham, Dahl and Fruge 2017), and against corruption (Beyerle 2014), among many other goals.

Non-violent resistance movements have been a major force for global political transformation. More than eighty political transitions have been primarily initiated through non-violent resistance since 1945 (Pinckney 2018). In the last twenty years, non-violent resistance was a major force in initiating the post-Soviet 'colour revolutions' (Bunce and Wolchik 2011), the 'Arab Spring' movements of 2011 (Roberts et al. 2016), a democratic transition in Burkina Faso (Harsch 2017) and the resignation of Algerian president Abdelaziz Bouteflika (Raghavan 2019). Many of the leading figures of these revolutions explicitly drew on the ideas and strategies of foundational authors of non-violent resistance such as Gene Sharp (Popovic 2015), and many also received training in non-violent resistance.

Non-violent resistance in the Velvet Revolution

Armenia's 2018 Velvet Revolution is thus a part of a widespread phenomenon. Leaders of the revolution such as current prime minister Nikol Pashinyan explicitly drew on the symbols and tactical repertoires of major non-violent resistance movements, seeking to take advantage of the tactics that had succeeded in achieving change non-violently in the past. The march from Gyumri to Yerevan echoed Gandhi's 1930 march to the sea in opposition to British salt taxes. The name 'Velvet Revolution' drew on the iconography of the 1989 uprising in Czechoslovakia that successfully ended that country's communist regime.

The Velvet Revolution has much to tell us about non-violent resistance. In particular, it highlights the transformative potential of what Peter Ackerman and Jack DuVall (2006) refer to as the three 'engines' of non-violent resistance: unity, strategic planning and non-violent discipline. The literature on non-violent resistance highlights how these three factors can allow non-violent resistance movements to bring about major political change even in the face of what appear to be prohibitively challenging circumstances (Ackerman and Kruegler 1994).

Unity in non-violent resistance movements is the articulation of a single set of goals and strategies among diverse constituencies. Unity increases movements' participation and thus points of leverage over their opponents. Unified movements present a popular alternative to authoritarian opponents and have many different potential avenues into the regime's pillars of support (Tilly 1994). Disunified movements struggle to articulate their demands and can be discredited by their opponents as simply reflecting a minority opinion.

Strategic planning is the intentional sequencing and execution of tactics to achieve the greatest leverage over the opponent with the lowest cost to the movement (Ackerman and Kruegler 1994). Strategic planning is crucial for movements to achieve success because movements often face a resource imbalance against their opponents. Resistance movements are typically working with whatever they can scrape together, while the state has extensive resources at its disposal to maintain its solidarity and divide and demobilize its opponents. Thus, if movements do not efficiently deploy their own resources to the greatest effect, the state is likely to be able to crush them simply because of its greater capacity for conflict.

Non-violent discipline involves the members of a movement not engaging in violence even when subjected to violent repression. Non-violent discipline helps non-violent resistance movements to succeed because it de-legitimizes government repression and encourages broader participation (Pinckney 2016). If movements combine violent and non-violent tactics, the state can easily bring its full coercive force to bear upon them with little danger of backfire. In contrast, even the most extreme totalitarian governments often hesitate to deploy violent repression against fully peaceful movements for fear of the consequences to their reputations and the loyalty of their pillars of support (Binnendijk and Marovic 2006; Hess and Martin 2006).

Many movements struggle to activate all three of these 'engines' of success, particularly because non-violent resistance movements are typically made up of many different groups with diverse goals that do not necessarily coordinate with one another. However, if achieved, these three factors can help movements achieve success even in the face of very unfavourable conditions. This is what we observe in the Armenian case. The situation in Armenia was unfavourable for a revolutionary movement for several reasons (Derluguian and Hovhannisyan 2018). First, the regime had proven itself robust to non-violent challenges in the past, most prominently the 2008 protests against the stolen election in which Serzh Sargsyan first became president (Gogia et al. 2009). Not only had the 2008 movement failed to prevent Sargsyan from coming to power, but the government's violent suppression of the movement had left many progressive forces in Armenia feeling that major change through action on the streets was impossible (Andreasyan et al. 2018).[6] In the months and weeks leading up to the 2018 protests, there was a feeling of inevitability, and a fear that Sargsyan could never be ousted (Abrahamian and Shagoyan 2018). The opposition forces that had confronted Sargsyan's predecessor, Robert Kocharian, in 2008 had almost completely disappeared. Their successors in the *Yelk'* ('Way Out') opposition alliance had largely been routed in the 2017 parliamentary election, receiving less than 8 per cent of the vote.

This robustness to challenge was evident in the hopeless atmosphere that pervaded the 'One Step' march from Gyumri to Yerevan and even the first few days of the protests in Yerevan (see Chapter 4). When Nikol Pashinyan and his followers entered the city on 16 April after more than two weeks of marching through the country attempting to rally support, less than 200 people were waiting for them. Members of the party joked that while the march had accomplished nothing, at least the hundreds of thousands of steps had been good for their health![7]

Second, the regime's primary patron, Russia, was a repressive autocracy rather than a liberal democracy. Close ties to liberal democracies have been argued to be one of the primary contextual factors facilitating the success of non-violent resistance movements (Ritter 2015). Conversely, connection to a powerful authoritarian patron – or what Steven Levitsky and Lucan Way refer to as a 'black knight' – able to sustain a struggling regime with external support has been crucial in facilitating the survival of several regimes facing non-violent revolutions (Levitsky and Way 2010). One powerful example of this were the columns of Saudi tanks rolling across the border to suppress the Arab Spring uprising in Bahrain. Even when international support does not directly crush a non-violent resistance movement, external financial incentives and the mere threat of external support can often keep movements from even getting started in the first place. In contrast to other movements in the region, the opposition in Armenia also lacked its own external supporters, with little to no linkage with Western patrons.

Third, the long-running Karabakh conflict with Azerbaijan had given rise to a highly-effective military and state security force, which had been successfully deployed to put down opposition forces in the past (Way 2008). The security forces were closely linked to Sargsyan and remained loyal to the regime throughout the uprising. Military fragmentation and defections are another factor shown to consistently facilitate non-violent resistance movement success (Chenoweth and Stephan 2011; Nepstad 2011). Without military defection, it is extremely difficult for non-violent movements to successfully oust a hostile regime (Nepstad 2013). While some small groups of soldiers joined the protests near the end of the movement, the military leadership severely criticized and punished these actions (MacFarquhar and Pérez-Peña 2018). Unlike in many other movements, the fact that the protests were not repressed appeared to be a matter of restraint on the part of the government, rather than disobedience or shirking on the part of the military.

Certain conditions also favoured the uprising. The Sargsyan regime had grown increasingly unpopular, with opinion polls indicating very low levels of public support.[8] President Sargsyan's attempt to remain in power past his two term limit by shifting himself into an empowered prime ministerial role was a classic mistake that served as a powerful focal point for mobilization. With few alternatives for legitimately expressing their grievances and expecting a genuine response, Armenians turned to the streets (Iskandaryan 2018)

This turn was made easier by over a decade of 'youth-driven, social media-powered, issue-specific' public protest campaigns (Paturyan and Gevorgyan 2016: 2; Ohanyan 2018). Other than the failed 2008 movement to prevent Sargsyan from taking office, these had been primarily on various 'non-political' issues such as the Save Teghut Forest movement, the 100 dram civic initiative against raising transport fees and the 2015 'Electric Yerevan' protests against increasing electricity tariffs (Avedissian 2015). Primarily spearheaded by youth activists, movements to preserve public parks, oppose government price increases and prevent environmental degradation had facilitated the growth of activist networks and had trained a generation of young protesters in creative ways to organize dissent and blunt the impact of repression. For instance, in the aftermath of the 2008 protests, civil society organizations planned 'public walks' as a means to get around a ban on public demonstrations (Ishkanian 2009: 24). These 'civic initiatives' largely stayed out of both formal opposition parties and organized NGOs,[9] both of which were widely discredited[10], and instead created a vibrant alternative mobilizational space in which the general public could become engaged with political issues (on this, see Chapter 4 in this volume, and Ishkanian 2015).

These movements were fuelled by the growth of the internet and social media in Armenia. Internet usage increased significantly in the years leading up to the revolution. When Serzh Sargysan was first elected president of Armenia in 2008, only around 6 per cent of Armenians were using the internet. By the time of the Velvet Revolution, that number had increased more than ten times to nearly 70 per cent (International Telecommunications Union 2018), and around half the population subscribed to Facebook (Elliott 2018). When the revolution broke out, the ubiquity of social media helped to both fuel mobilization and prevent repression as media and activist livestreams recorded many of the central events. The digital visibility of the movement was particularly crucial in a country with such a large and politically influential diaspora (Pearce 2018).

The Sargsyan regime's poor handling of the April 2016 'four-day war' with Azerbaijan was another factor that helped the 2018 movement.[11] The regime's inability to resolve the Armenian-Azerbaijani conflict in favour of Karabakh Armenians or to provide for their security, and the high number of Armenian casualties in the 2016 conflict undermined confidence in the government (Iskandaryan 2018). A small group of insurgents calling themselves *Sasna Tsrer* (the 'Daredevils of Sassoun', a reference to a medieval Armenian epic) exacerbated the situation when they took over a police station and demanded President Sargsyan's resignation. They failed to spark a revolutionary uprising, but widespread demonstrations in support of the attack significantly threatened the government (Silaev and Fomin 2018). This is another parallel between the Velvet Revolution and past incidents of non-violent revolutions. The non-violent movement that ousted the Argentine military regime in the 1980s was significantly spurred on by the country's defeat in the Falklands/Malvinas war in 1982 (Linz and Stepan 1996).

Several short-term factors also facilitated the movement's success. Prime Minister Sargsyan was hesitant to engage in violent repression because of the upcoming Francophonie summit to be held in Yerevan in October 2018.[12] In addition, the upcoming Armenian Genocide Remembrance Day may have provided a final push for Prime Minister Sargsyan to step down rather than have to create public images of peaceful protesters being violently suppressed on a day of such historic significance for the Armenian people.

Activating unity, strategy and non-violent discipline

The opposition movement thus certainly had some favourable raw material with which to work. Yet the unfavourable background conditions meant that bringing these favourable conditions to fruition was an uncertain enterprise at best. To bring the movement to its successful conclusion required significant strategic innovation on the part of Nikol Pashinyan and other movement leaders. This innovation involved the skilful deployment of all three of the key factors facilitating non-violent resistance movements' success: unity, strategy and non-violent discipline. Their deployment of these factors grew out of a process of strategic learning from past social movements in Armenia, but also represented a clear break from events of the past, something that indicates innovation and agency, rather than a straightforward following of past tactical repertoires.

First, there was a unifying message throughout the protests. The protests included almost all segments of Armenian society, and in particular were gender-balanced or sometimes even dominated by women (Makunts 2018). Opposition and civil society leaders intentionally encouraged participation from across society, and organized tactics anyone could safely participate in, even those unable to march or block a street. One of the most prominent of these was the timed banging of pots and pans at eleven o'clock each evening, a tactic drawn from the *cacerolazo* protests against Chilean dictator Augusto Pinochet (Huneeus 2009: 198).

Second, there were strong elements of strategic planning and learning from past mistakes. In the 2008 movement against Serzh Sargsyan's election, large crowds had gathered in Yerevan's central Opera Square. This increased visibility, but decreased their actual disruptive potential, and also made repression by security forces easier. In 2018, in contrast, activists employed a dispersed strategy, creating hundreds of small roadblocks throughout Yerevan and then rapidly redeploying to another road when police arrived to break up the blockade. The fluid, dispersed nature of the protest strained police capacity and meant that the protests had maximum disruptive potential. Kurt Schock identifies the ability of non-violent movements to shift between tactics of 'concentration', which gather large numbers of people in a single place, and tactics of 'dispersion', which spread people across many different locations, as a key indicator both of strategic sophistication within a movement and movement's likely success (Schock 2005). When major rallies did take place, the opposition relocated them from Opera Square to Republic Square, a location without the baggage of past repression, and leaders instructed participants to disperse when night came to avoid potential violent crackdowns.

Careful strategic choices also influenced the choices of public slogans and chants. Pashinyan's slogan: 'Take a Step' later blended with 'Reject Serzh'; both were simple, straightforward and easy for people to rally around. The fact that 'Reject Serzh' – in Armenian: *Merzhir Serzhin* – rhymes also made it a natural for chanting at rallies (Abrahamian and Shagoyan 2018). Simple, easy-to-remember slogans are powerful framing devices that have been central in many non-violent resistance movements. For instance, the Serbian youth organization *Otpor* used the slogans *Gotov je!* ('He's finished!') and *Vreme je* ('It's time') as unifying rallying cries in their successful campaign against President Slobodan Milošević (Nikolayenko 2013).

The description of the protests as a 'Velvet Revolution' was also carefully chosen. A more natural choice to describe the protests, based on recent history and regional precedent, might have been a 'colour revolution'. Yet leaders knew that calling on the precedent of the colour revolutions came with negative emotional salience, evoking Western geopolitical influence and social division. Hence, they reached back to the more obscure and less divisive imagery of the 'Velvet Revolution' in Czechoslovakia (Iskandaryan 2018).

Pashinyan and other leaders also emphasized non-violent discipline and went to great lengths to keep the protests entirely peaceful. Pashinyan loudly denounced any violence and threatened perpetrators of violent attacks with expulsion from the movement. This proclamation came out of a tradition of organizing throughout the years of protests leading up to the 2018 revolution, in which youth activists were careful to 'avoid violence … maintain a merry festive attitude, and generally attract the sympathetic attention of the citizens of Yerevan … no less importantly, the protesters engaged the police as "fellow Armenians" making mutual agreements to abide by the law' (Derluguian and Hovhannisyan 2018: 458).

The emphasis on non-violent discipline had many advantages that proved crucial in the movement's success. In particular, it bore fruit on 16 April when police repression of peaceful protesters in Yerevan sparked anger throughout the country, leading to a major loss of support for the Sargsyan regime and an increase in the size of the protests (Abrahamian and Shagoyan 2018). Most visibly, repression on this day led to Nikol Pashinyan's bandaged arm, which became a symbol of the protests for the remainder of the Revolution. This is a classic example of the 'backfire' dynamic in non-violent resistance struggles, when the exercise of repression rebounds against the one engaging in it because of the non-violent character of the ones repressed (Hess and Martin 2006). Backfire dynamics tend to only be triggered when movements are primarily or almost entirely non-violent. Breakdowns in non-violent discipline such as rioting or clashes with security services tend to undermine these dynamics since authorities can justify repression as necessary for maintaining public order, and ordinary people tend to be alienated from supporting the movement's goals.

Therefore, in the Velvet Revolution, we see success following the skilful deployment of unity, strategic planning (and learning) and rigid non-violent discipline. Of course, one cannot say with certainty what might have happened had any of these strategic factors been absent. Yet the parallels with the 2008 movement are illustrative. In both cases, an opposition force sought to oust an unpopular regime. In the first case, there was limited non-violent discipline, little strategic planning and a message that failed to unify because it focused on a polarizing and largely discredited former president, Levon Ter-Petrossian. The result was that the government was empowered to repress the movement, and after several deaths and arrests, the movement failed to achieve its key goal of preventing Serzh Sargsyan from becoming president of Armenia. In 2018, with the opposition having learned from its mistakes and a decade of both political and extra-political protest and mobilization under its belt, they were able to peacefully push Sargsyan from power and initiate a major political transformation.

Democratization after non-violent resistance

What can the non-violent resistance literature tell us about the likely future of Armenia's Velvet Revolution? The initial picture is cautious but encouraging. Non-violent resistance movements tend to initiate successful democratic transitions more often than any other form of regime breakdown (Karatnycky and Ackerman 2005; Celestino and Gleditsch 2013), and are particularly more effective in ushering in democracy than violent rebellions (Chenoweth and Stephan 2011). Yet it is not enough to simply usher in democracy. As the literature on democratic consolidation has highlighted, new democracies face an array of challenges before their new regimes are likely to endure (Linz and Stepan 1996; Schedler 1998; Svolik 2008). Similarly, there are several challenges that non-violent movements face when moving from opposing an authoritarian regime to establishing new democratic regime structures.

In particular, non-violent revolutions face the interconnected challenges of maintaining high levels of mobilization (and thus continuing pressure to push for democratic progress) while directing that mobilization towards building rather than breaking new political institutions (Pinckney 2018). If either of these challenges are not addressed, that is, if social and political mobilization drops off or if mobilization remains high but stays focused on revolutionary, institution-breaking goals, then democratic progress is unlikely. Yet if this pattern of high, yet institutionalized mobilization continues through a transitional period until new institutions can be formalized, then the likelihood of democratization is quite high.

When it comes to these challenges, the first year of transition in Armenia gave significant grounds for optimism. First, social and political mobilization remained quite high. Many civil society and activist groups, while they expressed significant confidence in the Pashinyan government, used the opportunity of a more sympathetic ear in Yerevan to expand rather than contract their public mobilization. This mobilization reflects the interplay of three distinct trends in Armenian civil society.[13] First, many activists left civil society to join the new government. Second, many of the remaining activists increased their criticism of government as they represented a more radical remaining fringe. And third, many activists reported that they were holding back from being overly critical of the new government because they were eager to see it succeed, but were also standing ready to hold the new leaders accountable (Andreasyan et al. 2018: 77).

One prominent example of these trends at work is the movement against the Lydian International Amulsar gold mine. Environmental activists had been engaged in pressure against the creation of the mine for several years. Yet they had always come up against major roadblocks from the Sargsyan administration, which was fully committed to moving forward with the mine's creation. In the immediate aftermath of the Velvet Revolution, young activists returning from Yerevan helped spearhead a series of demonstrations and road blockades to stop the mine. Many attributed their activism directly to the empowering example of the Velvet Revolution and the new, more sympathetic administration. As one activist said: 'If we protested during Serzh Sargsyan's rule, we would have been arrested right away. Now we, all of us Armenians, have overcome fear and created a democratic government. We can protect our rights' (Liakhov and Khudoyan 2018: 9). As of this writing, the protests have stopped the construction of the mine and have pressured the government to engage in a more systematic review of the mine's environmental impact.

Such mobilization no doubt represents a challenge for the Pashinyan government to address. Indeed, some referred to the Amulsar protests as Pashinyan's 'first major crisis' (Andreasyan et al. 2018: 76). Yet these kinds of mobilization are crucial for continuing to encourage democratic progress. Democracy relies on political elites knowing that they will be held accountable for their actions (Schmitter and Karl 1991). This is particularly true during transitions, when elites are establishing new norms of political behaviour. With civil society and ordinary citizens pushing back against the government, new political elites know that they must consider their opinions. Non-violent revolutions provide a powerful opportunity for increasing the vertical accountability of new regimes.[14] Yet for this opportunity to be realized, it must become obvious to new elites that people will engage in political action beyond the revolutionary moment. The Armenian public seems to be taking this lesson to heart, with encouraging signs for the future.

There have also been significant moves towards institutionalizing resistance, moving from the breakdown of old political structures to the creation of new ones. A major emphasis of Prime Minister Pashinyan and other leaders of the Velvet Revolution from the beginning has been a 'legalistic adherence to procedure' (Iskandaryan 2018: 480), and yet a willingness to direct extra-institutional mobilization towards achieving revolutionary goals when necessary. Pashinyan's road to the Prime Ministership is indicative of these twin emphases. After Prime Minister Sargsyan stepped down, Pashinyan was focused on achieving power through proper procedure, even though the domination of parliament by the Republican Party of Armenia (RPA) gave this long odds. When the parliament rejected his candidacy, he called people back to the streets to pressure it to give in, but maintained that the goal of the mobilization was to be realized through institutional channels. The general strike successfully pressured a significant chunk of the former RPA MPs to support Pashinyan's candidacy, and brought him into power.

Since that point, the call for snap elections and maintaining power through a parliamentary majority is another positive sign. The coalition of protest leaders, opposition figures, and technocrats seems ideally placed to further the goals of the revolution and move Armenia towards a more democratic future. The fact that the 2018 elections enjoyed broad public confidence and demonstrated compliance with international norms for free and fair elections is also another positive sign, expressing a new norm of accepting removal from power on the part of the RPA and the legitimacy of the new institutions.

Remaining challenges

Yet while the situation in Armenia gives significant grounds for optimism, it also provides significant grounds for concern. In addition to the challenges of continuing mobilization and shifting it towards institutional channels, which Pashinyan and the coalition of the Velvet Revolution seem to be handling quite well, there are many additional challenges that come with shifting a patronage-based political system towards one of higher democratic quality. The fight against corruption is one crucial question here. In particular, it remains to be seen whether the fight against corruption can be institutionalized into a new set of anti-corruption norms laws, rather than simply punishment of Pashinyan's former political rivals who are now out of power.

The Russian question also remains highly relevant for Armenia's future democratic progress (on this see also Chapter 7). From the revolution's beginning, Pashinyan has been clear that the sources of the Velvet Revolution are entirely domestic, that he and his government value close relations with Russia and that a shift to more democratic politics does not herald any kind of pro-Western shift in Armenia's foreign relations. Since becoming prime minister, Pashinyan has also been a frequent visitor to the Kremlin, and has gone to great lengths to reassure Russian president Vladimir Putin of his close alignment with Russia's interests (see, for example, Armenpress 2018). Thus, Putin and the Russian government have largely stayed out of Armenian politics since the revolution, since their greater concern is less with democracy or autocracy per se and more with geopolitics (Way 2018). Similar assurances by the Democratic Opposition of Serbia (DOS) helped ensure Russian abandonment of Serbian President Slobodan Milošević in that country's non-violent revolution (Bunce and Wolchik 2011). Yet considering that success in Serbia later rippled through Russia's sphere of influence, bringing in several more pro-Western regimes, Russia may be more hesitant to allow major changes in its geopolitical neighbourhood.

Effective domination of the new parliament by a single party and the near-complete rout of the old ruling party is also not an unalloyed good when considering Armenian democracy's future, particularly when tied with the extensive powers granted to the prime minister in the pre-revolutionary Armenian constitution. One of the crucial institutions for the growth of a new democracy is an institutionalized competitive party system (Mainwaring and Torcal 2006), with meaningful competition between political parties and an opposition able to effectively check the government. Without effective opposition, the example of past non-violent revolutions shows that even heroic protest movement leaders may shift in corrupt and authoritarian directions. For example, in 1991, a non-violent revolution led by the Movement for Multiparty Democracy (MMD) ousted Zambia's long-time single-party regime. The MMD's won Zambia's presidency by a three-to-one margin, and captured 125 out of 150 parliamentary seats, a similar proportion to Pashinyan's My Step and its allied Prosperous Armenia party. The lack of any effective political accountability mechanisms meant that MMD president Frederick Chiluba rapidly consolidated his own personal power, and engaged in very significant political corruption (Rakner 2003; Pinckney 2018). In contrast, many of the most successful transitions from authoritarian rule have been those in which authoritarian successor parties continue to serve as an effective opposition to the new regime (Loxton 2015). The effective domination of Armenia's politics by a single party could also prove problematic should the Nagorny Karabakh conflict with Azerbaijan heat up once again. Security emergencies are a frequent cause of democratic backsliding, as governments use the opportunity to crack down on political opponents in the name of national security.

Finally, there is the challenge of revolutionary disillusionment. The 'moment of madness' of the revolution past (Tarrow 1993), in many non-violent revolutions there is a painful waking up to underlying social and economic problems, and the realization that 'heroic' activists are unable on their own to resolve these problems. This can lead to backlash and even to nostalgia for an authoritarian past. Revolutionary leaders such as Prime Minister Nikol Pashinyan must transition to being politicians. Some leaders, such as Nelson Mandela, acquit themselves well during that transition. Others, such as Václav Havel or Mikheil Saakashvili, do less well.

Conclusion

The Armenian Velvet Revolution is the latest in a long line of non-violent revolutions that have challenged and frequently defeated authoritarian and quasi-democratic regimes in the twentieth and early twenty-first centuries. As such, it helps reinforce the insight that non-violent action can be a powerful tool to uproot entrenched power structures, even when conditions may be particularly unfavourable for political change. While revolutions typically seem inevitable when looked back on ex post, it is important to remember that even close observers rarely predict them ex ante. The same is true of the Velvet Revolution. In its aftermath, observers have identified many 'weaknesses' of the Sargsyan regime (see Chapter 3 of this volume), but these weaknesses on their own are insufficient to explain the revolution's success.

So what led to the Velvet Revolution's success? One key element was the skilful deployment of the three 'engines' of non-violent resistance: unity, strategic planning and non-violent discipline. The movement emphasized the common interests of all Armenians in ending a corrupt, patronal regime that had overstayed in power. It skilfully planned and deployed creative non-violent tactics and framing devices to maximize its impact, incentivize regime defection and mute or invert the impact of repression. Moreover, it kept its protests strictly non-violent, disincentivizing police repression and shifting public opinion in its favour. The combination of these three characteristics of successful non-violent resistance movements was sufficient to create a massive upswell of popular support for revolutionary change and force Prime Minister Sargsyan from power.

Will the Velvet Revolution result in greater democratization? Civil society is continuing popular mobilization and holding the new government accountable, while Prime Minister Nikol Pashinyan and the new generation of leaders now in power in Armenia appear to be skilfully navigating the political transition. Pashinyan has been careful to keep his pursuit of political goals within institutional confines, but has emphasized the incompleteness of the revolution thus far, keeping ordinary Armenians engaged in the political process and with strong reasons to continue mobilizing. Therefore, while many challenges remain, there are good reasons for optimism that the transition in Armenia will result in a regime of higher democratic quality.

What does the Velvet Revolution tell us about non-violent revolutions more broadly? The revolution has several important implications. First, it shows that it is possible to blend the diffuse, horizontal 'networked protest' of those connected by the internet with real institutional change. The Velvet Revolution was deeply integrated with the tools of digital and social media (MacFarquhar 2018). Yet it combined these tools with institutional pressure and integration with political elites to make not just symbolic but substantive change. This runs counter to a developing consensus that movements fuelled by the internet lack the structures to change long-term political outcomes (Tufekci 2017). Armenia demonstrates the possibility of combining the energy of tech-savvy youth activists with the institutional connections and hierarchy of opposition parties for a powerful blend of parliamentary and street politics (for a different expression of this argument, see Chapter 1 in this volume).

The Velvet Revolution also speaks to a debate in the literature on the international factors necessary for non-violent revolutions' success. Scholars have argued that both international diffusion and a friendly international patron may be necessary factors for the occurrence and success of non-violent revolutions (Lawson 2015; Ritter 2015). Yet the Velvet Revolution lacked both. Thus, it turns our attention away from external factors back towards domestic dynamics and the contingent decisions of the regime and opposition.

One thing is certain, we should not be too confident about the endurance of any single authoritarian regime. The history of non-violent resistance and of the Velvet Revolution in Armenia shows that even in unexpected and unfavourable circumstances, the tools of non-violent resistance, skilfully wielded, can lead to political transformation.

Notes

1 The views expressed in this chapter are solely those of the author and do not necessarily reflect the views of the U.S. Institute of Peace.
2 See, for example, the description of non-violent tactics in Amiryan (2018) and Abrahamian and Shagoyan (2018).

3   Because of this, non-violent resistance can also be pursued by any number
    of different kinds of political actors. It is perhaps most typically associated
    with social movements (Tarrow 1998; Della Porta and Diani 2009) and 'civil
    society', but can also be pursued by political parties, businesses and private
    individuals.

4   That is to say, 'a series of observable, continual tactics in pursuit of a
    political objective' (Chenoweth and Stephan 2011: 21).

5   Many of these movements are regularly profiled in the *Global Nonviolent
    Action Database* published by Swarthmore College at <https://nvdatabase.
    swarthmore.edu/>

6   Gevorg Ter-Gabrielyan, personal correspondence, 11 January 2019.

7   Interview with Vahram Ter-Matevosyan, 10 January 2019.

8   A 2017 poll indicated that only 8 per cent of the population believed
    Armenia was either 'definitely' or 'mainly' going in the right direction and
    less than 20 per cent of the population fully or partially trusted President
    Sargsyan (CRRC 2017).

9   Though there were informal partnerships between these civic initiatives and
    formal NGOs (Glasius and Ishkanian 2015; Paturyan and Bagiyan 2017).

10 The NGO sector in particular being viewed at least in part as a legacy of
    artificially-imposed foreign 'civil society' structures that had 'led to the
    depoliticization and taming of the emancipatory potential of civil society'
    (Ishkanian 2009: 10).

11 For more on the 2016 conflict, see Broers (2016).

12 Interview with Vahram Ter-Matevosyan, 10 January 2019.

13 Thanks to Laurence Broers for pointing these three trends out. See also
    Chapter 4.

14 For the classic discussion of the distinction between vertical and horizontal
    accountability see O'Donnell (1994).

References

Abrahamian, L. and Shagoyan, G. (2018) Velvet Revolution, Armenian Style.
    Demokratizatsiya: The Journal of Post-Soviet Democratization, 26 (4): 509–30.

Ackerman, P. and DuVall, J. (2006) The Right to Rise Up: People Power and the
    Virtues of Civic Disruption. *The Fletcher Forum of World Affairs*, 30 (2): 33–42.

Ackerman, P. and Kruegler, C. (1994) *Strategic Nonviolent Conflict, The
    Dynamics of People Power in the Twentieth Century*. Boston: Praeger.

Amiryan, T. (2018) Culture of Protest: The Symbols of Armenia's Velvet
    Revolution. *The Calvert Journal*. Available at: https://www.calvertjournal.com
    /articles/show/10318/culture-of-protest-symbols-of-armenia-velvet-revo
    lution (accessed 01 January 2019).

Andreasyan, Z., Ishkanian, A., Manusyan, A., Manusyan, S. and Zhamakochyan,
    A. (2018) *From Shrinking Space to Post-Revolutionary Space: Reimagining the*

Role and Relations of Civil Society in Armenia. Yerevan: Socioscope. Available at: http://socioscope.am/wp-content/uploads/2019/01/Socioscope-report _15.01_spread-eng.pdf (accessed 01 January 2019).

Armenpress. (2018) Armenia, Russia have Complete Understanding on Development and Strategic Directions of Bilateral Ties. *Armenpress.* Available at: https://armenpress.am/eng/news/959698.html (accessed 02 April 2019).

Avedissian, K. (2015) The Power of Electric Yerevan. *Open Democracy*, 6 July. Available at: https://www.opendemocracy.net/en/odr/electrified-yerevan/ (accessed 9 May 2019).

Bartkowski, M. J., ed. (2013) *Recovering Nonviolent History: Civil Resistance in Liberation Struggles.* Boulder: Lynne Rienner Publishers.

Bethke, F. S. and Pinckney, J. (2019) Nonviolent Resistance and the Quality of Democracy. *Conflict Management and Peace Science (OnlineFirst).* https:// doi.org/10.1177/0738894219855918 (accessed 6 April 2020).

Beyerle, S. M. (2014) *Curtailing Corruption: People Power for Accountability and Justice.* Boulder: Lynne Rienner Publishers.

Binnendijk, A. L. and Marovic, I. (2006) Power and Persuasion: Nonviolent Strategies to Influence State Security Forces in Serbia (2000) and Ukraine (2004). *Communist and Post-Communist Studies*, 39 (3): 411–29.

Brancati, D. (2016) *Democracy Protests.* New York: Cambridge University Press.

Bratton, M. and Van de Walle, N. (1997) *Democratic Experiments in Africa: Regime Transitions in Comparative Perspective.* Cambridge: Cambridge University Press.

Broers, L. (2016) *The Nagorny Karabakh Conflict: Defaulting to War.* London: Chatham House. Available at: https://www.chathamhouse.org/sites/default/fi les/publications/research/NK%20paper%2024082016%20WEB.pdf (accessed 11 February 2019).

Bunce, V. J. and Wolchik, S. L. (2011) *Defeating Authoritarian Leaders in Postcommunist Countries.* New York: Cambridge University Press.

Celestino, M. R. and Gleditsch, K. S. (2013) Fresh Carnations or All Thorn, No Rose? Nonviolent Campaigns and Transitions in Autocracies. *Journal of Peace Research*, 50 (3): 385–400.

Chenoweth, E. and Lewis, O. A. (2013) Unpacking Nonviolent Campaigns: Introducing the NAVCO 2.0 Dataset. *Journal of Peace Research*, 50 (3): 415–23.

Chenoweth, E. and Stephan, M. J. (2011) *Why Civil Resistance Works: The Strategic Logic of Nonviolent Conflict.* New York: Columbia University Press.

CRRC (Caucasus Resource Research Center) (2017) Public Perceptions on Political, Social, and Economic Issues in the South Caucasus Countries: Some Findings from the CRRC 2017 Data. Available at: http://www.crrc.am/ hosting/file/_static_content/barometer/2017/CB2017_ENG_presentatio n_final_.pdf (accessed 4 January 2019).

Cunningham, K. G., Dahl, M. and Fruge, A. (2017) Strategies of Resistance: Diversification and Diffusion. *American Journal of Political Science*, 61 (3): 591–605.

Della Porta, D. and Diani, M. (2009) *Social Movements: An Introduction.* Hoboken: John Wiley & Sons.

Derluguian, G. and Hovhannisyan, R. (2018) The Armenian Anomaly: Toward an Interdisciplinary Interpretation. *Demokratizatsiya: The Journal of Post-Soviet Democratization*, 26 (4): 441–64.

Elliott, R. (2018) Facebook Live Reshapes Election Campaigning in Armenia. *The Armenian Weekly*. Available at: https://armenianweekly.com/2018/12/05/facebook-live-reshapes-election-campaigning-in-armenia/ (accessed 4 April 2019).

Glasius, M. and Ishkanian, A. (2015) Surreptitious Symbiosis: Engagement Between Activists and NGOs. *VOLUNTAS: International Journal of Voluntary and Nonprofit Organizations*, 26 (6): 2620–44. DOI: 10.1007/s11266-014-9531-5

Gogia, G., Bouckaert, P., Gorvin, I., Kleshik, S. and Solvang, O. (2009) *Democracy on Rocky Ground: Armenia's Disputed 2008 Presidential Election, Post-election Violence, and the One-sided Pursuit of Accountability.* New York: Human Rights Watch.

Harsch, E. (2017) *Burkina Faso: A History of Power, Protest, and Revolution.* London: Zed Books.

Helvey, R. L. (2004) *On Strategic Nonviolent Conflict: Thinking about the Fundamentals.* Boston: Albert Einstein Institute.

Hess, D. and Martin, B. (2006) Repression, Backfire, and the Theory of Transformative Events. *Mobilization: An International Quarterly*, 11 (2): 249–67.

Huneeus, C. (2009) Mass Mobilization in Pinochet's Chile, 1983–88. In: Roberts, A. and Ash, T. G., eds, *Civil Resistance and Power Politics: The Experience of Non-violent Action from Gandhi to the Present.* New York: Oxford University Press, 197–212.

International Telecommunications Union (2018) *Individuals Using the Internet.* Available at: https://www.itu.int/en/ITU-D/Statistics/Pages/stat/default.aspx (accessed 4 April 2019).

Ishkanian, A. (2009) (Re)claiming the Emancipatory Potential of Civil Society: A Critical Evaluation of Civil Society and Democracy-Building Programs in Armenia Since 1991. *Armenian Review*, 51 (1): 9–34.

Ishkanian, A. (2015) Self-Determined Citizens? New Forms of Civic Activism and Citizenship in Armenia. *Europe-Asia Studies*, 67 (8): 1203–27.

Iskandaryan, A. (2018) The Velvet Revolution in Armenia: How to Lose Power in Two Weeks. *Demokratizatsiya: The Journal of Post-Soviet Democratization*, 26 (4): 465–82.

Karatnycky, A. and Ackerman, P. (2005) *How Freedom Is Won: From Civic Resistance to Durable Democracy.* Washington DC: Freedom House.

Kuran, T. (1991) Now Out of Never: The Element of Surprise in the East European Revolution of 1989. *World Politics*, 44 (1): 7–48.

Lawson, G. (2015) Revolution, Nonviolence, and the Arab Uprisings. *Mobilization: An International Quarterly*, 20 (4): 453–70.

Levitsky, S. and Way, L. A. (2010) *Competitive Authoritarianism: Hybrid Regimes after the Cold War*. New York: Cambridge University Press.

Liakhov, P. and Khudoyan, K. (2018) How Citizens Battling a Controversial Gold Mining Project are Testing Armenia's New Democracy. *OpenDemocracy*. Available at: https://www.opendemocracy.net/od-russia/peter-liakhov-knar-khudoyan/citizens-battling-a-controversial-gold-mining-project-amulsar-armenia (accessed 18 January 2019).

Linz, J. J. and Stepan, A. (1996) *Problems of Democratic Transition and Consolidation: Southern Europe, South America, and Post-communist Europe*. Baltimore: JHU Press.

Loxton, J. (2015) Authoritarian Successor Parties. *Journal of Democracy*, 26 (3): 157–70.

MacFarquhar, N. (2018) Behind Armenia's Revolt, Young Shock Troops From the Tech Sector. *The New York Times*, 15 October. Available at: https://www.nytimes.com/2018/05/19/world/europe/armenia-revolt-tech-sector.html (accessed 2 April 2019).

MacFarquhar, N. and Pérez-Peña, R. (2018) 'I Was Wrong': Armenian Leader Quits Amid Protests. *The New York Times*, 23 April. https://www.nytimes.com/2018/04/23/world/europe/armenia-prime-minister-protests.html (accessed 6 April 2020).

Mainwaring, S. and Torcal, M. (2006) Party System Institutionalization and Party System Theory after the Third Wave of Democratization. *Handbook of Party Politics*, 11 (6): 204–27.

Makunts, L. (2018) After Armenia's Velvet Revolution, New Colors and Vibes in Country's Politics and Society. ICNC. Available at: https://www.nonviolent-conflict.org/blog_post/armenias-velvet-revolution-new-colors-vibes-countrys-politics-society/ (accessed 4 January 2019).

Nepstad, S. E. (2011) *Nonviolent Revolutions: Civil Resistance in the Late 20th Century*. New York: Oxford University Press.

Nepstad, S. E. (2013) Mutiny and Nonviolence in the Arab Spring: Exploring Military Defections and Loyalty in Egypt, Bahrain, and Syria. *Journal of Peace Research*, 50 (3): 337–49.

Nikolayenko, O. (2013) Origins of the Movement's Strategy: The Case of the Serbian Youth Movement Otpor. *International Political Science Review*, 34 (2): 140–58.

O'Donnell, G. A. (1994) Delegative Democracy. *Journal of Democracy*, 5 (1): 55–69.

Ohanyan, A. (2018) Armenia's Democratic Dreams. *Foreign Policy*. Available at: https://foreignpolicy.com/2018/11/07/armenias-democratic-dreams/ (accessed 1 January 2019).

Paturyan, Y. J. and Bagiyan, A. (2017) NGOs and Civic Activism in Armenia: Four Case Studies. *Armenian Review*, 55 (3/4): 56–84.

Paturyan, Y. J. and Gevorgyan, V. (2016) Emergent Civic Activism: A New Phase of Transition for Post-Communist Armenian Civil Society? Paper Submitted to the 12th International Conference of the International Society for Third Sector Research.

Pearce, K. (2018) Livestreaming Armenia's 'velvet revolution'. *Eurasianet*. Available at: https://eurasianet.org/perspectives-livestreaming-armenias-v elvet-revolution (accessed 2 April 2019).

Pinckney, J. (2016) *Making or Breaking Nonviolent Discipline*. Washington DC: ICNC Press.

Pinckney, J. (2018) *When Civil Resistance Succeeds: Building Democracy after Popular Nonviolent Uprisings*. Washington DC: ICNC Press.

Popovic, S. (2015) *Blueprint for Revolution: How to Use Rice Pudding, Lego Men, and other Nonviolent Techniques to Galvanize Communities, Overthrow Dictators, or Simply Change the World*. New York: Spiegel & Grau.

Raghavan, S. (2019) Algerian Leader to Resign from Office by End of April after Weeks of Street Protests. *Washington Post*. Available at: https://www.was hingtonpost.com/world/algerian-leader-to-resign-from-office-by-end-of-april-after-weeks-of-street-protests/2019/04/01/776ed2f8-549b-11e9-aa8 3-504f086bf5d6_story.html (accessed 2 April 2019).

Rakner, L. (2003) *Political and Economic Liberalisation in Zambia 1991–2001*. Stockholm: Nordic Africa Institute.

Ritter, D. P. (2015) *The Iron Cage of Liberalism: International Politics and Unarmed Revolutions in the Middle East and North Africa*. New York: Oxford University Press.

Roberts, A., Willis, M. J., McCarthy, R. and Ash, T. G. (2016) *Civil Resistance in the Arab Spring: Triumphs and Disasters*. New York: Oxford University Press.

Schedler, A. (1998) What Is Democratic Consolidation? *Journal of Democracy*, 9 (2): 91–107.

Schmitter, P. C. and Karl, T. L. (1991) 'What Democracy Is. . . and Is Not'. *Journal of Democracy*, 2 (3): 75–88.

Schock, K. (2003) Nonviolent Action and Its Misconceptions: Insights for Social Scientists. *PS: Political Science and Politics*, 36 (4): 705–12.

Schock, K. (2005) *Unarmed Insurrections: People Power Movements in Nondemocracies*. Minneapolis: University of Minnesota Press.

Sharp, G. (1973) *The Politics of Nonviolent Action*. Boston: Porter Sargent.

Sharp, G. (1999) Nonviolent Action. In: Kurtz, L., and Turpin, J. E., eds, *Encyclopedia of Violence, Peace, and Conflict*. New York: Academic Press, 567–74.

Silaev, N. and Fomin, I. (2018) My Step Aside from Sasna Tsrer: The Dynamics of Protest Coalitions in Armenia, 2016 and 2018. *Demokratizatsiya: The Journal of Post-Soviet Democratization*, 26 (4): 483–508.

Svolik, M. W. (2008) Authoritarian Reversals and Democratic Consolidation. *American Political Science Review*, 102 (2): 153–68.

Tarrow, S. (1993) Cycles of Collective Action: Between Moments of Madness and the Repertoire of Contention. *Social Science History*, 17 (2): 281–307.

Tarrow, S. (1998) *Power in Movement: Social Movements and Contentious Politics*. New York: Cambridge University Press.

Tilly, C. (1994) Social Movements as Historically Specific Clusters of Political Performances. *Berkeley Journal of Sociology*, 38: 1–30.

Tufekci, Z. (2017) *Twitter and Tear Gas: The Power and Fragility of Networked Protest*. New Haven: Yale University Press.

Way, L. A. (2008) The Real Causes of the Color Revolutions. *Journal of Democracy*, 19 (3): 55–69.

Way, L. A. (2018) Why Didn't Putin Interfere in Armenia's Velvet Revolution. *Foreign Affairs*. Available at: https://www.foreignaffairs.com/articles/armenia/2018-05-17/why-didnt-putin-interfere-armenias-velvet-revolution (accessed 1 January 2019).

6

Armenia's transition

The challenges of geography, geopolitics and multipolarity

Richard Giragosian

Introduction

In October 2018, the new Armenian government of Nikol Pashinyan hosted a two-day Francophonie summit, with leaders from over forty mostly French-speaking countries. It was an opportunity for Pashinyan and his team to showcase their credentials as a committed and dynamic group of young reformers. Having displaced the incumbent ruling Republican Party of Armenia (RPA) after more than a decade in power, Pashinyan and his youthful team represented a validation of European values, despite their adamant rejection of geopolitical labels. The summit yielded the new Armenian government a significant degree of international recognition and respect. More importantly, the visits of French President Emmanuel Macron and Canadian Prime Minister Justin Trudeau, among other heads of state, to Armenia contributed unprecedented attention and unexpected admiration that only raised Armenia's profile globally. A subsequent visit to Yerevan by German Chancellor Angela Merkel further signalled international endorsement of Armenia's new democratic path and the country's elevated strategic significance.

These positive developments appeared to offer prospects of an assortment of new critical resources – domestic legitimacy, a genuine appetite for reform and an empowering stance from friendly outside actors – helping to mitigate the enduring challenges of Armenia's geopolitics. Ever since regaining its independence in the wake of the collapse of the Soviet Union, the Republic of Armenia has been challenged by a difficult and daunting combination of geography and geopolitics. This combination of multidimensional challenges has traditionally been defined by four distinct determinant factors, that each has simultaneously driven, delineated and discouraged the development of Armenia's sovereignty and statehood.

The first determinant is rooted in the historical rivalry between Russia and Turkey, which has often reduced Armenia to weathering a critical geopolitical choice between 'bad and worse'. That choice between two lesser evils, between the posture of submitting to Russian patronage and the peril of surrendering to Turkish mercy, has been Armenia's ultimate strategic dilemma, continuously undermining Armenian statehood and presenting a unique calculus for successive Armenian governments.

A second, but related, determinant has been the more recent threat stemming from a pan-Turkic alliance between Turkey and Azerbaijan. This again demonstrates Armenia's vulnerability as specifically rooted in its geography, whereby the country's location, interposing both between Turkey and Azerbaijan and mainland Azerbaijan and exclave Nakhichevan, is a double interruption to Turkish-Azerbaijani unity. And although the religious aspect of this threat was less of a factor in recent years, as seen by the absence of an Islamist angle to the Nagorny Karabakh conflict, it was an added driver for the anti-Armenian pogroms and massacres of the waning Ottoman Empire throughout the late nineteenth century and into the Armenian Genocide of the early twentieth century committed by the Young Turk leadership.

And as if the first two challenges were not serious enough, a third determinant of combined geopolitical and geographic restraints – which also represent a deeper combination of the two earlier factors – is rooted in the current confrontation between Russia and the West. This was more clearly pronounced during the long-term Cold War posture of entrenched competition and rivalry between the Soviet Union and the United States, with a broader arena pitting the Soviet bloc and its proxy states against the West and its allies. For Armenia, this Cold War context imposed seven decades of isolation within the Soviet Union that forcibly subsumed Armenian sovereignty and independence. The pressures of Russian-Western confrontation were lessened during the temporary 'unipolar moment' following the end of the Cold War, but resumed with its retrenchment since the late 2000s with the Georgian and Ukrainian crises.

A fourth and more subdued challenge is that of making the best of Armenia's relations with the two remaining neighbours with whom it does share open borders, Georgia and Iran. Each presents challenges of its own, however. Georgia confronts multiple challenges from its own geography and geopolitics, being committed to a Euro-Atlantic path while facing two secessionist challenges in Abkhazia and South Ossetia and remaining vulnerable to Russia's geopolitical pressure. Armenia's border with Iran potentially offers a small window into a nation and culture with which Armenians have historically had a warm relationship. Yet under the current conditions of Iranian-Western confrontation over nuclear and other issues, and sanctions from Euro-Atlantic powers, the leeway for this window to open is very narrow indeed. Georgia and Iran confront Armenian foreign policy with the problem of 'override', whereby Yerevan's relations with each are nested within overarching geopolitical relations with Russia and the West that tend to override the opportunities that are potentially available.

Revisiting the ABCs of Armenian strategy: Adaptation, balancing and 'complementarity' – and velvet

Against that harsh backdrop, modern Armenia continues to face a similar combination of challenges that generally conform to that same multidimensional quartet of determinants and that reflects the same intensity of past threats. Regardless of regime or leader, Armenian statehood since independence was forced to respond adroitly and adeptly, with a resulting policy of strategic innovation comprised of three elements.

First, reflecting the necessity of an unexpected independence at the moment of collapse of the Soviet system, Armenia was already at war with Azerbaijan over Nagorny Karabakh ('Artsakh'). Beyond the need to manage the Soviet legacy, this state of war from the outset of the country's early period of independence triggered an urgent response of adaptation, whereby Armenia sought to contain and mitigate the burdens of an energy crisis after the collapse of natural gas supplies and the disruption of electricity transmission, the imposition of a blockade arising from the closure of borders with Azerbaijan and Turkey that disrupted core trade and transport links, and a scarcity of goods that saw the replacement of a command economy with a more primitive short-term system of 'conflict economics'. Nevertheless, there was a degree of adaptation, both on the political and personal level in those early, dark years of Armenian independence. Although defined more by improvisation and necessity, the resulting siege mentality was able to garner an impressive degree of national unity and shared sacrifice as a wartime coping mechanism for national survival.

Beyond such improvised adaptation, Armenia also responded by seeking greater strategic balance between Russia, as a partner for security, and the West, as a supporter and donor of reforms. This search for more balance included a related effort to seek greater options in what became known as the policy of *complementarity*, a term largely attributed to Armenia's former foreign minister Vartan Oskanian (serving for a decade from 1998 to 2008) (Oskanian 2008). Over time, and well into the two-term presidency of Serzh Sargsyan, complementarity served as a fundamental pillar of Armenian foreign policy, although marked by a mixed record of profit and loss (Socor 2013).

Armenia's 2018 Velvet Revolution shook up the received wisdom about Armenia's foreign policy options. Bolstered by both international attention and the recognition of the country's greater strategic significance, the Velvet Revolution immediately offered the prospect of a critical addition to the ABCs of Armenian strategy: a significant degree of 'soft power'. Traditional 'hard power' elements of foreign policy rely on military force and national power to coerce and command, most often utilizing pressure and threats in pursuit of national interest. Armenia is endowed with few of these hard power assets, however. Given the additional limits of small size and population, a remote and isolated location and the burden of unresolved yet simmering conflict, it must pursue a more innovative and flexible 'small state' strategy of leveraging soft power by applying elements of persuasion and attraction. Bringing velvet to Armenia's foreign policy implies a 'small state, soft power' formula that speaks to both Armenia's needs and actual assets.

First, the implications of a policy preference for soft power are positive, as Armenia's prioritization of 'soft' over 'hard' elements of its foreign policy results in an elevation of diplomacy and negotiation over threat and the force of arms (McConnell, Megoran and Williams 2014). This is befitting for a small state locked in a simmering conflict with a larger neighbour in a difficult neighbourhood. Armenia has an opportunity and an imperative to differentiate itself from illiberal or authoritarian modes of managing conflict (Lewis, Heathershaw and Megoran 2018). Authoritarian conflict management requires higher levels of coercive power and evasion of democratic oversight that Armenia has neither the capacity nor the appetite for after the Velvet Revolution. Furthermore, even if contained to specific policy areas, illiberal practices tend to diffuse across political systems, signifying a threat to the broader project driving the Velvet Revolution. Lastly, exercising soft power also offers its own diplomatic dividends, especially in contrast to Azerbaijan, which has more traditionally emphasized its rhetoric of aggressive and bellicose language based on its surging military spending. Coupled with Azerbaijan's entrenched oil-driven corruption, such a tactical reliance on threats and military force has only further damaged Azerbaijan's status and standing over the longer term.

Reliance on soft power assets as instruments of Armenian foreign policy is also more effective and more attentive to the dividends of harnessing its global diaspora and the benefits of culture and national 'branding'. The

Armenian diaspora has played diverse roles in post-Soviet Armenia's political trajectory (see Chapter 9). The potential for celebrity power to impact on Armenia's profile was showcased by the intense media interest in the 2015 visit to Armenia of the Kardashians, image-savvy reality TV stars, whose brief time in the country resulted in a massive flurry of attention and coverage. Whatever the negative aspects of the celebrity culture driving the Kardashian phenomenon, their visit provided an unplanned public relations coup and a fresh new celebrity 'brand' promoting Armenia.

Multipolarity and a new crisis of confidence

Nearly every assessment of Armenian foreign policy focuses on the danger of the country's over-dependence on Russia (see Chapter 7). And although such a focus is both accurate and necessary, a new, unexpected challenge to Armenian foreign policy emerged in the first year of the Pashinyan government. This surprising challenge came from the United States, against the backdrop of an emergent multipolar order no longer defined by American hegemony and consistency. The United States directly threatened and pressured Armenia in two separate areas of foreign policy. Despite a long-standing and stable bilateral relationship, the United States was especially outspoken and aggressive in its criticism of Armenia for its ties to Iran and over its operational deployments to Syria. While the American attacks against Armenia were softened by promises of support and assistance, the sudden and assertive tone of US criticism sparked an unprecedented crisis of confidence, with some concerns over the possibility of US sanctions against Armenia. While the threat of US sanctions on Armenia over its ties to Iran was not new (Shaffer 2003), in light of the more impulsive and seemingly aggressive policies of the Trump administration, this new situation was more serious for Armenia than ever before.

Bolton's 'Iran offensive'

The first sign of this new crisis of confidence came in October 2018, during the visit of then US National Security Adviser John Bolton to Armenia. As an American political figure well known for his hard-line, neoconservative views, Bolton was both brisk and brash in meetings with Armenian officials, where he warned that Armenia's relationship with Iran was under greater scrutiny in Washington. Interestingly, Bolton emphasized higher US expectations of the new Pashinyan government, noting that the Trump administration was much less tolerant of any failure by Armenia to engage Azerbaijan in moving faster towards a negotiated resolution to the Karabakh conflict, especially given Armenia's newly minted democratic credentials, and urging the Armenian premier to take 'decisive steps' in that direction (Radio Free Europe/Radio Liberty 2019). The warning to Armenia, an example of the Trump administration's 'divisive diplomacy', was also very much in line with Washington's now common habit of angering friends and allies while placating or appeasing rivals and opponents (Giragosyan 2017; Global Risk Insights 2016). Furthermore, the message from the Trump administration, as articulated by Bolton, was to put Armenia on notice that the United States seeks to apply 'maximum pressure' in order to 'squeeze Iran', warning that Washington also intends to enforce tightened sanctions 'very vigorously' and noting that the Armenian border with Iran will be 'a significant issue' (for more see Giragosian 2018a).

Seeking to somewhat soften the tone of Bolton's threats, other American officials sought to reassure Armenia, highlighting a very different and more positive message. That more positive and predictable message came in mid-October 2018 when, at the close of a visit to Armenia, George Kent, the US Deputy Assistant Secretary of State for European and Eurasian Affairs, promised that although Washington already provided Armenia with $14 million in additional aid after the change of government in 2018, further support would be provided for the Armenian government's anti-corruption efforts and programmes to diversify the Armenian economy, including a focus on improving the country's investment climate.

Yet a second, subsequent episode of such 'bluff and bluster' from the Trump administration came later, in reaction to a December 2018 statement by Armenian Prime Minister Pashinyan promising to 'deepen not only economic but also political relations with Iran', despite the challenge of US sanctions that were re-imposed by the Trump administration. This was also followed by quiet, behind-the-scenes American diplomacy seeking to pressure the Armenian government to crack down on Iranian airlines and banks operating in Armenia.

Warnings over Syria

Another significant area of confrontation was over Syria, as Armenia initiated a 'humanitarian mission' that was widely perceived in the West as a deployment in support of Russian military operations in the Syrian theatre. In fact, no matter what the precise context, the US State Department issued an unusually assertive statement in February 2019 stressing that Washington did not support 'any engagement with Syrian military forces' or 'any cooperation between Armenia and Russia for this mission'. In response, Armenian Foreign Ministry spokeswoman Anna Naghdalyan stated that although the Armenian government 'took note of the statement' by the US State Department, the deployment of some eighty-three Armenian army medics, sappers and other personnel to Syria was solely a 'humanitarian' mission.

In an additional clarification in support of Armenian government policy, Ruben Rubinian, the chairman of the parliamentary committee on foreign relations, added that 'sending a team of specialists to Syria is very important for us because it is first of all aimed at ensuring the physical security of our compatriots living there and second of all the security of peoples living in Syria', and represented 'a purely humanitarian move'.

For its part, however, Russia seized the opportunity to embarrass the United States and quickly took advantage of the rather undiplomatic American move, with Russian Deputy Foreign Minister Grigory Karasin warning that the United States was actively interfering in Armenia's internal affairs and stressing that Moscow expected 'that the current leadership of Armenia, which received a necessary mandate in the parliamentary elections, will have the courage to resist the unhidden external blackmail and pressure and will defend its sovereign right to independently make decisions based on national interests'. Karasin further added that the 'tragic fate' of Ukraine and Georgia, which he said were 'let down' by the West, 'must serve as a warning' to Armenia. Although Karasin's crude rhetoric obviously failed to impact Armenian policy, it did complicate Armenia's bid to avoid deeper entanglement in Russia's confrontation with the West.

Changes in American policy?

From a broader perspective, US policy towards Armenia has long been defined and driven by a perspective on relations with Armenia as being a subset of issues within a broader context of US–Russian relations. Such a view was generally consistent through both the Bush and the Obama administrations, and larger considerations, such as Turkey and Iran, also added to the dominant perspective of a Russian-centric view of Armenia. But given the unpredictable and unorthodox nature of the Trump White House and President Trump's rather suspicious personal ties and commercial dealings in Russia, the traditional American approach to Armenia has changed, with fresh questions over the precise view of Armenia actually held by the Trump administration.

What is also different in US policy, however, is the end to the past practice of the United States 'looking the other way' as Armenia deepened its ties and trade with Iran, despite the fact that Armenia has consistently conformed to previous sanctions and only saw Iran as an essential alternative to counter its over-dependence on Russia. And given Washington's primitive zero-sum approach to Iran, a new physics applies, where for every positive action by Armenia to engage Iran, there is a danger of an American negative reaction. This is the challenge of the new multipolarity, refracting in unpredictable ways to challenge the scope and vectors of Armenia's foreign policy.

The necessity of engaging Iran

For all countries, geography does not normally change, and for Armenia, with two of its four borders closed, relations with Iran are essential, as a secondary but significant alternative to Georgia's near-monopoly as Armenia's primary trade route. The imperative of engaging Iran is also bolstered by the economic benefits, as evident in the fact that in 2018, Armenian trade with Iran soared by over 40 per cent, reaching $364 million. Although there are limits to Armenia's opportunities to emerge as a 'bridge' to Iran, Yerevan does have some strategic advantages to leverage as it seeks to deepen and develop its relations with Iran.

One such strategic advantage stems from the fact that Armenia is Iran's only stable and friendly neighbour in the region, making it uniquely positioned to offer Iran an avenue to mitigate its own isolation. A second advantage is rooted in Armenia's membership in the Eurasian Economic Union (EAEU), which allows Armenia to offer Iran an important transit platform to reach the much larger markets of EAEU member states. Similar dividends from providing for transit can also be seen in Armenia's role as a platform for Western engagement in the untapped Iranian market.

A third advantage is that, although Iran has the options of maritime trade with Russia through the Caspian Sea and with the West through its Persian Gulf ports, only Armenia offers a reliable overland route, a position especially attractive to Iran given the stark contrast to the tension with Azerbaijan. That overland route offers real potential for expanding road and railway links and developing a broader energy infrastructure network, with the operational natural gas pipeline between Iran and Armenia serving as a foundation for the further expansion of energy transport and Armenian exports of surplus electricity to Iran.

In terms of energy, however, the challenge is actually from Russian opposition, which is natural due to the overwhelming dominance of Russia's

Gazprom in the Armenian domestic market, which drives the reality that Gazprom would not willingly allow any new competition from Iranian gas supplies. Currently, Armenia imports roughly 500 million cubic metres of Iranian gas annually in a barter or swap agreement, in exchange for Armenian exports of electricity to Iran. By contrast, annual Armenian imports of natural gas from Russia total about two billion cubic metres and, most importantly, are purchased at significantly cheaper, subsidized prices. Beyond the disparity in gas supplies, the relatively narrow diameter of the existing Armenia-Iran gas pipeline prevents any re-export of gas beyond Armenia and requires the construction of an additional or twin gas pipeline in order to achieve any significant increase in the volume of gas from Iran (Oxford Analytica 2015). At the same time, any possible expansion of Armenian imports of gas from Iran would also mandate a new contract to replace the current barter arrangement and would most likely be based on higher world prices.

From a more practical perspective beyond energy, the more realistic and still attractive commercial areas for expanding Armenian trade and investment with Iran include the information technology (IT) sector and as a key component in the supply chain for Iran's imports of scarce automotive and aircraft parts and supplies, as well as high-end consumer goods, whose commercial opportunities are significantly enhanced by years of pent-up demand and the promise of high profit margins (for more see Giragosian 2015a) .

What comes next?

Based on the threats and criticism from the Trump administration over aspects of Armenian foreign policy, there were genuine concerns over the possible imposition of sanctions or other related punitive measures by the United States. Nevertheless, Armenia is not in violation of existing American sanctions against Iran and remains committed to maintaining its strict adherence to the existing restrictions in place covering banking, aviation, terrorism and money laundering (Oxford Analytica 2015). But as Washington seems intent on further tightening sanctions as part of its attempt to undermine the Western nuclear deal with Iran, there is a risk of some form of American retribution as Armenian trade with Iran follows its natural course of expansion.

Yet the threat of American sanctions against Armenia is still unlikely, for several reasons. First, despite the aggressive posture of the Trump administration, Armenia is not the centre of its concerns over Iran. This is due to the fairly limited scale of trade with Iran and because of the absence

150   *Armenia's Velvet Revolution*

of any significant military or security-related elements of the bilateral relationship. A second factor that discourages such a sanctions scenario stems from the powerful political position of the Armenian-American lobby, whose influence within the US Congress may be sufficiently powerful to counter any move against Armenia by the White House.

And a third factor making the risk of sanctions against Armenia unlikely is the broader strategic context, as US foreign policy is distracted by developments elsewhere, challenged by proliferation concerns in North Korea and diverted by its stated goals to withdraw from Syria and Afghanistan. Thus, although the unprecedented American critique of aspects of Armenian foreign policy does pose a challenging 'crisis of confidence', the danger of American sanctions or punishment of Armenia seems unlikely.

The imperative of a 'small state strategy'

For a small country like Armenia, one of the more critical challenges is to attain a degree of relative relevance and strategic significance. As a landlocked country located in a rather remote region, garnering recognition and relevance has been a difficult task. In addition to the lingering tension with Turkey, the simmering conflict with Azerbaijan and the mounting unreliability of Russian patronage, the imperative of an effective Armenian foreign policy is also defined by its historical role as a state founded on the survival of genocide. Armenia requires more than simple recognition of its statehood; rather, the country must also seek greater strategic significance. It is precisely this set of challenges, however, that necessitates an innovative and active foreign policy (Giragosian 2018b). Against this backdrop, Armenian foreign policy has been fairly successful and consistent, further bolstered by the political influence and sophistication of the global Armenian diaspora and its lobbying and advocacy organizations (Zarifian 2014). At the same time, however, far too many of the successes of Armenia's foreign policy have been due to the mistakes and weaknesses of its opponents and rivals, rather than as a derivative of its own diplomacy.

For both the defence and development of Armenian statehood, there are several fundamental limits and challenges. The first of these limits is seen in the country's unforgiving geography, as the lack of assured access to either the Black or Mediterranean Seas has contributed to landlocked isolation (Collier 2007). Second, the limits of geography also pertain to neighbouring countries, as two of Armenia's four borders remain closed. While this has only magnified the importance of Georgia as the main route for Armenian exports and imports, especially given the limits of using Iran as an effective alternative, it has also led to the development of a 'siege mentality' within Armenia.

This reality of inherent limitations and challenges has spurred the need for Armenian foreign policy to seek greater space or room for manoeuvre, demonstrated by the strategy of complementarity, which as noted earlier strives for strategic balancing and greater options. And despite some obvious setbacks and mistakes, this 'small state' strategy has generally been successful in mitigating the damage from gradual over-dependence on Russia and in maximizing opportunities. The latter success in seizing opportunities was most evident in Armenia's rare second chance to regain and restore strategic relations with the European Union (EU), for example, with the successful negotiation and conclusion of the Armenia-EU Comprehensive and Enhanced Partnership Agreement (CEPA) in November 2017 (for more see Giragosian and Kostanyan 2017). And as a country coerced to sacrifice its earlier association agreement and related Deep and Comprehensive Free Trade Area (DCFTA) with the EU in favour of joining the Russian-dominated EAEU, this was a particularly important achievement (Giragosian 2014).

A second important aspect of the efficacy of this 'small state strategy' is the Armenian policy of engagement as an active member in multilateral organizations and as a committed contributor to regional and international security. The country's engagement in multilateral diplomacy is also based on parity, being active in such diverse Western organizations as the Council of Europe and NATO's Partnership for Peace (PfP) programme while also maintaining its role as a member of the Russian-oriented Collective Security Treaty Organization (CSTO) and the Commonwealth of Independent States (CIS), as well as the more neutral United Nations. This parity also applies to the security arena as well, as seen by Armenia's contributions to NATO and UN peacekeeping missions, including deployments to Kosovo (KFOR), Iraq, Afghanistan (ISAF), and even southern Lebanon (UNIFIL), while serving as a founding member of the Russian-led CSTO (for a more detailed assessment of Armenian peacekeeping deployments, see: Giragosian 2015b). Armenia's multilateral engagement is also broader than simply the political or security fields, however, and includes membership in the World Trade Organization (WTO), as well as key partnerships with the International Monetary Fund (IMF) and the World Bank.

Transforming 'soft power' into 'smart power'

For Armenia, the complexity of challenges and the daunting nature of the threat environment nevertheless require more than a simple reliance on soft power. What is needed is a more advanced and ambitious strategy that seeks to transform soft power into 'smart power'. Such a transformation implies a graduation of policy that can utilize the soft power tools of persuasion and attraction, backed and bolstered by underlying threats of coercion and pressure of hard power. It is this 'push–pull' application of a hard–soft power combination that constitutes 'smart power'. In practical terms for Armenia, this requires a more coordinated foreign policy framework that includes elements of public diplomacy, with an added use of celebrity promotion (as seen in the examples of the Kardashians and the positive legacy of the late Charles Aznavour, among others) for positive image and national branding, as well as networking based on the political influence and lobbying/advocacy power of the Armenian diaspora.

Yet the task of forging such smart power is not as easy as it seems and depends on several prerequisites for success. First, it requires a degree of political will that has been generally missing in recent years. And although the peaceful change of government and an important free and fair election in December 2018 have done much to improve governance and democratization, the new government has not yet demonstrated enough political will and sufficient statesmanship to any lasting degree. A second key requirement for attaining effective smart power in Armenia is strategic vision, or at least the articulation of a clear and coherent long-term strategy for the country. And in this area too, despite the enthusiasm and energy of the idealistic new government, there is still an absence of demonstrable strategic vision. The outlook, however, is promising, and the lack of strategic vision and a desired end state may be due more to inexperience and inattention than to any inability or unwillingness to define what sort of 'New Armenia' is envisioned by the Pashinyan government.

A new economic statecraft

In addition to the need to transform soft power into a more innovative smart power, Armenian foreign policy should also add a new element of economic statecraft. Such an expansion of focus in foreign policy to include a more creative emphasis on economic statecraft would match the Pashinyan government's current programme of countering corruption and overturning the country's oligarchic system. In the face of looming 'over-the-horizon' threats to Armenia, economic statecraft would help in three distinct ways.

First, in the absence of a coherent strategic vision for the country, economic statecraft would help in the formulation of such a vision for Armenia, based on the identification and prioritization of specific targets, metrics and long-term goals for the sustainable development over strategic time periods (over five-, ten- and twenty-year periods for example). In the case of the Armenian government's worldview, this would entail an emphasis on forging a new, knowledge-based economy, driven by a new growth model that rewards technological innovation and results in the necessity of 'creative destruction' from entrepreneurship and private sector risk-taking.

This would also offer an important new opportunity for the Armenian government to better define and defend its stated goal of implementing an 'economic revolution', which to date has been overly ambitious but vague in its promises, and seriously short on presenting specific policies or measures. For example, there would be an opportunity to further expand defence-related research and development (R&D), evident in such areas as the domestic production of drone and unmanned aerial vehicle (UAV) technology, advances in military electronics and navigational systems. The gains in defence R&D could then be leveraged for a set of new policies to offer incentives to, and exploit the synergy with, the defence sector for the country's under-funded and neglected science and technology (S&T) sector, for example with related benefits then available for university-based research, technology and IT-related job training programmes, and other cases of such 'dual use' technology between military and civilian research.

The second benefit from such economic statecraft would stem from the preparation of a defensive policy posture capable of mitigating the negative impact from the economic spillover on the Armenian economy from external shocks, such as from a decline in the Russian economy, a decrease in remittances or the demise of subsidized energy. Economic statecraft in this context would mean the start of scenario-based simulations to explore policy alternatives to defend against such external shocks, while also expanding tools to defend against the vulnerabilities and weaknesses of sectors in the Armenian economy.

A recommendation for adopting economic statecraft would also include significant attention to the national security-related implications from the issue of foreign investment and outright ownership of control over key strategic sectors of the economy, such as the energy, mining and telecommunications sectors, as well as the national railway network, as some notable examples. A practical result, therefore, would be the creation of a state entity to review future foreign investment projects that could impact national security or that would have strategic implications for Armenian national security. Such an entity would also be expected to assess the implications of past foreign investment deals, while also addressing the new national security considerations of, for example, membership in the EAEU.

And a third important dividend from such economic statecraft could be derived from a more ambitious effort to deepen economic growth through the expansion of exports into new markets, and the rebuilding of a more modern and forward-looking new manufacturing base, conforming to world standards. This would also assist in the state's efforts to end the inordinate market share and dominance of the commodity-based cartels prevalent in the previous oligarchic system, and to help establish a more level playing field for business where barriers to market entry are reduced, if not eliminated. This third area of economic statecraft would also help to improve the country's investment climate, which despite the change of government, has been undermined by a serious decline in investor confidence, largely due to the ongoing disruption of the mining sector.

Economic statecraft would also be essential to begin to better manage and overcome the limits to growth imposed by external constraints, including closed borders, a weak manufacturing base and a readjustment of the country's direction of trade after joining the EAEU. The latter factor is especially serious, as a set of initial exemptions from the higher tariffs required by members of the EAEU have already begun to expire in January 2020 and will continue to be phased out over the coming few years. The necessity for adopting higher trade tariffs to conform to EAEU standards will apply to some 800 Armenian goods and products, triggering an obvious blow to the Armenian economy (Giragosian and Kostanyan 2017). Moreover, this impact may be further exacerbated by the lack of a government strategy to manage or at least mitigate the economic harm from such a move. To date, the Armenian government has not yet decided whether to fight the expiration of the exemptions and seek to renegotiate, or to formulate a plan to counter the economic impact on exporters.

Therefore, the recommendation to add an expanded and enhanced role for economic statecraft to Armenian foreign policy offers a set of varied advantages and various opportunities. And the real promise and potential are also evident in the country's underlying stability, as seen in monetary policy, for example, with the Pashinyan government demonstrating admirable prudence in both safeguarding the independence of the Central Bank and empowering the Finance Ministry to maintain sound monetary policy free of political interference. Additionally, the country's blossoming IT sector also provides an important pre-existing foundation or platform for such an ambitiously innovative policy shift that would not be hindered by closed borders, marginal market access, limited trade and transport, or relative geographic isolation.

At the same time, Armenia can rely on economic statecraft to pursue the new strategic opportunities inherent in its position as a member of the EAEU, presenting itself as a 'bridge' between the EAEU and the West, and with the EU more precisely. Such a bridging role would be bolstered by the EAEU's need to garner greater legitimacy and credibility, as Armenia could leverage its CEPA deal with the EU as an avenue for institutional engagement and cooperation between the EAEU and the EU. And for a small landlocked state like Armenia, such a potential bridging role would be further advanced by transforming Armenia's geography from a liability into an asset, which despite lacking any land borders with the EAEU itself, offers alternative avenues to leverage Armenia's relations with Iran, proximity to the Middle East and even interest in the potential benefits from the possible reopening of its closed border with Turkey.

Engaging China

Simultaneously, in order to attain a greater strategic balance, Armenia's economic statecraft could also be based on the subtle and stealthy pursuit of engagement with China (Giragosian 2019). While this eastward embrace might seem surprising, given the disparity in size and remote connections between Armenia and China, it does conform to both Armenian and Chinese interests. For China, the small country of Armenia is recognized as a stable and promising element of a much larger landscape, whose position at the intersection of the Caucasus and the broader Middle East offers a pivotal bridgehead for China. From an Armenian perspective, the appeal of drawing closer to China stems from the opportunities in positioning itself within China's Belt and Road Initiative (BRI). Although Armenia is far too small and remote to take on individual significance for China, as part of this bigger picture, the country has appeared on the Chinese agenda of expanding trade and infrastructure, thereby enhancing China's influence and prestige.

Once again multipolarity poses a potentially serious challenge, however, for the outlook on Armenia's strategic embrace of China and its pursuit of deepened military ties to China. That challenge stems neither from Yerevan or Beijing, and, interestingly, not even from Washington. Rather, it may be Moscow that will come to resent being upstaged by a new rival. Yet China's presence and position in the South Caucasus remains far less than other regional powers, in contrast to Russia, Turkey and even Iran. And given the limits of Chinese interests in the region, it seems unlikely that China would seek to challenge Russia for dominance. Nevertheless, Moscow has been watching Beijing closely and with a degree of trepidation. Although Russia remains Armenia's most important security partner, for the Armenian government, the country's pronounced over-dependence on Russia necessitates a course correction, based on garnering greater balance. Yet this engagement of China may still work for Armenia, as ties to China are still less threatening to Russia than any embrace of the West. Multipolarity, in this sense, works both for and against Armenia.

Conclusion: Promise and peril

From a broader perspective, in the wake of Armenia's Velvet Revolution, there is a contradictory context of promise and peril in the country's geopolitics. The promise of the evolution of a more innovative Armenian foreign policy based on the application of smart power stems from three main factors. The first, more encouraging factor is the inherent advantage accruing from state legitimacy (Ohanyan 2018b). Backed by a wave of popular support and bolstered by a democratic parliamentary election in December 2018, the Armenian government is now endowed with a degree of institutionalized legitimacy that was seriously missing in previous governments, given the lack of any popular mandate from free and fair elections (Ohanyan 2018a). Institutional legitimacy is a critical advantage, offering the government an avenue to rebuild public trust and confidence in the state while also providing a fresh sense of accountability and ownership among ordinary citizens. The advantage of such legitimacy is also a source for both political will and statesmanship, as the leadership will be able to adopt bolder reforms and assume politically risky policies that can shape rather than follow public opinion.

At the same time, however, there is an equally important set of concerns that present a degree of peril for Armenia. Despite a lasting degree of popularity, the largely inexperienced government and an even less seasoned parliament face dangerously high public expectations, constituting crucial tests of leadership and political maturity. And as impressive as the forced resignation and defeat of the old regime was, the real demands of governance, including the necessity for compromise and concession, represent much more daunting and difficult challenges for the Armenian leadership. At the same time, coming challenges and crises in foreign policy will undoubtedly exert pressure and pose tests of resolve for the government.

Contributing both promise and peril to the outlook for Armenia is the broader trend of multipolarity and the devolution and diffusion of diplomatic power. This trend is both global and regional, with serious implications for a smaller player like Armenia. On the one hand, devolution and diffusion has contributed to the rise of new non-state actors, such al-Qaeda and the Islamic State, with highly negative impacts for regional and global stability. But this trend is also grounded in the diffusion of diplomacy that has seen the demise of an international order structured around a bipolar superpower dimension and the rise of BRICS (the term referring to a grouping of five major emerging national economies: Brazil, Russia, India, China and South Africa). This trend of diffused diplomacy is also continuing, if not increasing. Most recently, for example, the power and prestige of traditional global leaders have suffered a serious decline. This is based on more than the rise of either right-wing populism in Europe or the American retreat sparked by US president Donald Trump. Moreover, the decline of Western leadership has been matched by a profound shift in 2018, with a global survey covering 130 countries revealing that the United States now holds an approval rate of a mere 31 per cent, barely exceeding a 30 per cent approval rate for Russia, and seriously undermined by China's 34 per cent rating (Pew Research Center 2018).

While this measure of 'approval' does not cover power or influence, it does show just how badly global public opinion perceives the West, beyond the reaction to Trump to include the lowest numbers for France and Germany, which respondents gave 9 per cent and 10 per cent approval ratings, respectively. Interestingly, the survey's rating of the 'job performance of the leadership of the United States' in the South Caucasus has mixed results. In Armenia, the positive view of American leadership decreased by 7 per cent over the 2017 survey, with an approval rating of 31 per cent and a 32 per cent disapproval rating. In Azerbaijan, the rating was similar, with only 33 per cent approving, but with as many as 48 per cent disapproving. In Georgia, however, US leadership enjoyed a 44 per cent approval rating, with only a 25 per cent disapproval rating (Pew Research Center 2018: 19).

For Armenia, the shift in global leadership is important for two reasons. First, despite its rather marginal role in the global clash of interests, the indirect impact is serious. For example, not only could Russia's confrontational posture against the West place Armenia in a difficult and exposed position as a Russian ally, but American moves against Iran can also complicate Armenia's need for stable relations and expanded trade with its southern neighbour. A second reason underlying the relevance to Armenia of such a global shift is the possible resulting opportunity to better leverage its position as a platform or bridge between much larger powers, acting as a conduit for Chinese engagement in the region, or between Russia and the Europe, for example. At the same time this diffusion of power and leadership on a global scale also confirms the maxim that in diplomacy, as in politics, perception is as important as reality.

References

Collier, P. (2007) *The Bottom Billion: Why the Poorest Countries Are Failing and What Can Be Done About It*. Oxford: Oxford University Press.

Giragosian, R. (2014) *Armenia's Strategic U-Turn*. European Council on Foreign Relations (ECFR) Policy Memo, ECFR/99, April. Available at: https://ww

w.ecfr.eu/page/-/ECFR99_ARMENIA_MEMO_AW.pdf (accessed 11 June 2019).

Giragosian, R. (2015a) Armenia as a Bridge to Iran? Russia Won't Like It. *Al Jazeera English*, 30 August. Available at: www.aljazeera.com/indepth/opin ion/2015/08/armenia-bridge-iran-russia-won-150830063735998.html (accessed 11 June 2019).

Giragosian, R. (2015b) Peacekeeping Contributor Profile: Armenia. *Providing for Peacekeeping*, November. Available at: www.providingforpeacekeeping.o rg/2015/12/14/peacekeeping-contributor-profile-armenia/ (accessed 11 June 2019).

Giragosyan, R. (2017) Тревожное невмешательство. Как американо-российские отношения повлияют на Южный Кавказ [Anxious Non-Interference. How US-Russian Relations Affect South Caucasus]. *Internationale Politik und Gesellschaft*, 17 February. Freidrich Ebert Stiftung (FES). Available at: https://www.ipg-journal.io/regiony/evropa/statja/show/t revozhnoe-nevmeshatelstvo-225/ (accessed 11 June 2019).

Giragosian, R. (2018a) Trump Administration Plants US Flag in Armenia. *Asia Times*, 26 October. Available at: www.atimes.com/article/trump-administrat ion-plants-us-flag-in-armenia/ (accessed 11 June 2019).

Giragosian, R. (2018b) Small States and the Large Costs of Regional Fracture: The Case of Armenia. In: Ohanyan, A., ed., *Russia Abroad: Driving Regional Fracture in Post-Communist Eurasia and Beyond*. Washington DC: Georgetown University Press, 103–17.

Giragosian, R. (2019) Armenia Adds Beijing to Its Delicate Balancing Act. *Asia Times*, 14 January. Available at: www.atimes.com/article/eastward-embrace-beijing-added-to-a-delicate-balancing-act/ (accessed 11 June 2019).

Giragosian, R. and Kostanyan, H. (2017) EU-Armenian Relations: Charting a Fresh Course. Centre for European Policy Studies (CEPS) Commentary, 15 November. Available at: www.ceps.eu/publications/eu-armenian-relation s-charting-fresh-course (accessed 11 June 2019).

Global Risk Insights. (2016) Trump's Plans: The Outlook for U.S. Foreign Policy Towards Eurasia, 29 November. Available at: http://globalriskinsights.com/ 2016/11/trump-foreign-policy-eurasia/ (accessed 11 June 2019).

Lewis, D., Heathershaw, J. and Megoran, N. (2018) 'Illiberal Peace?' Authoritarian Approaches to Conflict Management. *Cooperation and Conflict*, 23 April. DOI: 10.1177/0010836718765902

McConnell, F., Megoran, N. and Williams, P., eds (2014) *The Geographies of Peace: New Approaches to Boundaries, Diplomacy and Conflict Resolution*. London: I.B. Tauris.

Ohanyan, A. (2018a) A Very Potent Protest Movement Is Emerging in Armenia. *Al Jazeera*, 21 April. Available at: https://www.aljazeera.com/indepth/opinio n/potent-protest-movement-emerging-armenia-180419135116999.html (accessed 11 June 2019).

Ohanyan, A. (2018b) What's Next for Armenia's Protest Movement? *Al Jazeera*, 1 May. Available at: https://www.aljazeera.com/indepth/opinion/armenia-protest-movement-180501091308469.html (accessed 11 June 2019).

Oskanian, V. (2008) *Speaking to Be Heard: A Decade of Speeches*. Yerevan: Civilitas Foundation.

Oxford Analytica. (2015). Armenia Could Be 'Bridge' if Iran Opens to the World. Oxford Analytica Daily Brief, 12 November. Available at: https://da ilybrief.oxan.com/Analysis/DB206641/Armenia-could-be-bridge-if-Iran-op ens-to-the-world (accessed 2 February 2020).

Pew Research Center. (2018) Global Attitudes Survey. Available at: www.gallup .com/analytics/247040/rating-world-leaders-2019.aspx (accessed 11 June 2019).

Radio Free Europe/Radio Liberty (RFE/RL). (2019) Bolton Voices U.S. Support for Pashinian. RFE/RL Armenian Service, 24 January. Available at: https:// www.azatutyun.am/a/29728982.html (accessed 11 June 2019).

Shaffer, B. (2003) Iran's Role in the South Caucasus and Caspian Region: Diverging Views of the US and Europe. In: Whitlock, E., ed., *Iran and Its Neighbors. Diverging Views on a Strategic Region*. Berlin: SWP, 17–22.

Socor, V. (2013) The End of 'Complementarity' in Armenia's Foreign Policy. *Eurasia Daily Monitor*, 10 (165), 18 September. Available at: https://jamesto wn.org/program/the-end-of-complementarity-in-armenias-foreign-policy/ (accessed 11 June 2019).

Zarifian, J. (2014) The Armenian-American Lobby and Its Impact on US Foreign Policy. *Society*, 51 (5): 503–12.

7

Preserving the alliance against tall odds

Armenia's Velvet Revolution as a challenge to Russia

Pavel K. Baev

Introduction

What makes Armenia's Velvet Revolution unique among the not inconsiderable number of civil uprisings starting back in the incredible year of 1989 is the imperative – unquestionable for the vast majority of participants in the uprising – of preserving the military-security alliance with Russia. Armenia has not only been locked in an intractable conflict with Azerbaijan from even before its existence as an independent state began but also is severely affected by hostile relations with Turkey. Russia is consequently seen as the only effective and irreplaceable security guarantor. In the majority of successful and unsuccessful mass uprisings in the wider European region, perhaps with the exception of the second Kyrgyz revolution in April 2010, the desire to come closer to and become a part of the West was a major driver, as symbolized by the raising of the European Union (EU) flag on the parliament building in Chisinau, Moldova, on 7 April 2009 (Kramer and Hill 2009). Yet the leaders, as well as the rank and file, of the Armenian revolution took great care not to declare and demonstrate their pro-Western feelings, even if such causes as extermination of corruption, advancement of economic reforms or building of truly democratic institutions were most certainly resonant with an agenda of rapprochement with the EU (Zolyan 2018a). But the reassurances of unwavering commitment to upholding ties with Russia eagerly issued by Nikol Pashinyan both at the many street rallies and from the hard-won position of prime minister have not secured him much trust in the Kremlin.

Russia's response to the overthrow of what the Kremlin recognized as legitimate authorities in Armenia by street protests was uncharacteristically hesitant and ambivalent, and this chapter examines this puzzling incertitude (Baev 2018a). Three different drivers interacted in the decision-making process in Moscow regarding the Armenian revolution and its aftermath: (a) Russia's geopolitical perceptions of the South Caucasus and ambitions in the region; (b) Russian policy's characteristically counter-revolutionary ideological stance; and (c) the impact of the popular uprising's anti-corruption ethos on personal attitudes in the Kremlin. This chapter will deal with each of these three drivers after assessing the scope and asymmetry of ties between Russia and Armenia, and before taking stock of Russian–Armenian bilateral relations over the year following the revolution and pondering over their prospects.

An asymmetric partnership shaped by security dependency

The trajectory of Russian–Armenian relations in the post-Soviet period remained remarkably stable despite the initial severe turmoil and further complex interplay of geopolitical interests in the wider Caucasian region. From the moment of the break-up of the USSR in late 1991, the fledgling Armenian government recognized that only Russia could provide critically important and reasonably effective security guarantees, and so in May 1992, Armenia signed the Collective Security Treaty (Tashkent Treaty) with Russia and four Central Asian states and has remained a fully committed member of this security alliance through its uneasy history (Weitz 2018). It was the violent conflict in Nagorny Karabakh that shaped the foreign and security policy of the newly reborn Armenian state, and responding to its request, Moscow negotiated a ceasefire agreement in May 1994 that still holds, despite the rejection by Azerbaijan of the Russian plan for a peacekeeping operation (de Waal 2013).

Armenia also signed the Treaty on Friendship, Collaboration and Mutual Aid with Russia in August 1997, and remained a loyal ally through the calamity of the two Chechen wars and during the upheaval of the Russia-Georgia war in August 2008 (Asmus 2010). The security alliance is consolidated by a permanent Russian military presence on Armenian territory: The 102nd base near Gyumri was re-established from the Soviet facility in mid-1992 and it presently hosts up to 5,000 troops as well as various weapons systems, redeployed there after the withdrawal of bases in Georgia (Akhalkalaki and Batumi) in the mid-2000s (102nd Military base... 2015). Recurrent incidents spark local protests against this base, but it is broadly perceived as necessary for ensuring Armenia's security (Goble 2018).

Strong security ties determine the priority orientation of Armenia's economic connections towards Russia. In the late 1990s, Azerbaijan insisted that the strategic oil and gas pipelines delivering its hydrocarbons to Western markets would go around Armenia, which still has to rely exclusively on Gazprom for covering its demand (Could a pipeline... 1995). Armenia was not a member of the Russia-led Eurasian Economic Community (2000–14), but joined its successor – the Eurasian Economic Union (EAEU) – in late 2014. In order to make this move, Armenia had to withdraw from well-advanced negotiations with the EU on an association agreement, but it managed to repair this damage by signing late in 2017 a Comprehensive and Enhanced Partnership Agreement (CEPA), which envisages essentially the same level and intensity of cooperation, without irritating Moscow (Poghosyan 2018). While trade with the EU now accounts for nearly a quarter of Armenia's export and import, Russia is still the largest trade partner and the main source of investment. Import of energy from Russia is the key component of Armenia's large trade deficit, and remittances from labour migrants in Russia constitute some 10 per cent of its GDP, so the plan for launching an 'economic revolution' can only succeed with Russia's acquiescence (Mejlumyan 2019).

The irreducible security vulnerability and high level of economic dependency have formed a firm conviction in Moscow that Armenia is doomed to remain Russia's loyal ally, even if it abstains from recognizing the legitimacy of the annexation of Crimea. This tendency towards taking Armenia for granted translates into a rather relaxed attitude to Yerevan's cautious but consistent course towards the expansion of ties with the EU and NATO.

Eroding Russian dominance over Caucasian geopolitics

Russia had engaged in conflict management in the Caucasus, engulfed by the turmoil accompanying the collapse of the USSR, already in the early 1990s, but the peace-enforcement/keeping operations established in that early era had little geopolitical significance. Indeed, Russia – weakened and perturbed as it was – had to take responsibility for improvising imperfect compromises and monitoring ceasefires, and dubious decisions taken by President Boris Yeltsin under serious duress happened to have lasting, if mostly unintended, impacts on regional dynamics (Baev 1997). What turned Russian engagement in local ethno-territorial conflicts into the composite fragments of a wider geopolitical competition was the development of the Caspian Sea hydrocarbon resources, interpreted in Washington (rather erroneously, in the wisdom of hindsight) as a major game changer in global energy markets (Starr and Cornell 2005). The much-vaunted yet ultimately overestimated 'great game' continued into the early 2000s, fuelling the competition between the *Nabucco* and the *South Stream* pipeline projects – until both failed (Baev and Øverland 2010).

As the perceived importance of Caspian oil and gas was declining, the geopolitical picture in the Caucasus was dramatically altered by the short but intense Russo-Georgia war in August 2008 (Asmus 2010). Unlike the construction of hydrocarbon 'corridors', which all circumvented Armenia, that Russian exercise in using military power as an instrument of policy had direct impact on its position in the region. Russia asserted, at least temporarily, the status of dominant power in the Caucasus, and Armenia, as Moscow's loyal security ally, also improved its standing, even if the line of communications through Georgia was interrupted and losses to the Armenian economy were severe. After the initial shock, the United States and the NATO allies tried to turn the page on the Russo-Georgian war by initiating a 'reset' with Russia, but the present Russian aggression against Ukraine made the lessons of that war very relevant indeed (Kofman 2018).

Except for consolidating its control over Georgia's breakaway regions of Abkhazia and South Ossetia and formally recognizing them as 'states', Russia did not try to exploit its dominant position in the Caucasus, and the next reconfiguration of the geopolitical constellations came only in spring 2014, with the annexation of Crimea. This direct Russian aggression against Ukraine produced little resonance in the Caucasus in terms of re-energizing the unresolved conflicts, but the power balance in the wider Black Sea region has shifted significantly in its favour (Tucas 2017). The heavily militarized Crimea has become the central position from which Russia could enjoy superiority in any confrontation with NATO in the Black Sea theatre. The intervention in Syria, meanwhile, established a strategic connection between this theatre and the Eastern Mediterranean, and increased Turkey's reluctance to engage in NATO's plans and operations aimed at containing Russia's activities (Delanoe 2019). The mini-battle near the Kerch Strait in December 2018, in which two Ukrainian ships and a tugboat were captured by Russian forces, demonstrated Moscow's readiness to utilize its naval capabilities for political aims (Petersen 2019).

Russia's concentration on the confrontation with the West, as well as the sustained stress of the Syrian intervention, have resulted in a relative but steady decline of its dominance over the Caucasus (de Waal 2018a; Broers 2018). Georgia, for that matter, is able to cultivate its relations with NATO with little or no reaction from Moscow, except for some hollow warnings (Peel and Foy 2018). Azerbaijan tested Russia's capacity for forceful conflict management by launching an offensive in Nagorny Karabakh in April 2016, opting not to go too far but sufficient enough to keep up the pressure (ICG 2017). Turkey feels free to build closer ties with Azerbaijan not only in oil and gas transportation but also in security matters expecting that Moscow would raise no objections and would prioritize its own 'strategic partnership' with Ankara, brittle as it is. Armenia has good reasons to worry about Russia's diminishing attention to, and shrinking resources for, controlling power manoeuvring in the Caucasus, even as Yerevan also seeks to diversify its international relations and diminish its dependency on Moscow (Iskandaryan 2019). One low-cost way for Yerevan to demonstrate compliance with Russia's international agenda is to provide symbolic contributions to its intervention in Syria, and this rare support is indeed appreciated in Moscow (Kucera 2019).

In the absence of any significant moves by the United States in the Caucasus and given the low content of the EU ties to this neighbourhood, Moscow is not particularly concerned about the shortage of its own power-projection capabilities. Yet, it seeks to limit the freedom of manoeuvre for the three South Caucasian states in order to avoid developments requiring a more concentrated effort to be directed at geopolitical competition in this region.

Russia's unwavering stance against revolutions

It is typical for authoritarian regimes to live in fear of public uprisings that could disrupt their control over political processes and bring their very existence to an abrupt end. The evolution of Russian President Vladimir Putin's regime from a pseudo-democracy to rigid authoritarianism, in which heavy reliance on the enforcement of 'order' is softened only by an all-penetrating corruption, leads to its progressively deeper concerns about revolutions and correspondingly increasing efforts aimed at their prevention and suppression. This natural evolution is distorted and is at times propelled by the impact of external events, particularly in the immediate neighbourhood, which could sharply increase the impact of the 'fear factor', so that the intensity of the counter-revolutionary campaigns in Moscow oscillates.

Subsumed under the moniker of 'colour revolutions', the first wave of public unrest arrived in the early 2000s, when Putin's regime was gaining strength and growing more confident in its own future. Consequently, disapproval rather than fear shaped its responses. Yet Moscow invested significant resources in countering the 'Orange Revolution' (or the *Maidan* uprising) in Ukraine in late 2004 – and suffered a humiliating defeat (Åslund and McFaul 2006). The main lesson Moscow learned from that experience was that more 'competitive' regimes allowing for both more openness in political dynamics and more Western influence were most at risk of explosions of public unrest, typically triggered by anger against fraudulent elections (Baev 2006). More rigid authoritarian regimes, like that in Uzbekistan, faced the risk of local rebellions (like that in Andijan in May 2005), but were presumed to be much safer against the threat of regime-shaking revolutions (Ó Beacháin and Polese 2010).

The first wave of colour revolutions subsided in the second half of the 2000s, and from Moscow's perspective, the election of Viktor Yanukovych (barred from taking office by the *Maidan*) as the president of Ukraine in early 2010 signified a decisive victory over this menace (Kuzio 2010). The 'spectre of revolution' still loomed behind the rallies in Chisinau, Moldova in April 2009 and the violent clashes in Bishkek and Osh, Kyrgyzstan, in April–May 2010, but the weakening of President Mikheil Saakashvili's government in Georgia by protests in 2009 and 2011, before its defeat in the parliamentary elections in October 2012, was interpreted in Moscow as an effective minimization of this threat (Baev 2011). What turned that relaxed attitude into a sharp new panic attack was the coinciding of the explosion of turmoil in the Middle East, dubbed the 'Arab Spring', and the series of mass protests in Moscow in from December 2011 to June 2012, triggered by crudely rigged parliamentary elections.

This overlap of two unconnected trends led to a drastic re-evaluation of the threat posed by domestic discontent to the survival of Russia's quasi-competitive but inherently authoritarian regime. The impression from the crowds occupying Tahrir Square in Cairo probably convinced Vladimir Putin of the imperative to reinstate himself as Russia's president, a manoeuvre he quite probably had in any case already planned, but the crowds in Bolotnaya Square in Moscow showed the disappointment and discontent with that 'natural' restoration. His obsession with the danger of sudden eruption of mass protests is related to the psychological trauma of witnessing the angry rallies in Dresden back in 1989, when his modest career in the KGB was interrupted by the irresistible movement for German reunification (see Hill and Gaddy 2015, Chapter 6). Putin therefore felt compelled to assume the role of a global champion for the counter-revolutionary cause, and the military intervention in Syria launched in September 2015 and aimed at rescuing the beleaguered Bashar al-Assad regime consolidated this role (Dannreuther 2014). Before this still ongoing enterprise was set in motion, however, Moscow suffered an unexpected and shocking setback from the victory of the 'Euro-Maidan' uprising in Kiev, which initially appeared to be manageable and even marginal. Putin's response to that shocking defeat in the struggle against revolutions was swift and severe, and the aggression against Ukraine locked Russia into inevitable and asymmetric confrontation with the West. The latest manifestation of the ideological conflict in this confrontation is Russia's 'principled' support to Nicolás Maduro's regime in Venezuela, shaken by mass protests that are encouraged by the United States and accepted as legitimate by the EU (Dabagyan 2019).

In this wider regional and global Russian campaign against revolutions, the Caucasus, rather counter-intuitively – given its track record of popular uprisings – remained peripheral. Yet the street protests in Armenia against the increase in fuel prices in summer 2015 attracted some reproachful attention in Moscow (Andreasyan and Derluguian 2015). While the Armenian authorities managed the crisis very carefully, avoiding forceful suppression, Russian propaganda blamed US interference for sponsoring what it termed the 'electro-Maidan', a blend of the Armenian 'Electric Yerevan' and Ukrainian 'Euro-maidan' tropes (Sergeev 2015). There were also some rallies and disturbances in 'independent' Abkhazia in 2015–6, but Moscow felt confident that the situation in that satellite statelet remained firmly under control (Roks 2016). Severe repressions against the opposition in Azerbaijan were a much better fit with Russia's counter-revolutionary drive, and Putin has maintained cordial personal relations with the hereditary president Ilham Aliyev (Kauzlarich and Kramer 2018).

By the start of 2018, concerns in Moscow about a new wave of revolutions had largely dissipated, and Putin had planned confidently on extending his occupancy of the Russian presidency for another term without incurring any public protest. Armenia's Velvet Revolution appeared as an unwelcome fly in the ointment, bucking the presumed trend of the decline of unrest in the 'Eurasian street'.

Extensive Russian use of political corruption

Democracies are by no means immune to corruption, but in authoritarian regimes, the blending of political power and illicit fortunes acquires an overwhelming, even grotesque, character and becomes an organic feature rather than a fault of the political system. Putin inherited from Boris Yeltsin a system of power weakened by feeble political control over the predatory behaviour of key economic actors, and he managed to turn corruption into a major lever of strengthening the re-centralization of power. The merciless prosecution of Mikhail Khodorkovsky and the expropriation of his Yukos oil company was a means of disciplining Russia's 'oligarchs', some of whom (such as Viktor Vekselberg or Mikhail Fridman) were allowed to keep their fortunes provided they deferred to orders from the Kremlin, while others (such as Oleg Deripaska) were even brought closer to the centre of power (Mikhail Freedman... 2018; Fedorinova 2018). More important, however, was the policy of empowering new bosses of state-owned companies, such as Gazprom (Alexey Miller) or Rosneft (Igor Sechin), as well as granting opportunities for enrichment to dubious entrepreneurs (such as Gennady Timchenko or Arkady Rotenberg), all of whom were impeccably loyal to Putin (Åslund 2019). These characters have gained significant influence over Russian foreign policy-making, and if Sechin plays a key role in Venezuela, Miller's Gazprom remains a major player in the Caucasus (Gabuev 2019).

The steady climb of oil prices up to the crisis of 2008–9 vastly increased the volume of money circulating in the shadows of the Russian economy and made it possible to elevate systematic corruption to the level of state policy, particularly in the North Caucasus. Severe suppression of insurgent/terrorist networks in this chronically unstable region went hand-in-hand with generous financing of local elites and their patronage structures, which to all intents and purposes was a form of corruption. Since the onset of the crisis in Russian-Western relations in 2014–6, it has become impossible for the federal centre to sustain these financial flows, which has led to forceful removal of several political clans, first of all in Dagestan (Biurchiev 2018). More recently, the high-resonance arrest of Rauf Arashukov, a 'senator' from Karachaevo-Cherkessia in the chamber of the Federation Council was also presented as a case of the struggle against corruption, while in fact it was a sign of escalating local squabbles for shrinking resources (Stanovaya 2019).

What makes the latter theatrical 'special operation' particularly interesting is the direct involvement of Gazprom, since the father of the young 'senator', Raul Arashukov, was also detained and accused of massive fraud in executing his responsibility for the distribution of gas supplies across the North Caucasus organized by Gazprom's subsidiary Mezhregiongaz (Romanova 2019). The energy giant Gazprom has since the start of the 'Putin era' grown into a high-impact political instrument, and corruption is one of the key means for advancing its business interests in Europe (Mammadov 2018). There is no need here to elaborate on these well-researched activities, but what is relevant is Gazprom's abuse of its monopoly on gas supply to Armenia. Yerevan's profound dependency on this source makes it very difficult for the new Armenian authorities to investigate the networks of gas corruption (Mejlumyan 2018). Georgia, for that matter, has managed to rid itself of the gas import from Russia, and this has been one of the key factors in its success in the struggle against corruption (Dalakishvili 2017).

What hampers the efforts of Pashinyan's team at curtailing gas-driven corruption is the looming wider context: In the course of the evolving confrontation between Russia and the West, the corruption issue has been elevated to the level of a major 'hybrid' threat and thus effectively 'securitized'. Indeed, many European states, and particularly the United Kingdom, has identified Russian export of corruption as a profound security threat, and American sanctions have targeted billionaires in Putin's 'inner circle' very personally (Moscow's Gold 2018; Åslund 2018). Moscow finds it necessary to counter this pressure and has provided various means of financial support to the sanctioned 'oligarchs' (Bazanova, Sterkin and Sinitsina 2018). This clash of policies over matters belonging to the problem-area of financial crime has had severe repercussions for anti-corruption campaigners in Russia such as Alexei Navalny (Thaler 2017). It also had significant consequences for shaping the attitude and responses in the Kremlin to the revolution in Armenia.

Russian responses to the Velvet surprise: Shock and ambivalence

Moscow appeared to respond to the explosion of street protests in Yerevan with uncharacteristic indifference and self-restraint, but what could have been taken for a wise political choice not to interfere was in fact anything but. The main feature of the Armenian revolution that determined Russian ambivalence was timing. In spring 2018, the Kremlin was exceedingly busy managing President Putin's re-election for yet another term. The attention span within the limited group of courtiers enjoying access to the nervous and egocentric autocrat was consequently severely limited, particularly given the additional complication of organizing such a high-profile mega-event as the World Cup. Putin's team (distracted with their own jockeying for post-election promotions) was eager to follow their leader's impression that the situation in Armenia was firmly under control, interpreting the early signs of what was in fact a brewing uprising as the usual minor disturbances of a disaffected minority that had accompanied nearly every election in this particular country (Polovinko 2018). Putin called Serzh Sargsyan and congratulated him on his appointment as the prime minister a week prior to his resignation on 22 April, which came as a shocking surprise for the Russian authorities, who had been reassured by Pashinyan's arrest and detention two days previously (Zolyan 2018b). After Sargsyan's unexpected political capitulation, it was definitely too late to interfere forcefully. What seemed to be a considered and deliberative decision to embrace rather than condemn what was from almost any Kremlin perspective an undesirable series of events, was in fact the inescapable consequence of a major oversight in risk assessment (Baev 2018b).

It would be a mistake to assume that Russia's capacity for intervening was limited by the difficulty of transporting reinforcements to the 102nd military base near Gyumri; in fact, a direct military intervention was entirely out of the question. Moscow, however, had at its disposal a vast arsenal of various 'hybrid' means, from the FSB 'assets' in the Armenian National Security Service to newly established 'troll factories' ready to execute dirty cyber-attacks, yet these capabilities remained idle (Grigoryan 2018). It took about eight months for Pashinyan to legitimize his unexpected grasp of power, and during that time Russia remained content to monitor the twists and turns of the Armenian political crisis without any pro-active steps towards influencing its outcome. The interplay between the three main drivers in the decision-making in the Kremlin was fluid, and some disapproving noises were emitted now and again, but the decision to refrain from pulling strings and pushing the revolution back stayed solid (Galstyan 2018).

The reasonable assessment of geopolitical risks as low and manageable is presumed to be the main underpinning of this decision, neutralizing the negative attitude towards victorious 'street power' (Way 2018). Observation of the absence of any anti-Russian feelings among the protesters was indeed supplemented in many analyses in Moscow think-tanks by the argument that US involvement had been insignificant (Kortunov 2018). Many analysts argued at length that because of the absence of Western sponsorship, the turmoil in Armenia should be neither defined as, nor mistaken for, a 'colour revolution' (Markedonov 2018a). Even liberal commentators pointed out the unique features of Armenian society, which made the revolution a unique case that could not be reproduced in Russia (Krasheninnikov 2018). There was indeed no tangible resonance from the protracted protest activity in Yerevan across the wider Caucasian region, so Moscow was reassured of the low demonstration effect of this isolated case of victorious revolution (Barabashin and Souleimanov 2018).

Having reluctantly accepted a 'colourless' revolution in Armenia as an exception from its principled policy of opposing civil uprisings, the Kremlin was then irked by the aggressive anti-corruption campaign unleashed by the new authorities in Yerevan. Their swift investigations of abuse of power by the 'Sargsyan clan' were taken as the 'normal' political punishment of defeated opponents, but Putin attempted to draw the line at the detention of former president Robert Kocharian (Khalatyan and Mareeva 2018). A couple of phone calls from the Kremlin encouraged Kocharian to announce his 'return to politics' in direct opposition to Nikol Pashinyan's inexperienced government (Solovyev 2018). Another strong signal to Yerevan was the rejection of its claim for the appointment of an Armenian as new secretary general of the Collective Security Treaty Organization (CSTO) to replace

Yury Khachaturov, who was under the same investigation as Kocharian. The Kremlin opted rather to leave the post temporarily vacant (Kolesnikov 2018).

Putin may or may not have any particular sympathy for Kocharian, but he definitely excels in the exploitation of gas exports as an instrument of policy. Hence, the investigation of corruption within Gazprom's subsidiaries in Armenia was another 'red line' for the Russian president. This line was firmly established by the 10 per cent increase of the price on gas imported from Russia, which created a difficult problem for Pashinyan's government as it struggled to prove to its support base that the revolution produced immediate positive economic results (Khalatyan and Mordyushenko 2019). The draft Anti-Corruption Strategy published for open discussion might have convinced *The Economist* to name Armenia as its 'Country of the Year 2018', but it also convinced the Kremlin that the struggle against corruption was aiming too far ('Ovation nation' 2018). Putin found no time for a meeting with Pashinyan, who travelled to Moscow in January 2019 for a session of the EAEU (Simonyan 2019).

As Armenia entered the post-revolution period at the start of 2019, the attitude in the Kremlin had hardly become more agreeable. While Yerevan's geopolitical loyalty was taken for granted, Moscow's strong aversion to street protests was reinforced by suspicions about the political aims of the Armenian anti-corruption campaign.

Possible Russian manipulations of post-revolutionary Armenia

The contemporary picture of Russian–Armenian relations may appear rather static, but there are major drivers of change, some of which have to be left out of this analysis. The domestic situation in Russia at the middle of Putin's supposedly last presidential term may deteriorate and give rise to mass protests, which would bring about an empowerment of counter-revolutionary ideology, so that Armenia would be perceived in the Kremlin as a 'storm-bringer'. The smouldering and by no means frozen war in eastern Ukraine may escalate to large-scale hostilities, and not necessarily on Moscow's initiative, as was the case in the Kerch Strait crisis of November 2018, and the Caucasus may be affected by this military confrontation. The Russian intervention in Syria, which appears to be stable and successful, may suddenly turn into a complex disaster, including a new bitter quarrel with Turkey, that would have heavy consequences for Armenia. It is entirely possible that all three of these calamities could happen simultaneously, but it is rather improbable that none of them would occur.

Assuming that Moscow in the near future would grant some attention to the Caucasus, we can expect a cautious rather than blunt use of geopolitical levers to ensure Armenia's continuing dependency upon its stern 'security guarantor'. The Armenia–Azerbaijan conflict, which was – perhaps counter-intuitively – unaffected by the revolution, presents plentiful opportunities for such pressure (de Waal 2018b). Many Azerbaijani analysts argue that the weakening of Russian–Armenian ties increases Baku's leverage in the power play around this protracted deadlock (Huseynov and Rzaev 2018). Seeking to pre-empt attempts to exploit the conflict for undermining his reforms, Pashinyan initiated several rounds of talks with Azerbaijani president Ilham Aliyev, but his space for compromises, necessary for achieving real progress towards a settlement, is in fact quite limited (Shirinyan 2019). Moscow has indirectly but effectively upped tensions around this seat of conflict by negotiating for the delivery of a squadron of 12 Su-30SM fighter-bombers to the Armenian air force. Yerevan felt obliged to pursue this offer, even if this purchase would necessitate a significant increase of its defence budgets in 2019–21 (Dronina 2019).

Russia has already started using geopolitical tools in combination with various 'soft power' means to influence the trajectory of the inexperienced post-revolutionary Armenian authorities and will certainly proceed with this control-building. Moscow expects this trajectory to follow the 'natural course' of gradual consolidation of a personalistic quasi-democratic regime with a pronounced tendency towards authoritarianism (Markedonov 2018b). Economic ties, in which corruption is an essential element, will be used to compromise the promised economic reforms and engage the key figures in the new government. The Armenian diaspora in Russia, which has remained rather distant from the revolutionary mobilization, could be an important resource for the Kremlin policy, even if this numerous diaspora is not that well represented in the high echelon of Putin's elite and accounts for only one entry (Samvel Karapetyan) in the *Forbes'* list of 100 richest businessmen in Russia (Forbes rating… 2018). Where the 'russified' Armenians are remarkably prominent is in the Russian propaganda machine (Margarita Simonyan, editor-in-chief of the RT television network, has become an internationally notorious figure, and dubious media-manager Aram Gabrelyanov perhaps also deserves a mention), and this tool will certainly be employed to the maximum effect on Armenian society (Mandraud 2017). Putin's personal relations with Kocharian will be utilized to keep Pashinyan nervous about his ability to communicate with the Kremlin, and extra-cautious in making any 'offensive' steps towards the reduction of dependency on Russia by exploring the Western vector. At the end of the day, Moscow always has the powerful lever of gas supplies at its disposal (Avakov 2018).

A more difficult and disagreeable option for Russia is an Armenia that breaks with the pattern of authoritarian retrenchment and persists with democratic reforms. Even if the leadership of such an Armenia would go a long extra mile in upholding the strategic alliance with Russia, the Kremlin would still see it as a security challenge. It is not only that progress in building a modern state would be applauded in Europe and attract Western investors, so that Armenia would become an unreliable ally. More important is the precedent of achieving success by discarding the corruption-infested 'competitive authoritarian' model (Levitsky and Way 2010). Moscow treats the Georgian case as an exception that proves the general rule of adherence to softer or more rigid variations of such a model, but a democracy-building Armenia could disprove the quasi-ideological proposition that Russia can only exist as an authoritarian police state (Surkov 2019). Growing irritation with South Caucasian 'deviations' might tempt the Kremlin to resort to more forceful measures for restoring control over this close neighbourhood, particularly if domestic discontent in Russia would foment perceptions in the Kremlin that another 'patriotic' mobilization was needed. Georgia constitutes the most feasible target for such an exercise in power projection, and a Russian intervention in exposed western Georgia (which could be an expanded version of the amphibious operation in August 2008) would deliver the Armenian leadership into an impossible situation of either cooperating with naked aggression or condemning a demonstration of irresistible force. This kind of thinking about the unthinkable may appear to make a leap too far, but Russia needs to convert its position of power in the Black Sea theatre into tangible victories, and the success in conquering Crimea has made a deep imprint on its strategic culture.

Conclusion

Russia could have strongly opposed the Armenian revolution and could have organized or even led its forceful suppression – but it did not, and timing is the most probable explanation of this indifferent attitude. In hyper-centralized authoritarian systems, like Russia's, all key decisions can only be taken at the top, and in the crucial week of April, the Russian 'decider' happened to be busy with his own re-election, and in the weeks that followed, he did not want to spoil the perfect spectacle of the 2018 World Cup. To Putin's credit, he did not attempt any 'hybrid' operations, for which the resources were easily available, when the optimal moment was already gone, and he accepted – however grudgingly – the new political reality in Armenia.

As of this writing, Moscow is reassured of the geopolitical loyalty of post-revolutionary Armenia, but the irritation with Yerevan's determined struggle against corruption revives the Kremlin's intrinsic abhorrence of toppling authoritarian regimes through street protests. Russia seeks to maintain control over the management of the long-deadlocked Armenian-Azerbaijani conflict and assumes that Pashinyan's ability to design a meaningful initiative for its settlement is limited. The sale of a squadron of Su-30SM multi-role fighters is organized by Moscow as means of sustaining tensions between Armenia and Azerbaijan. At the same time, raising the price of natural gas exported to Armenia is intended to deny the new government the chance of delivering some tangible economic benefits to the gradually demobilizing populace.

Moscow expects Armenia's post-revolutionary government to follow the 'natural' trajectory of regressing to a personalized authoritarian regime, and it applies a range of economic and propaganda means to stimulate such a degradation. If Armenia breaks with the pattern of 'competitive authoritarianism' and insists on progressing with democratic reforms, mounting angst combined with the urge to achieve a new 'victory' in order to dispel domestic discontent might prompt Putin's court to resort to a new military adventure in the Caucasus. The bottom line is that Russia wants the Armenia's Velvet Revolution to fail – and seeks to ensure that it will – by producing just another corrupt pseudo-democratic regime, which goes directly against the longing of the Armenian people and the intentions of its new leadership.

References

Andreasyan, Z. and Derluguian, G. (2015) Fuel Protests in Armenia. *New Left Review*, 95 (September–October): 29–48.

Åslund, A. (2018) Want to Hit Putin Where It Hurts? Target His Friends. *The Hill*, 9 February. Available at: https://thehill.com/opinion/international/404 524-want-to-hit-putin-where-it-hurts-target-his-friends (accessed 6 May 2019).

Åslund, A. (2019) *Russia's Crony Capitalism: The Path from Market Economy to Kleptocracy*. New Haven: Yale University Press.

Åslund, A. and McFaul, M., eds (2006) *Revolution in Orange: The Origin of Ukraine's Democratic Breakthrough*. Washington DC: The Carnegie Endowment.

Asmus, R. D. (2010) *A Little War that Shook the World*. New York: Palgrave Macmillan.

Avakov, A. (2018) The Kremlin Wants to Frighten Pashinyan with Increase of Gas Price. *Moskovsky komsomolets*, (in Russian) 28 December. Available at: https://www.mk.ru/politics/2018/12/28/kreml-khochet-napugat-pashinyana -gazom-povysiv-ego-stoimost.html (accessed 6 May 2019).

Baev, P. K. (1997) *Russia's Policies in the Caucasus*. London: The Royal Institute of International Affairs, 7 August. Available at: https://www.chathamhouse. org/publications/books/archive/view/63316 (accessed 6 May 2019).

Baev, P. K. (2006) Turning Counter-Terrorism into Counter-Revolution. *European Security*, 15 (1): 3–32.

Baev, P. K. (2011) A Matrix for Post-Soviet 'Color Revolutions': Exorcising the Devil from Details. *International Area Studies Review*, 14 (2): 3–22.

Baev, P. K. (2018a) What made Russia Indifferent to the Revolution in Armenia. *Caucasus Analytical Digest*, 104 (July): 20–4. Available at: http://www.laen der-analysen.de/cad/pdf/CaucasusAnalyticalDigest104.pdf (accessed 6 May 2019).

Baev, P. K. (2018b) What Explains Russia's Uncharacteristic Indifference to the Revolution in Armenia? *Order from Chaos*, Brookings Institution, 7 May. Available at https://www.brookings.edu/blog/order-from-chaos/2018/05 /07/what-explains-russias-uncharacteristic-indifference-to-the-revolution-i n-armenia/ (accessed 6 May 2019).

Baev, P. K. and Øverland, I. (2010) The South Stream versus Nabucco Pipeline Race: Geopolitical and Economic (Ir)rationales and Political Stakes in Mega-projects. *International Affairs*, 86 (5): 1075–90.

Barbashin, A. and Souleimanov, E. A. (2018) A Color Revolution Russia can Live with. *The American Interest*, 7 June. Available at: https://www.the-amer ican-interest.com/2018/06/07/a-color-revolution-russia-can-live-with/ (accessed 6 May 2019).

Bazanova E., Sterkin, F. and Sinitsina, I. (2018) Russian Authorities Seek to Establish Off-Shore Entities to Help the Sanctioned Oligarchs. *Vedomosti* (in Russian), 10 April. Available at: https://www.vedomosti.ru/economics/artic les/2018/04/10/764372-ofshori-oligarham (accessed 6 May 2019).

Biurchiev, B. (2018) How the Kremlin's Anti-corruption Agenda Masks Federal Control in the North Caucasus. *Open Democracy*, 18 April. Available at: https://www.opendemocracy.net/od-russia/badma-biurchiev/federal-contro l-in-the-north-caucasus (accessed 6 May 2019).

Broers, L. (2018) The South Caucasus: Fracture without End? In: Ohanyan, A., ed., *Russia Abroad: Driving Regional Fracture in Post-Communist Eurasia and Beyond*. Washington DC: Georgetown University Press, 81–102.

'Could a Pipeline bring Peace?' (1995) *The New York Times*, 15 February. Available at: https://www.nytimes.com/1995/02/15/business/could-a-pip eline-bring-peace.html (accessed 6 May 2019).

Dabagyan, E. (2019) Russia Challenges USA in the Western Hemisphere. *Nezavisimaya Gazeta* (in Russian), 26 March. Available at: http://www.ng.ru/ kartblansh/2019-03-26/3_7540_kart.html (accessed 6 May 2019).

Dalakishvili, N. (2017) Georgia, Gazprom Agree to New Transit Terms. *VOA News*, 12 January. Available at: https://www.voanews.com/a/georgia-gazpro m-agree-new-transit-terms/3674663.html (accessed 6 May 2019).

Dannreuther, R. (2014) Russia and the Arab Spring: Supporting the Counter-Revolution. *Journal of European Integration*, 37 (1): 77–94.

Delanoe, I. (2019) Russia Extends Black Sea Control. *Le Monde Diplomatique*, 8 February. Available at: https://mondediplo.com/2019/02/08black-sea (accessed 6 May 2019).

Dronina, I. (2019) Su-30SM Fighters will take the Armenian Sky Under Control. *Nezavisimaya Gazeta* (in Russian), 11 February. Available at: http://www.ng.r u/armies/2019-02-11/8_7504_su.html (accessed 6 May 2019).

Fedorinova, Y. (2018) Deripaska's Hard Times Help Oligarch Weather Trump Sanctions. *Bloomberg*, 22 December. Available at: https://www.bloomber g.com/news/articles/2018-12-22/deripaska-s-hard-times-help-oligarch-we ather-trump-sanctions (accessed 6 May 2019).

Forbes' Rating of 200 Richest Businessmen in Russia. (2018) *Forbes.ru*. Available at: https://www.forbes.ru/rating/360355-200-bogateyshih-biznesmenov-r ossii-2018 (accessed 23 April 2019).

Gabuev, A. (2019) Russia's Support for Venezuela has Deep Roots. *Financial Times*, 3 February. Available at: https://www.ft.com/content/0e9618e4-23c8 -11e9-b20d-5376ca5216eb (accessed 6 May 2019).

Galstyan, A. (2018) Post-revolution Armenia Needs to Work on Mistakes. *Analytics & Comments* (in Russian), Russian International Affairs Council, 17 January. Available at: http://russiancouncil.ru/analytics-and-comments/ analytics/postrevolyutsionnoy-armenii-trebuetsya-rabota-nad-oshibkami/?s phrase_id=25311221 (accessed 6 May 2019).

Goble, P. (2018) Armenians Call for Russian base at Gyumri to be Shut Down. *Eurasia Review*, 27 December. Available at: https://www.eurasiareview.com/ 27122018-armenians-call-for-russian-base-at-gyumri-to-be-shut-down-ope d/ (accessed 6 May 2019).

Grigoryan, A. (2018) Armenian Revolution Aided by Restraint of Military, Security Services. *Eurasia Daily Monitor*, 15 (69), 7 May. Available at: https ://jamestown.org/program/armenian-revolution-aided-by-military-securit y-services-restraint/ (accessed 6 May 2019).

Hill, F. and Gaddy, C. G. (2015) *Mr. Putin: Operative in the Kremlin*, second edition. Washington DC: Brookings Press.

Huseynov, V. and Rzaev, A. (2018) The 'Velvet Revolution' Is Affecting Armenia's Ties with Russia. *EurActiv*, 23 October. Available at: https://ww w.euractiv.com/section/global-europe/opinion/the-velvet-revolution-is-affec ting-armenias-ties-with-russia/ (accessed 23 April 2019).

ICG (International Crisis Group). (2017) *Nagorno Karabakh's Gathering War Clouds*. Report No. 244, 1 June. Brussels: International Crisis Group. Available at: https://www.crisisgroup.org/europe-central-asia/caucasus/nag orno-karabakh-azerbaijan/244-nagorno-karabakhs-gathering-war-clouds (accessed 23 April 2019).

Iskandaryan, A. (2019) Armenia-Russia Relations: The Revolution and the Map. *Russian Analytical Digest*, No. 232, 22 February. Available at: http://www.css. ethz.ch/content/dam/ethz/special-interest/gess/cis/center-for-securities-st udies/pdfs/RAD232.pdf (accessed 23 April 2019).

Kauzlarich, R. and Kramer, D. J. (2018) Azerbaijan's Election Is a Farce. *Foreign Policy*, 11 April. Available at: https://foreignpolicy.com/2018/04/11/azerbaij ans-election-is-a-farce/ (accessed 23 April 2019).

Khalatyan, A. and Mareeva, Y. (2018) Serzh Sargsyan Befriended the Wrong People. *Kommersant* (in Russian), 27 June. Available at: https://www. kommersant.ru/doc/3669474 (accessed 23 April 2019).

Khalatyan, A. and Mordyushenko, O. (2019) Yerevan Will not Increase the Gas Price. *Kommersant* (in Russian), 9 January. Available at: https://www. kommersant.ru/doc/3849687 (accessed 23 April 2019).

Kofman, M. (2018) The August War, Ten Years on: A Retrospective on the Russo-Georgian War. *War on the Rocks*, 17 August, Available at: https://wa rontherocks.com/2018/08/the-august-war-ten-years-on-a-retrospective-on -the-russo-georgian-war/ (accessed 23 April 2019).

Kolesnikov, A. (2018) Dear Comrade Secretary General. *Kommersant* (in Russian), 9 November. Available at: https://www.kommersant.ru/ doc/3793999 (accessed 23 April 2019).

Kortunov, A. (2018) We Shouldn't Take the Protest Against Sargsyan for a Protest against Russia. *Analytics & Commentary* (in Russian), Russian International Affairs Council, 24 April. Available at: http://russiancouncil.ru/ analytics-and-comments/comments/nelzya-skazat-chto-protest-protiv-sarg syana-eto-protest-protiv-rossii/?sphrase_id=25269238 (accessed 23 April 2019).

Kramer, D. J. and Hill, W. H. (2009) Moldova: The Twitter Revolution That Wasn't. *Open Democracy*, 28 May. Available at: https://www.opendemocracy .net/article/email/moldova-the-twitter-revolution-that-wasn-t (accessed 23 April 2019).

Krasheninnikov, F. (2018) Why Russia Is Not Armenia. *New Times* (in Russian), 6 May. Available at: https://newtimes.ru/articles/detail/161862/ (accessed 6 May 2019).

Kucera, J. (2019) Armenia Sends Military Deminers and Medics to Support Russian Mission in Syria. *Eurasianet*, 8 February. Available at: https://eurasia net.org/armenia-sends-military-deminers-and-medics-to-support-russian- mission-in-syria (accessed 23 April 2019).

Kuzio, T. (2010) The Russian Factor in Ukraine's 2010 Presidential Elections. *Eurasia Daily Monitor*, 7 (9), 14 January. Available at: https://jamestown.or g/program/the-russian-factor-in-ukraines-2010-presidential-elections/ (accessed 6 May 2019).

Levitsky, S. and Way L. A. (2010) *Competitive Authoritarianism: Hybrid Regimes After the Cold War*. Cambridge and New York: Cambridge University Press.

Mammadov, R. (2018) Russia Putting the Pieces Together to Maintain Its Gas Stranglehold on Europe. *Eurasia Daily Monitor*, 11 April. Available at: https

://jamestown.org/program/russia-putting-the-pieces-together-to-maintai
n-its-gas-stranglehold-on-europe/ (accessed 6 May 2019).

Mandraud, I. (2017) Margarita Simonian ou le visage d'une propaganda russe
decomplexée. *Le Monde*, 14 January. Available at: https://www.lemonde.fr/eu
rope/article/2017/01/14/margarita-simonyan-ou-le-visage-d-une-propagan
de-russe-decomplexee_5062601_3214.html (accessed 6 May 2019).

Markedonov, S. (2018a) Country Born from Protest: Why the Events in
Armenia only Superficially Resemble 'Colour Revolution'. *Profil* (in Russian),
29 April. Available at: https://profile.ru/politika/item/125561-strana-roz
hdennaya-protestom (accessed 6 May 2019).

Markedonov, S. (2018b) Post-election Puzzle in Armenia: The Claim on
'wide support' for Pashinyan Is Dubious. *Sputnik Armenia* (in Russian), 10
December. Available at: https://ru.armeniasputnik.am/analytics/20181210/16
172434/poslevybornyj-pasyans-v-armenii-argument-o-vseobshchej-pod
derzhke-pashinyana-okazalsya-spornym.html (accessed 23 April 2019).

Mejlumyan, A. (2018) Armenian Investigation of Gazprom again Tests Ties
with Russia. *Eurasianet*, 16 November. Available at: https://eurasianet.org/
armenian-investigation-of-gazprom-again-tests-ties-with-russia (accessed 6
May 2019).

Mejlumyan, A. (2019) Armenia adopts plan for 'economic revolution'.
Eurasianet, 15 February. Available at: https://eurasianet.org/armenia-adop
ts-plan-for-economic-revolution (accessed 6 May 2019).

Mikhail Fridman Shows the Downside of being a Russian Oligarch. (2018) *The
Economist*, 6 December. Available at: https://www.economist.com/europe/20
18/12/08/mikhail-fridman-shows-the-downside-of-being-a-russian-oligarch
(accessed 6 May 2019).

Moscow's Gold: Russian Corruption in the UK. (2018) London: House of
Commons, Foreign Affairs Committee, 15 May. Available at: https://publica
tions.parliament.uk/pa/cm201719/cmselect/cmfaff/932/93202.htm (accessed
6 May 2019).

Ó Beacháin, D. and Polese, A., eds (2010) *The Colour Revolutions in the Former
Soviet Republics: Successes and Failures*. London: Routledge.

Ovation Nation: The Economist Country of the year 2018. (2018) *The
Economist*, 22 December. Available at: https://www.economist.com/leaders/2
018/12/22/the-economists-country-of-the-year-2018 (accessed 6 May 2019).

Peel, M. and Foy, H. (2018) Georgia Pledges to Forge Ahead with NATO
Ambitions. *Financial Times*, 24 July. Available at: https://www.ft.com/conten
t/e1a48320-8e53-11e8-b639-7680cedcc421 (accessed 6 May 2019).

Petersen, M. (2019) The Naval Power Shift in the Black Sea. *War on the Rocks*, 9
January. Available at: https://warontherocks.com/2019/01/the-naval-power-
shift-in-the-black-sea/ (accessed 6 May 2019).

Poghosyan, B. (2018) *Tailor-Made Cooperation? Armenia's New Partnership
Agreement with the EU*. Policy Brief. Brussels: European Policy Center, 15
February. Available at: http://www.epc.eu/pub_details.php?cat_id=3&pu
b_id=8275 (accessed 6 May 2019).

Polovinko, V. (2018) Not Saakashvili: What Nikol Pashinyan will do as Prime Minister and How Moscow Will Treat Him. *Novaya Gazeta* (in Russian), 10 May. Available at: https://www.novayagazeta.ru/articles/2018/05/10/76420-t ochno-ne-saakashvili (accessed 6 May 2019).

Roks, Y. (2016) Khadzhimba Remains President of Abkhazia. *Nezavisimaya Gazeta* (in Russian), 11 July. Available at: http://www.ng.ru/cis/2016-07-1 1/6_abhazia.html (accessed 6 May 2019).

Romanova, O. (2019) Dramatic Arrest in the Senate, or How Alexei Miller Won over Igor Sechin. *Commentary* (in Russian), Carnegie Moscow Center, 1 February. Available at: https://carnegie.ru/commentary/78267 (accessed 6 May 2019).

Sergeev, D. (2015) Maidan in Yerevan: Who Benefits from the Replay of the Ukrainian Collapse? *TV Zvezda* (in Russian), 25 June. Available at: https://tv zvezda.ru/news/vstrane_i_mire/content/201506250733-3jxr.htm (accessed 6 May 2019).

Shirinyan, A. (2019) What Does 2019 Hold for the Nagorno Karabakh Conflict? *ISPI Commentary*, 6 February. Available at: https://www.ispionline.it/en/ pubblicazione/what-does-2019-hold-nagorno-karabakh-conflict-22138 (accessed 6 May 2019).

Simonyan, Y. (2019) Unfortunately for Pashinyan, Putin has no Time for a Meeting. *Nezavisimaya Gazeta* (in Russian), 24 January. Available at: http:// www.ng.ru/cis/2019-01-24/5_7491_armenia.html (accessed 6 May 2019).

Solovyev, V. (2018) That Call was a Big Support: Interview with Robert Kocharian. *Kommersant* (in Russian), 19 September. Available at: https:// www.kommersant.ru/doc/3745275 (accessed 6 May 2019).

Stanovaya, T. (2019) Senator's Arrest Exposes Cannibalization of Russia's Power Vertical. Commentary, Carnegie Moscow Center, 6 February. Available at: https://carnegie.ru/commentary/78295 (accessed 23 April 2019).

Starr, S. F. and Cornell, S. E., eds (2005) *The Baku-Tbilisi-Ceyhan Pipeline: Oil Window to the West*. Washington DC: Johns Hopkins University-SAIS. Available at: https://www.silkroadstudies.org/resources/pdf/Monograph s/2005_01_MONO_Starr-Cornell_BTC-Pipeline.pdf (accessed 6 May 2019).

Surkov, V. (2019) Durable Putin's State. *Nezavisimaya Gazeta* (in Russian), 11 February. Available at: http://www.ng.ru/ideas/2019-02-11/5_7503_surkov.ht ml (accessed 6 May 2019).

Thaler, G. (2017) Enemy of the State – Putin's Loudest Critic. *CBS News*, 7 August. Available at: https://www.cbsnews.com/news/enemy-of-the-state-pu tins-loudest-critic/ (accessed 6 May 2019).

Tucas, B. (2017) NATO and Russia in the Black Sea: A New Confrontation? Russia's Design in the Black Sea: Extending the Buffer Zone. *Commentary*. Washington: CSIS, 6 March and 28 June. Available at: https://www.csis.org /analysis/nato-and-russia-black-sea-new-confrontation (accessed 6 May 2019).

de Waal, T. (2013) *Black Garden: Armenia and Azerbaijan Through Peace and War*. 2nd edn. New York: New York University Press.

de Waal, T. (2018a) The Caucasus: No Longer Just Russia's Neighborhood. *Strategic Europe*. Brussels: Carnegie Europe, 18 December. Available at: https ://carnegieeurope.eu/strategiceurope/77992 (accessed 6 May 2019).

de Waal, T. (2018b) Armenia's Revolution and the Karabakh Conflict. *Strategic Europe*. Brussels: Carnegie Europe, 22 May. Available at: https://carnegieeuro pe.eu/strategiceurope/76414 (accessed 6 May 2019).

Way, L. A. (2018) Why Didn't Putin Interfere in Armenia's Velvet Revolution? *Foreign Affairs*, 17 May. Available at: https://www.foreignaffairs.com/articles/ armenia/2018-05-17/why-didnt-putin-interfere-armenias-velvet-revolution (accessed 6 May 2019).

Weitz, R. (2018) *Assessing the Collective Security Treaty Organization: Capabilities and Vulnerabilities*. Carlisle Barracks: Strategic Studies Institute, US Army War College.

Zolyan, M. (2018a) What to Expect from Armenia's New Leader. Commentary, Carnegie Moscow Center, 16 May. Available at: https://carnegie.ru/ commentary/76365 (accessed 6 May 2019).

Zolyan, M. (2018b) What Is Happening in Yerevan? *Analytics & Comments,* The Russian International Affairs Council (in Russian), 17 April. Available at: http://russiancouncil.ru/analytics-and-comments/analytics/chto-proiskh odit-v-erevane/?sphrase_id=25269238 (accessed 6 May 2019).

102nd Military base of the Russian Group of Forces in the Caucasus. (2015) *Kavkazsky uzel* (in Russian), 3 April. Available at: https://www.kavkaz-uzel.e u/articles/152315/ (accessed 6 May 2019).

8

Political patriarchy

Gendered hierarchies, paternalism, and public space in Armenia's 'Velvet Revolution'

Tamar Shirinian

Feminist activists who had decided to participate in Armenia's 'Velvet Revolution' were already exasperated early on by the ways in which what is often termed patriarchy (*hayrishkhanut'yun* in Armenian) was playing out in the movement. Lusine Sargsyan, a grassroots activist who had been involved in queer and feminist work for a number of years, explained this exasperation: 'You get tired, you know? Not only are you out there all day, running around the city, and trying to do something, but then here are these men who are also getting in your way and sometimes even destroying (*k'andum en*) the work that you have done.' Anna Nikoghosyan, a feminist activist who had been involved in a number of initiatives prior to the Velvet Revolution, explained to me that 'this was a very patriarchal movement, which was expected. ... But in all of this, I think that there were many moments of micro, and maybe even macro, feminist victories, which I have been able to initiate with a group of women over the duration of these events.'

Nikoghosyan was referring to *Aghchiknots'*, or 'Girls' Place', a Facebook chat among women interjecting collectively formed voices and interventions into the movement and beyond, which she and Ruzanna Grigoryan, another grassroots activist who had been involved in organizing in Armenia for a number of years prior to the Velvet Revolution, had initiated. The *Aghchiknots'* chat is not necessarily a 'feminist' platform, nor is it a 'group', in that it includes various women with diverse political perspectives and goals, but with the common purpose of gathering women's voices and acting as women. The chat is still active today – a space in which women regularly share information about political goings-on and organize actions. When Nikoghosyan and Grigoryan began participating in the movement (14 April for Nikoghosyan and 13 April for Grigoryan), they found that – as in previous social movements in which men felt entitled to dominate public space, give orders to women and direct their actions, and place women under their 'protection' – patriarchal norms were being reproduced within the Velvet Revolution's time and space of action. The *Aghchiknots'* initiative was prompted largely because of the problem that they, along with other women within the movement, saw as this constant interruption of their work by men. These forms of interruption were not only demeaning and irritating but were also counterproductive to the solidarity they saw as critical for action. The Facebook chat was initiated on 15 April, and throughout the days of the movement, and afterwards, more and more women were added who could now organize actions together as well as create spaces within the movement through which they could, together, hold ground against men's interruptions.

In this chapter, I explore the work of *Aghchiknots'* and grassroots feminist activists during the Velvet Revolution to make sense of the problem of patriarchy in Armenia. In my use of patriarchy, I refer to a system of kinship based on father's right – *patria potesta* (Borneman 2004). Father's right organizes how we might understand 'traditional' Armenian kin-relations in which decision-making capacities – the 'traffic' in (Rubin 1975) or 'exchange' (Levi-Strauss 1969) of women, the ordering of space, land use and so on – are held by the father of the family, usually the most senior father within a *gerdasdan*, or the extended family unit that includes a father, all of his sons and their wives (Luzbetak 1951; Hoogasian Villa and Matossian 1982; Shirinian 2018a).

Patriarchy is a kin-based system of sexual oppression in which women are mothers, domestic labourers and consumers (Eisenstein 1979); thus, patriarchy produces ideologies regarding gender. In Armenia, normative ideologies regarding gender place men and women within different roles and separate capabilities, understood both as 'traditional' and often 'natural': men are strong and women are fragile; men take care of public obligations outside of the home, where they are also to deal with other men, while women organize private spheres, but also at the larger directorship of men. Within these two senses of patriarchy, systems that reflect one another and that also work simultaneously, gendered subjectivities are formed, in which men feel a naturalized superiority over women and women also feel, or are expected to feel, inferiority to men. This is particularly apparent in the ideological dictum that men expect and are expected to care for women (mothers, sisters, wives, etc.) through a paternal relation, but one that also comes with rights to make decisions about and for women and in which women *need* to be cared for, or are expected to feel such a need.

However, patriarchy must also be understood as something much larger than kinship and its associated ideological dimensions – both in Armenia and beyond. Feminist scholars have shown how gendered hierarchies structure relations in spheres much wider than the private and the domestic, such as in property rights in capitalism (with pre-capitalist roots) (Barrett 1989; Engels 1985), divisions of labour (Sacks 1989; Enloe 2014), political rights and access to political decision-making (Murray 1995), as well as citizenship and national belonging (Alexander 1994; Peterson 1999). Here, I am interested in pointing to these gendered ideologies and practices as patriarchal in structure, highlighting how patriarchy plays a major role within the sphere of the political, spanning the spectrum from the very grassroots up to highly institutionalized forms and environments. I take heed from my Armenian feminist interlocutors who often refer to these practices, ideologies and values within the public sphere as 'patriarchy'.

I term this latter sense of patriarchy – in which decision-making practices rooted in the home and father's right transcend that space and become a larger national or state-claimed form of right – *political* patriarchy. Political patriarchy might consequently itself be understood as a concept of multiple scales. From its most local expressions, political patriarchy is a system that informs the private relationships between husband and wife, husband and children, and so on. On its most global scale within the social realm, patriarchy informs the relationships between president or prime minister and citizens, or what John Borneman has termed *political fatherhood*, most apparent in authoritarian regimes (2004). In between these local and global scales, however, are multiple other expressions of the everyday public encounters between citizens among themselves, between citizens and state apparatuses (the police, for instance), and among protesters within a social movement.

I have previously argued that Armenia as a nation, especially within the Republic of Armenia, must be understood as a *nation-family*, in which rather than the relations of strangers within and among the public, one finds intimate encounters between those who have never met yet nevertheless hold 'familial expectations' towards one another. I have shown how this sense of a nation practiced as a family is most visible from the perspective of queer subjects. Queer subjects who – by way of disrupting expectations of what is proper for the nation – feel the burden of having to constantly be approached and reproached by others within the nation for their behaviours and practices. As such, Armenia as a nation-state might be understood as a body politic that is practiced as an extended family (Shirinian 2018b). These forms of public intimate encounters allowed for the possibilities of social trust, sustaining solidarity and collective effervescence for the Velvet Revolution. Yet, as I will show throughout this chapter, when expressed in their patriarchal and paternalist forms, these intimate encounters also broke down senses of solidarity and trust. Important to this iteration of the nation as an extended family is the way in which rights are also distributed according to gendered hierarchies that stem from kinship norms. Political patriarchy is, similar to the nation-family itself, most visible and tangible from the perspective of those who feel its effects most intensely – in the case of social movements in Armenia in general and the Velvet Revolution in particular, women who attempted to break from its rules of order. In other words, the sphere of the political was highlighted as one ordered by patriarchal structures in moments of disruption, as when women refused patriarchal (and/or paternalist) interruptions or when they demanded to use public space autonomously from men.

Investigating the Velvet Revolution in Armenia through performances of – and contestations against – patriarchy, and especially political patriarchy, furthers feminist analyses of social movements. This approach takes seriously the liminal space and time of social movements, in which many acts of disruption – including ideological disruption – occur, which might be tangential to the main objective of struggle or fall conceptually outside of it altogether. Furthermore, understanding the sphere of the political by way of the ideological system of patriarchy also allows for a deeper understanding of the ways in which patriarchy works within political fields and how it is countered within feminist frameworks of action. Engagement of these questions contributes to scholarship that aims to understand the role of gender in political transitions (Ishkanian 2008; Verdery 1996; Waylen 1994), especially by homing in on the organization of public space, gendered relations, and interventions on the social and ideological reproduction of patriarchal norms in the midst of a political movement that led to transition.

I arrived in Yerevan on 17 May to begin research on the revolution, and especially women's' participation within it. I collected twelve oral histories in the form of recorded interviews with women activists, most of whom identified with the category 'feminist', but also some who interrogated the easiness with which this term is often applied. All of my interlocutors, however, were women who had, in previous political work, problematized gender in some capacity. Thus my interlocutors were all women who had at least a few years of experience in previous social and political movements in Armenia who had also interjected into those movements gendered and sexual analyses – problematizing patriarchy, heterosexism and questions of propriety.

As my arrival in Yerevan came a couple of weeks after the events of the Velvet Revolution had ended, and order was beginning to take shape again, many of my oral history interviews turned to reflection on that liminal moment. Alongside formal interviews, this chapter also draws on informal discussions that took place during my fieldwork from 17 May to 11 July 2018, and participant observation among those who had participated in the movement. What I found through oral histories, discussions, conversations and often arguments regarding the movement was that much of what women activists found compelling was the work they had done not only towards the ousting of Serzh Sargsyan from power but also towards countering everyday forms of patriarchy that erupted within political actions. I examine the ways in which political patriarchy played out during the movement, as well as the various ways in which it was countered, to argue that while the Velvet Revolution was not a feminist movement by any measure, it produced encounters and moments through which larger, ideological, feminist work was being done.

Decentralized protest and gendered hierarchies

In April 2018 – through massive protests, strikes and shut downs of streets and roads all over the country – Armenians successfully forced the resignation of Prime Minister Serzh Sargsyan, who had been in power for ten years as president until he pushed for a constitutional referendum that would allow him to stay in power as prime minister after the end of his second legal term as president (see the Introduction). Nikol Pashinyan, a journalist, activist and also, at the time of the movement, a member of parliament had begun a march on foot from the city of Gyumri in the north of the country towards Yerevan.

Unlike previous attempts at mass mobilization of the Armenian population, including Pashinyan's own previous attempts, this time, he insisted on a decentralized – *apakentronats'vats* – model, in which Yerevan as the capital city would not be the centre of the movement and everyone everywhere in the country would join. Pashinyan's call for decentralized protest demanded civil disobedience in all sectors of life – from student strikes, to workers' strikes to a shutdown of streets and roads in order to halt movement of the status quo, and for every citizen to do their part no matter in what region, city or village they lived. Furthermore, decentralization would mean civil disobedience by all, no matter what age or gender they were. These forms of decentralization were understood by most of my interlocutors as key to the success of pushing for the resignation of Serzh, as Sargsyan was colloquially called, from power. First, decentralization meant that everyone was involved and it became quite apparent – especially by around 20 April – that the regime did not have legitimacy. Second, as a tactic of protest, it meant that police, special forces and the military would not be able to locate the movement in any one place, making it near impossible to squash. *K'ayl ara, merzhir Serzhin* ('Take your step, reject Serzh') became the main slogan of the movement, hailing as its audience every person in Armenia.

This demand for everyone to take their own step meant that public and political action were no longer containable as masculine space. Karine Aghajanyan, one of my interlocutors who was an active participant in the Velvet Revolution and who had been active in a number of prior social movements, explained the importance of this demand in regards to gender:

> Women were at least equal participants in all of the actions and no one within the movement would say to them, 'why are you participating?' ... In my experience during the 100 dram actions [a 2013 movement that successfully campaigned against a price rise in public transportation from 100 Armenian drams to 150 drams] or Electric Yerevan [see Chapter 2], or other such protests, in that time they would just very directly say to women 'Don't come here, this is not for you. Why are you out here in the street? You are a girl.' You understand? And here they were saying, 'Come out into the streets! Everyone!' It [your gender, age, etc.] didn't matter.

While Aghajanyan also admitted that many instances of patronizing comments and disruptions by men did occur during the movement, as I discuss further, Pashinyan's call for everyone to participate capped the possibilities of discourses laying exclusive claim to public and political space for men.

Social movements, which rely on some sensibility of 'the people', raise the question of the gender of 'the people', sometimes prompting the emergence of revolutionary reconfigurations of gender and sexuality (Hasso and Salime 2016) vis-à-vis embodied practices and performative acts in assembly (Butler 2015). Within their analysis of the Arab Spring, Frances Hasso and Zakia Salime ask, 'Even at the level of language, were girls, women and nonconformists included in the people? Does *regime* refer only to governments, or does it include other controlling systems that require felling? Why did conflict so often take sexualized forms on men's and women's bodies?' (Hasso and Salime 2016: 2). Pointing to how it was not just political regimes that were disrupted or toppled, but ideologies and orders of subjectivization – with gendered and sexual dimensions – as well, they argue that the revolutions within the Arab world 'publicly disputed gender and sexual orders in novel, unauthorized, and often shocking ways, even as a range of forces actively worked to reassert order and respectability boundaries. This is a permanent legacy that will continue to roil sexual and gendered orders in the region' (Hasso and Salime 2016: 2–3).

Gender and sexuality are integral parts of social movements, not just on the level of symbolism and representation, but within the realms of praxis and action. During the 2011 Arab Spring, women in Tunisia, Egypt and Libya struggled equally alongside men even while their own bodily integrity and honour was being directly targeted by police forces – something that exceeded the threats of violence against their male counterparts (Johansson-Nogues 2013). The insecurity that women faced during the movements, Elisabeth Johansson-Nogues argues, continued in the aftermath of the movement when women have faced more attacks on their rights and violence against women has been on the rise (2013). The Arab Spring and the 2013 Gezi Park movement in Turkey became sites in which women – through art, graffiti, blogging and performance – inserted their own voices within the movement while also simultaneously critiquing the reproduction of widespread patriarchal ideologies within the very workings of those movements (Gokariksel 2016; Benyoussef 2016). These gendered dimensions all played roles within the goings-on of Armenia's Velvet Revolution too, and all were linked to the already-existing gendered imaginaries and practices of Armenia prior to the movement – imaginaries and practices that feminist activists most often refer to as 'patriarchy'.

Nikoghosyan and Grigoryan, becoming witness to how the Velvet Revolution was a site in which patriarchal imaginaries and practices were being socially and ideologically reproduced, and being in conversation with other women who were also becoming exasperated by these processes, formed the *Aghchiknots'* chat. As Nikoghosyan explained, in the first few days of the protests, many people were busy shutting down streets in order to prevent the flow of traffic and to disrupt the workings of the nation-state as a part of Pashinyan's call for decentralized civil disobedience. But in doing this work, there were many moments of having to confront masculine occupation of public space and the disruption of women's actions by men. As Nikoghosyan explained:

> Because when really angry drivers would get there [to streets shut down by protesters] … they would target the men because for them the women did not exist. They did not address you as a woman. They would first come to the man next to you and speak to him: 'Brother, there is a sick person at home, I have to get home' and you know, all kinds of things, [telling him], 'you have to open up this street right away.' And those men, the men protesters, they were playing the role of negotiator and they were

starting to try to convince us that we have to let the road open for this one car, because this is an exception, and so on. And, thus, they would start to debate and argue with us. But we were much more guarded and sure of our position there and we didn't let them ... . Generally, this is how gender would play out during this movement. Men were more likely to give in (*harmarvogh ein*) and women, [even] women who might have even been 1,000 kilometres far away from feminism, their feelings about this seemed to be much stronger – the sense that no, we are closing this street and no one can tell me otherwise. Women, in this sense, were much more uncompromising and unbreakable.

Through the roles of 'negotiator' and 'guard', Nikoghosyan here addresses the gendered differences between men and women when it came to shutting down streets. Importantly, her point about women's uncompromising role related not only to women who were feminists but also to women in general – even those women who did not or would not identify their political position as 'feminist', or who might even have been opposed to such a politics. The problem was not just that men often undid the work of women – which, as many of my interlocutors would explain, was a major problem – but also that considerable time was spent in these first couple of days arguing with fellow men protesters instead of acting in solidarity to get political work done. In these senses, political patriarchy produces gendered hierarchies within actions of protest, standing in the way of social solidarity among citizens.

These moments of male disruption, however, also sometimes became moments in which new strategies could be created. Nikoghosyan, for instance, also narrated one moment, among many, in which this very problem of the difference between masculine negotiation and feminine guardianship was rendered one of democratic decision-making. In this one instance, she explained,

One of the drivers got so angry that we were on the verge of a fight and there the men were telling us that we had to let him go and were arguing with us and my friend, Ruzanna [Grigoryan], and I, we suggested to them that we have a discussion and come to a consensus about whether we were going to continue to close the street or if we were going to let this car through. And for the young people there, this was a very new practical skill. And so we started talking, everyone expressed some opinion on the matter. We were saying no, we won't let him through, the men were saying that we have to let him through and then I suggested that we take a vote and the majority there voted that we should open up that street and I said okay, the majority thinks we should let the street open, but I am abandoning this space, this street, because I feel like right now we are going against the decentralized civic initiative and message, because we are going against the need to make people feel uncomfortable, because that is the whole point of this, for people to experience discomfort (*anharmarut'yun*). If you constantly help people out when they feel troubled, you'll never get to your goals. And so, we left and went to another intersection. And in many intersections, these same things have occurred.

While Nikoghosyan and Grigoryan left this particular intersection eventually, this moment that could have caused a total break in solidarity became an opportunity to move towards something else. Moments like these introduced practices, such as those that Ernesto Laclau and Chantal Mouffe have termed 'radical democracy': forms of collective processes that move towards equality and freedom, and that point to the reflexivity and always unfinished work demanded by democratic modes of praxis (2014). These were new ways of negotiating and making use of public space that went beyond not only patriarchal modes of power that maintained decision-making in the hands of men but also surpassed liberal democratic forms as grassroots mechanisms emerging out of actually existing circumstances rather than top-down structures.

The problem of propriety

Patriarchy not only establishes gendered hierarchies but also creates and permits particular roles and possibilities – senses of propriety – outside of which action is censured or reproached. Many of my interlocutors pointed to ways in which these notions of the 'proper' worked within street actions during the movement. Political patriarchy, thus, might be understood as a form of power that necessarily attempts to exclude women from the realm of the political because what is defined as political in this context demands actions that are deemed impermissible – or 'improper' – for women.

Nikoghosyan, for instance, described what happened while she was working to shut down a street at one point during the movement and encountered a car with a pregnant woman inside. A man who was also out on the street with her approached her as she was blocking the road and not allowing that car or any other to pass and asked her, '*Qeznic inch kin?*' ('What kind of woman are you?'). She explained that she looked into the car and saw that there was a pregnant woman inside, but that this woman looked perfectly fine, sitting quietly in the car. This did not stop various other protesters from approaching her and explaining to her that the woman was pregnant and that she was not well and that Nikoghosyan needed to let this car pass. Here, we see that the expectation of gender plays both ways. First, Nikoghosyan is condemned for not being a proper woman, because she is not invested in the plight of motherhood. Second, however, we also see that the pregnant woman herself bears the burden of being unwell and not being able to withstand political disruption. While this scene might have been a quite different one were the pregnant woman herself to approach Nikoghosyan – what may have become an act of solidarity between women – political patriarchy cuts between women's solidarity and instead places each of them within a 'proper' slot of 'woman', something both of them were seen as disrupting. 'And I said', Nikoghosyan continued narrating this event, laughing, '"I am the kind of woman who doesn't give way to a pregnant woman. So, get used to that." And he was turning red and angry.' Nikoghosyan and other women who acted in these ways during the Velvet Revolution were seen as disrupting notions of what is proper for women, but they also took up this sense of being disruptive and ran with it, finding power within it. 'These kinds of examples', Nikoghosyan explained, 'show how we were playing on the very fine threads of what it means to be a woman. And that we were crossing over onto the other side of the boundary of what it meant to be a woman.'

At the time that the Velvet Revolution began, various feminist activists in Yerevan had organized some actions of solidarity with Asya Khachatryan, a young woman from Yerevan who had been living in Stepanakert in Karabakh and who had experienced police harassment there as a reaction against her 'impropriety' as a young woman. Asya, whose hair was dyed blue and who went out into the city at night by herself and who had beer bottles in her home, had become something incomprehensible to Karabakh police and thus became the object of harassment, including overnight detention in a police station and continued harassment after she was let go, prompting her to move back to Yerevan. Various women activists in Yerevan had dyed their hair blue to make a statement about femininity and autonomy. Thus, during the first couple of days of street actions as a part of civil disobedience during the Velvet Revolution, Nikoghosyan's hair still had some remnants of blue in it. As she explained, people were often staring at her and commenting on her appearance, which also acted as a way of dismissing her as a political actor. 'They were looking at me and saying "Look at this one's hair, her appearance. Have you even ever looked at yourself in the mirror? My stomach turns looking at you" and a lot of other really hurtful things.' At one point, Nikoghosyan told me, she was not only insulted directly about her 'ugly' appearance but that one woman had even suggested to her that her place is in Tsereteyin, a neighbourhood known for having many sex workers.

'She was basically telling me that I was a whore. She didn't realise, however, that this was not hurtful for me,' she told me, laughing. In other words, while the comment was meant as an insult, it did not work on Nikoghosyan as she embraced sex positivity and did not find sex work demeaning as most Armenians might.

Moments like these also sometimes engendered solidarity with other women. Nikoghosyan told me that at one point, when her blue hair was being commented upon by a man in the street, another woman approached her and said, 'Don't listen to him. You are very beautiful. You are ideal.' At this point in the interview, Nikoghosyan laughed gleefully, continuing, 'And there was this kind of solidarity between women. Indescribable solidarity between women who were within the movement. It was happening in all kinds of ways and it was so touching [*shat huzich er*], very touching.'

This sense of being emotionally touched by witnessing and being a part of street actions was a major theme in my interviews. Nearly every one of my interlocutors came to a point in the interview where they gave me a glimpse of a moment that had stuck with them, touched them, making them feel something extraordinary. These moments often incited feelings of something transcendent from the here and now, of the possibilities beyond the usual and, as such, they were often moments in which what was proper was disrupted in ways that seemed to challenge the world as it was previously known. For instance, Aghajanyan told me about one morning in particular when she experienced such a feeling. 'I think it was the morning of 20 April,' she began,

and a girl had closed the street with her own car right here on Gulbenkian St. [near where Aghajanyan lived in Yerevan] . . . . The police were telling this girl to open up the street. So, she's in the street in her car, blocking traffic and she just pushes the electric button raising the windows on the car in an act of 'Fuck you', you know? [laughs]. And the police, I mean, I don't know, they start to say things like 'My dear sister, open the street now', and so on and she says 'No, I am doing something here' and then they start talking to her in a more legal language: 'You have blocked traffic in a public space, you have no right to do this, you are breaking the law' and she says that she is not violating anything. That she is carrying forth an act toward her citizen duties. And when she realizes that they're talking, talking and threatening to arrest her she says, 'None of you have the right to touch my car.' And then again, she presses the button and the window comes up again. And then those police officers try to push that car out of the way, scare her, tell her they're going to arrest her, etc.

This moment was, for Aghajanyan, a realization of how women were undoing various forms of social expectations, norms and laws regulating feminine propriety. She continued,

> Things like this were happening, and they were just bringing me so much pleasure [*k'efs berum er*]. I was watching this scene and thinking *jan* [my dear life], where have you been? Where have women like this been? In all these years, I was thinking that in Armenia active and politically informed women made up one group – at the most about 500 people. But during this widespread protest, I saw women whom I did not recognize, who don't fit within my concept of being aware of rights, advocate for their own rights, in their own casual ways, self-aware and confident – that in all these years I have been tearing myself apart fighting with police officers but still afraid of those police officers ... and here was this girl who was not afraid. And for me it was just shocking how she could just be so unafraid.

The massive protests and decentralized public acts of disobedience in the Velvet Revolution brought out into highly visible public space, and into contact with one another, those who had not previously met and who would not otherwise have encountered one another in such ways. Aghajanyan found a great deal of inspiration in such women's acts of resistance.

My interlocutors often described these moments – seeing the work that others were doing, and being entrenched in so many moments of resistance – as inspirational, because of their own personal realization of numbers. Gayane, another one of my interlocutors who was a young queer activist, told me that the social movement became, for many visibly queer persons, an opportunity for others to harass them collectively. However, she also conveyed that it was a time of great joy, precisely because coming out into the streets daily meant encountering various other queer men and women whom they did not previously know. 'There were moments when I would look around and see so many women, for example, holding hands or cuddling each other in the streets and think 'What is this? Are we growing in number?' I thought I knew all of the non-heterosexual women in this city and then I realized that I probably don't.' Lara Aharonian, a feminist activist and the director of the Women's Resource Center, teared up when I interviewed her as she discussed the ways in which she saw young women taking initiative. 'I found strength in it, you know? If they were out there, risking so much, I knew that I could keep going and that I had to,' she told me. 'Seeing all of these young women who were willing to risk so much made me really see that things in Armenia were changing and that this new generation would be different and was already bringing in so much difference,' she continued.

Fearlessly and visibly disrupting propriety in public sometimes also had the effect of producing a level of threat that was not to be messed with lest it cause even further disruptions. On 20 April, for instance, the *Aghchiknots'* group had organized an action in which they marched down various streets of central Yerevan chanting *Serzhě mer papan chi, menk' papa chunenk'!* ('Serzh is not our daddy, we do not have a daddy!'), publicly criticizing not only Serzh Sargsyan as an illegitimate leader but also, simultaneously, the entire order of political patriarchy. During this action, Nikoghosyan, along with a few others, were arrested, dragged into a police van and taken to the police station. She discussed her interaction with the police while she was at the police station:

> There were a lot of gendered problems there too, with the police. Because, first of all, when you are a woman they want to make you feel bad as if, like, what kind of woman are you when you are doing things like this? There was a woman [police officer] there who was asking me questions like this and it was completely fine with her that I didn't want to give her any information, but when the police officers were men and they asked you something and you refused, it was like their ego became deflated and they all of a sudden got really aggressive, as if, how could it be that they were demanding something from a woman who was refusing this. This is a very authorial [*ishkhanakan*] thing and you could really feel it in these instances. Also, at the police station I was sitting with my legs just spread open [performs this during the interview], with pleasure [*havesov*], and men would be brought into the police station and I would quickly tell them what to say and what not to say and what their rights were and then I would get yelled at by the police officers and then respond that I was just telling them their rights and then I would become the target of their attention, 'Look at the way she's sitting. What is this?' And then at some point their biggest boss came in, I was sitting on the floor. He said, 'Let me bring you a chair to sit on.' I said 'I don't want a chair.' 'Well, wouldn't that be more convenient?' I said, 'No, this is very convenient for me.' ... And then he said to me, 'But does an Armenian girl sit that way, the way in which you are sitting right now?' and I said, 'Why? How am I sitting? I will sit however I want to sit.' And then he looked at me and said, '*Shar a esi, hani steghits*' ['This one is trouble, get her out of here'] and they took me out of the police station. And, like that, I was released hours before I really should have been. It was great, that moment. [laughs]

Thus, while Aghajanyan was shocked that so many women she did not know and who would not have previously fit within her conceptualization of politically informed and active women had fearlessly acted publicly and confronted police officers, Nikoghosyan's experience at the police station highlights some of the ways in which this may have been operating. By highlighting the 'authorial' dimensions of these encounters, Nikoghosyan points to the ways in which the male police officers are concerned not only with the bureaucratic process but also with insisting on their power and their authority – sometimes acting and speaking purely for the purposes of creating a sense and aura of power. Being a fearless woman within a context of political patriarchy places Nikoghosyan under threat – garnering particular attention from the authorities, who challenge her not only for her actions of civil disobedience but also for her impropriety in doing so as a woman.

Fearlessness, however, also threatens. A woman who speaks and acts defiantly – in other words daring to move so far beyond the prescriptive and proper sensibilities of shyness, coyness, modesty and fragility – is a woman who threatens the very foundations of the logics through which police officers know how to act. Nikoghosyan's defiance of propriety within the police station reminded me of the loud public scenes of Member of Parliament Zaruhi Postanjyan from the *Zharangut'yun* ('Heritage') Party. In 2013, for instance, Postanjyan publicly questioned President Sargsyan's expenditure at casinos in Europe during a Council of Europe Parliamentary Assembly in Strasbourg, leading to her removal from the Armenian delegation. She is known for public protests, often yelling and screaming while being dragged off by police officers, sometimes marking her as 'crazy' and thus easier to dismiss as a political actor, but also often marking her as threatening to the very orders in which a woman is expected to behave within public space: quietly, invisibly.

Political/public space and paternalism

Political patriarchy, founded upon gendered hierarchies and senses of propriety, also informs understandings of spatialization, especially that of public space as a masculine domain. 'You have to feel comfortable in public space and even when you really don't, you have to pretend that you do. You have to insist that you belong here, because you do,' Lusine Sargsyan reprimanded me as we were walking along the crowded Mashtots Avenue on a Friday evening in June 2018. After various encounters with groups of men who took over the entire width of the sidewalk, she expressed annoyance towards the next group. 'Excuse me, we are trying to pass. The street does not belong to you,' she asserted as she grabbed my hand and moved us through. As we passed, we heard snickers and, sensing my discomfort, she proceeded to lecture me on the importance of making a claim to public space. Lusine saw the occupation of public space in this sense as a feminist act on its own terms. 'Men think that public space belongs to them and they will continue to think so unless women do something about it,' she explained.

This sensibility of public space as masculine space is not unique to Armenia. Public and private have commonly been theorized as split across gendered and sexual lines (Fraser 1990; Chatterjee 1993; Warner 2005). In the context of political action, such as the Velvet Revolution, public and private are not only split in these ways, but become visible as ordered by way of paternalist patriarchy in its political realms. Public space, in other words, is a space in which paternal and patriarchal relations – transcending the space of the domestic and the familial – take shape as a strategy of men speaking and acting on behalf of women, for their own good.

Aghajanyan explained the gendered dimensions of Armenian political worlds as produced, even structurally, as patriarchal since most police officers are men and 'because they are men, they relate to women not only on professional terms but also in that patriarchal way – sister, brother, on that platform', in an *akhparavari* (brotherly) way. She pointed out that it was this very patriarchal structure that forced men, even her friends who would otherwise be supportive of her, to intervene on behalf of her and other women. While men interrupt women's actions without women's consent, Aghajanyan highlighted the ways in which they do this because of a larger political patriarchy based on paternalism, in which men see it as necessary to protect their women comrades from patriarchal police officers and other patriarchal men. The assumption is, of course, that women cannot handle patriarchal male police officers on their own.

During my interview with Aghajanyan, Ishkhanuhi, a friend of hers who had come over at the same time the day that Aghajanyan and I had set aside time for the interview, was present in the room. As Aghajanyan spoke about men's interruptions as coming from a place of care and protection, Ishkhanuhi interrupted:

> I'm sorry, but I have to say something. Men would come so that when drivers showed up and were being confrontational, they would deal with the situation in their *akhparavari* way ... to be in solidarity with one another as men. Not that they were coming to surround their women and protect them, and stand with them, they couldn't care less [*tk'ats unein*] about those women. ... They kept a solidarity with one another.

They did not break this solidarity. ... 'Let him go, my sister dear, let him go.' How are they supposed to close streets in this way?

Ishkhanuhi's interruption here brings into focus the ways in which paternalism is a form of patriarchy, and in this case, political patriarchy. In response to Ishkhanuhi, Aghajanyan confirmed that in her experience, there was almost no woman-and-police officer or woman-and-driver interaction that was not, without any request for such an interruption, interrupted by men. 'Because it is public, it is their space, and even if there are women making use of that public space now, they have given her *permission* [emphasis mine – T.S.] to be there,' Aghajanyan added.

While the kin-language of 'sister' (*k'ur jan,* 'dear sister', or *k'uyriks,* 'my sister') and 'brother' (*akhper* or *akhpers,* 'my brother') expresses forms of care and kin-solidarity, these forms are caught up in systems of power in which 'sister' and 'brother' are not equal and do not have equal access to rights. In this context, this question of access to rights becomes a political question rather than one of the solely intimate private realm of family. Kin-language, seeping out from the private intimate realm, from the relational framework between men and women, and into a context of political solidarity, disrupted the very forms of solidarity it was meant to evoke in these moments. As such, paternalism expressed as solidarity erupted into moments of inequality and became challenged within the political sphere.

Nikoghosyan told me of one moment towards the beginning of the movement when she had woken up really early in the morning and had prepared a text – a call to action regarding anti-capitalism, wages and the importance of strikes – that she had brought with her and wanted to read in front of a crowd that had gathered at a closed-off intersection. There was another protester, a man, at that intersection, who had a loudspeaker. She asked to use the loudspeaker so that she could read the text that she had prepared. 'Give it to me. Let me see,' this man had responded, referring to the text, to which Nikoghosyan had asked 'Why?' 'So that I can see if it's okay for you to read it.' Nikoghosyan was angry and also surprised, asking him, 'But who are you to tell me if I should or should not read something?' She decided that she did not need his loudspeaker and began to speak loudly, reading her prepared text. After a couple of minutes, this man had handed her the loudspeaker anyway.

Moments like these highlight the way in which patriarchy, paternalism and gendered hierarchies were not only being reproduced but also actively disputed and countered during the days of the movement. Understanding the Velvet Revolution as a decentralized movement that brought multiple voices and forms of difference towards a centralized call that demanded that everyone come out into the public means understanding it as a time and space where various other regimes, orders, logics and ideologies were being contested. While the social movement was a site for the reproduction of patriarchal norms, especially the reproduction of these values and expectations within public and political space, it was also a space of constant, everyday, challenges of those forms of patriarchy.

Conclusion

One hot afternoon in July 2018, Lusine Sargsyan and I had been walking through central Yerevan and decided to take a breather and cool down in Mashtots Park. The park is structured by walkways lined with grass and trees on one side, a small square of benches in the centre and a privatized café on the other side nearest Mashtots Avenue. The public benches were all occupied, so we decided to make use of the patches of green grass that lined one side of the park, setting down our bag and backpack as pillows and lying down. This quickly became a contested act as multiple times men passing by made comments and threw disapproving looks our way. 'You know,' Lusine began, 'during the movement, everyone was sitting on the ground – on street curbs, steps of buildings, and on patches of grass. Women, too'. Lusine had been someone who had always worked to challenge notions of propriety, and saw her claim to public space as her feminist act. She now explained her feeling of shock when in April and May, during the liminal period of the Velvet Revolution, she saw that what she had always done as an act of protest had become normal and everyday. By July, however, it was clear that this was no longer appropriate behaviour, especially for young women.

I was becoming uncomfortable with the glares of passers-by, so I sat up as Lusine questioned my behaviour. 'Are you scared?' she laughed. At that very moment, a middle-aged man, wearing a '*dukhov*' t-shirt – an artefact of the movement, celebrating Pashinyan as someone whose charisma came from his masculine style and high spirits – was passing by, and stopped to ask us a question. '*Sirum ek' mer Nikoli nor Hayastanĕ?*' ('Do you like our Nikol's New Armenia?'). Annoyed, and knowing what was about to come next, Lusine responded, 'No.' 'But why don't you like it? He's made it possible for us to live in a new, clean, democratic country. And look how you're treating this new country,' he responded, referring to our improper form of occupying public space. Lusine's response got right down to the contradictions in the ideological reproduction of propriety in this so-called 'New Armenia': 'Well, that's the kind of people we are, we make space dirty. There is now room for all kinds of people in the New Armenia, isn't there?' The man, now a bit annoyed, began to walk away, saying *'Chisht chek' anum'* ('You're not doing what is right').

The Velvet Revolution produced time and space as a wellspring of challenges to existing social, cultural and ideological norms. But this time and space was a liminal one. Once the revolution and social movement came to an end, power as gendered, patriarchal and paternal returned largely to its 'normal', pre-revolutionary, state. One of the major concerns that feminist activists and other women who struggled and fought within the movement had after the 'Velvet moment' had passed was the gendering of appointments to ministries. Prime Minister Pashinyan only appointed two women among the twenty ministerial positions, signifying a return to the 'normal', the patriarchal, in everyday practices that was concerning to many women. While many feminist activists acknowledged from the very beginnings that that movement was in itself a largely patriarchal one, they also experienced everyday and very real moments of having countered and struggled against patriarchy. What many of my interlocutors would point out, however, is that as the movement had produced the grounds for dialectical work on gendered ideologies, it had also produced new subjects, ones who were less willing to submit to the previous world's regulations of their bodies, voices and access to public space.

References

Alexander, M. J. (1994) Not Just (Any)*Body* Can Be a Citizen: The Politics of Law, Sexuality, and Postcoloniality in Trinidad and Tobago and the Bahamas. *Feminist Review*, 48: 5–23.

Barrett, M. (1989) *Women's Oppression Today: The Marxist/Feminist Encounter*. New York: Verso.

Benyoussef, L. (2016) Gender and the Fractured Mythscapes of National Identity in Revolutionary Tunisia. In: Hasso, F. S. and Salime, Z., eds, *Freedom Without Permission: Bodies and Space in the Arab Revolutions*. Durham: Duke University Press, 51–79.

Borneman, J. (2004) Introduction: Theorizing Regime Ends. In: Borneman, J., ed., *Death of the Father: An Anthropology of the End in Political Authority*. New York: Berghahn Books, 1–32.

Butler, J. (2015) *Notes Toward a Performative Theory of Assembly*. Cambridge, MA: Harvard University Press.

Chatterjee, P. (1993) *The Nation and Its Fragments: Colonial and Postcolonial Histories*. Princeton: Princeton University Press.

Eisenstein, Z. (1979) *Capitalist Patriarchy and the Case for Socialist Feminism*. New York: Monthly Review Press.

Engels, F. (1985) *The Origin of the Family, Private Property and the State*. New York: Penguin Books.

Enloe, C. (2014) *Bananas, Beaches and Bases: Making Feminist Sense of International Politics*. Berkeley: University of California Press.

Fraser, N. (1990) Rethinking the Public Sphere: A Contribution to the Critique of Actually Existing Democracy. *Social Text*, 25/26: 56–80.

Gokariksel, B. (2016) Intimate Politics of Protest: Gendering Embodiments and Redefining Spaces in Istanbul's Taksim Gezi Park and the Arab Revolution. In: Hasso, F. S. and Salime, Z., eds, *Freedom Without Permission: Bodies and Space in the Arab Revolutions*. Durham: Duke University Press, 221–58.

Hasso, F. S. and Salime, Z. (2016) Introduction. In: Hasso, F. S. and Salime, Z., eds, *Freedom Without Permission: Bodies and Space in the Arab Revolutions*. Durham: Duke University Press, 1–24.

Hoogasian Villa, S. and Matossian, M. K. (1982) *Armenian Village Life Before 1914*. Detroit: Wayne State University.

Ishkanian, A. (2008) *Democracy Building and Civil Society in Post-Soviet Armenia*. London and New York: Routledge.

Johansson-Nogues, E. (2013) Gendering the Arab Spring? Rights and (In) security of Tunisian, Egyptian, and Libyan Women. *Security Dialogue*, 44 (5–6): 393–409.

Laclau, E. and Mouffe, C. (2014) *Hegemony and Socialist Strategy: Toward a Radical Democratic Politics*. New York: Verso.

Levi-Strauss, C. (1969) *The Elementary Structures of Kinship*. Boston: Beacon Press.

Luzbetak, L. J. (1951) *Marriage and the Family in Caucasia: A Contribution to the Study of North Caucasian Ethnology and Customary Law*. Vienna: St. Gabriel's Mission Press.

Murray, M. (1995) *The Law of the Father? Patriarchy in the Transition from Feudalism to Capitalism*. New York: Routledge.

Peterson, V. S. (1999) Sexing Political Identities: Nationalism as Heterosexism. *International Feminist Journal of Politics*, 1 (1): 34–65.

Rubin, G. (1975) The Traffic in Women: Notes on the 'Political Economy' of Sex. In: Reiter, R., ed., *Toward an Anthropology of Women*. New York Monthly Review Press, 157–210.

Sacks, K. (1989) Toward a Unified Theory of Class, Race, and Gender. *American Ethnologist*, 16 (3): 534–50.

Shirinian, T. (2018a) A Room of One's Own: Woman's Desire and Queer Domesticity in the Republic. *Armenian Review*, 56 (1–2): 60–90.

Shirinian, T. (2018b). The Nation-Family: Intimate Encounters and Genealogical Perversion in Armenia. *American Ethnologist*, 45 (1): 48–59.

Verdery, K. (1996) *What Was Socialism and What Comes Next?* Princeton: Princeton University Press.

Warner, M. (2005) *Publics and Counterpublics*. New York: Zone Books.

Waylen, G. (1994) Women and Democratization: Conceptualizing Gender Relations in Transition Politics. *World Politics*, 46 (3): 327–54.

9

Democratization and diaspora

The Velvet Revolution and the Armenian nation abroad

Kristin Cavoukian

The Armenian diaspora's role in home-state politics is a perennial topic of conversation in the Republic of Armenia. As such, the 2018 events known as the 'Velvet Revolution', in which peaceful protests forced the resignation of Serzh Sargsyan and ultimately brought Nikol Pashinyan to power, were notable in that the diaspora had very little influence. Instead, the Velvet Revolution, which unfolded on the streets of Yerevan and throughout the Republic of Armenia, was almost entirely a home-grown phenomenon. While some diasporans exhibited a high degree of *engagement* with the events as they unfolded, as a whole, most had little actual *involvement* in those events.[1]

The diaspora's relative lack of involvement may seem counter-intuitive, given the vast literature on diasporas engaging in what Benedict Anderson has called 'long-distance nationalism' (Anderson 1992). And given the long-standing tendency within Armenia, dating back to Soviet times, to view the diaspora as politically meddlesome, it seems natural to look to that diaspora as a key player in the peaceful popular uprisings that ultimately brought down a government. However, the Velvet Revolution largely caught the sizeable and diverse Armenian diaspora by surprise. The overall diaspora response was cautious, with great enthusiasm in some quarters dwarfed by trepidation in others about the potential of disaster should foreign actors – namely, Russian or Azerbaijani elites – react negatively or take advantage of the country's power vacuum. Specifically, while support for the Velvet Revolution was to be found among younger diasporans, newer organizations and a few celebrities, the larger, more established diaspora organizations responded with extreme caution, with most withholding comment until Sargsyan's resignation was a fait accompli. Interestingly, while there had generally been a great deal of critique within the diaspora of Armenia's diaspora engagement institutions under previous governments, challenges and changes to those institutions in the aftermath of the Velvet Revolution were met with a surprisingly alarmist diaspora reaction.

This chapter situates the Armenian diaspora's response to the events unfolding in Armenia in 2018 within the general pattern of state-diaspora relations since Armenia's independence in 1991. Despite expectations to the contrary, the diaspora has generally acted as a conservative, risk-averse force in Armenian politics. Most diasporans have preferred to engage with Armenia financially, rather than taking a more active part in its transformation, and their financial engagement has tended to lend support and legitimacy to the government of the day, regardless of its domestic track record.

The diaspora's passion for Armenian politics has largely focused on foreign policy, and issues pertaining to sovereignty, territory and national identity. With respect to these concerns, Western diasporans have been very vocal in their criticism of the government, unlike Armenians living in the former Soviet space, who have typically showed more deference to Armenia's ruling elites. To reduce this irritant, the Armenian state engaged in a process I call 'identity gerrymandering', a rhetorical strategy aimed at cultivating and elevating the status of a pliant and compliant post-Soviet Armenian diaspora, especially in Russia, to counterbalance and hopefully serve as a model for the Western diaspora. In doing so, Armenian elites stressed the differences between the organizational types found in the West and in post-Soviet states.

The diaspora responses to the Velvet Revolution, however, reveal significant commonalities – large organizations in both Russia *and* the West exhibited no enthusiasm for the events, while individuals, smaller groups and especially young diasporans broke with these large organizations to support the protests in Armenia as they unfolded. This, coupled with the apparent Western diaspora acceptance of the Ministry of Diaspora – the institution central to the gerrymandering project – suggests that the state may have been at least partially successful in producing convergence between the Russian and Western diaspora's organizational behaviours and in disciplining the Western diaspora's more unruly impulses. However, it also hinted that the more salient diaspora cleavage, twenty-seven years after Armenia's independence, was perhaps between large diaspora organizations and a new generation of diasporans who no longer feel represented by them. The Velvet Revolution, which presented an opportunity to put the Republic of Armenia on a new political footing, also laid the groundwork for a more genuine state-diaspora relationship, one in which the institutional architecture in the home state, and the organizational landscape in the diaspora, might be revisited.

Diasporas and pro-democracy revolutions?

Within comparative politics, the study of diasporas has drawn largely from the literatures on nationalism and ethnicity, with diasporic behaviour often seen as a 'long-distance' variant of ethnic politics (Anderson 1992). Movements to secure or restore an ethnic homeland have not only included diaspora participants (Smith 2010: 4) but also often originated among diaspora elites (Kapur 2007: 97). Diasporas have been involved in recruitment, arming and financing for political, military and terrorist operations (Cohen 1996: 516, 519; Kapur 2007: 98; Sheffer 1994: 65; Smith 2010: 4–5). Diasporic nationalism can take the form of repatriation movements, as well as attempts to intervene in the political, social or economic life of the home state in order to strengthen a specific vision of national identity (Tölölyan 2007b: 221; Shain and Sherman 2001: 5–6). However, much diaspora home-state interaction takes the form of financial flows such as economic aid, philanthropy, and increasingly, remittances, which reached a record high of $689 billion globally in 2018, vastly exceeding foreign direct investment in most states (World Bank 2019).

According to Tölölyan, diasporas wield 'stateless power' that, unlike the more materially decisive power typically exercised by states (as in taxation and coercion), takes the form of 'a set of relations that can constrain or enable' (Tölölyan 2007b: 219). Some of this stateless power may be directed towards home states in transition, where Western diasporas are often assumed to prefer more democratic outcomes, and may thus attempt to import ideas and institutions of governance gleaned from their host states (Safran 2009: 83; Tölölyan 2007b: 221), as well as lobby their host-state governments to influence the home state. In fact, diaspora attempts to influence United States (US) foreign policy in this way are so ubiquitous that Shain considers them 'one of the clearest indications that an ethnic community has 'arrived' in American society' (Shain 1999: 8).

There are important variations in diaspora involvement in home-state politics, however, with sovereignty, territorial integrity or physical security issues generally prompting more intense diasporic responses than domestic political matters (Shain 1999: 66). Koinova notes that post-communist diasporas have displayed varying support for liberal democracy and democratization movements. Thus, for example, the Serbian diaspora by and large did not support the *Otpor* movement demanding regime change in the late 1990s, while the Ukrainian diaspora was much more supportive of the 2003 Orange Revolution (Koinova 2009: 42–3, 56–7).

It is important to specify what is meant by diaspora 'support' for democratization movements, especially in the former Soviet space, where the strong Russian reaction to so-called 'colour revolutions'[2] has included the perennial accusation that protests seen as contrary to Russian interests are the product of foreign influence (see Chapter 7 of this volume). Ukraine's two popular uprisings, both of which resulted in the resignation of the country's leadership and new elections, are worth considering in this regard. Prior to the 2003 Orange Revolution, Koinova claims that many established Ukrainian diaspora organizations, including the Ukrainian World Congress, had effectively been apologists for the corrupt Kuchma regime. However, as the fraudulent election of 2003 unfolded, many Ukrainians sounded the alarm in their host states regarding electoral irregularities, raised money to support the protests via a network of credit unions and served as election observers in the eventual repeat runoff election (Koinova 2009: 56). During the 2013–14 Euromaidan movement, Krasynska notes that Ukrainians around the world were inspired to participate digitally, such as by tweeting, posting on social media, and translating articles into English and other languages, as well as holding solidarity protests in their host states. While doing so generated a heightened sense of national pride and interconnectedness among diasporans, it is unclear how much of an impact this activity had on the success of the movement (Krasynska 2015: 186; Fujiwara 2015: 204). In both cases, the diaspora clearly played a minor, supporting role, and within the diaspora, individuals and emergent groups, rather than established organizations, led the charge.

Identity gerrymandering: The Armenian state's approach to diaspora relations

Diaspora home-state influence is not unidirectional. My previous work had focused on the ways in which home states attempt to construct diaspora identities for their own purposes. In the Armenian case, I have suggested that Armenian elites engaged in a process of 'identity gerrymandering', attempting to engineer a loyal constituency of co-ethnics abroad (Cavoukian 2016: 12).

Post-Soviet Armenia needed to manage relations with a large, influential diaspora, mostly living in the West, whose relationship with the state was more commemorative than it was kin-based or economic (Boyarin and Boyarin 2002: 11), and who were perceived as out of touch and culturally foreign.[3] Independent Armenia's contentious relationship with the Western diaspora – doubly 'Western' in that most of its members traced their roots to Western Armenia (Eastern Turkey), and had settled in Western states

– is well documented (Panossian 2003; Tölölyan 2007a). It can be traced to Soviet-era vilification of the diaspora-based Armenian Revolutionary Federation (ARF, or Dashnaktsutyun) as well as post-independence conflicts between Armenia's first president Levon Ter-Petrossian and the ARF, who began contesting Armenian elections as a domestic political party. But while the conflict was in part over the proper role of the diaspora (and the ARF) in Armenian politics, an equally salient irritant was the Western diaspora's penchant for vocal criticism of Armenia's government.

Unruly public disagreement with Armenia's ruling elites was much less common among ethnic Armenians living in the post-Soviet space, where public deference to the republic's elites, and the unquestioned acknowledgement of their authority, was the norm. An example of this contrast was seen during Serzh Sargsyan's 2009 tour of major diaspora centres to promote the Turkey-Armenia Protocols, a controversial agreement to normalize relations between the two states.[4] Sargsyan was met with public protests in New York, Paris and Beirut, but not in the Russian city of Rostov-on-Don, where there was far less criticism, and it was expressed privately (Sanamyan 2009).

Armenian elites gerrymandered diasporan identity by rhetorically enlarging the global pool of 'diasporans' to include the more deferent and less culturally foreign Armenians in Russia and the other former Soviet states. These post-Soviet Armenians abroad had previously never conceived of themselves as part of the diaspora, and the majority were in fact relatively recent migrants from Armenia (Cavoukian 2016: 13–14). Armenia's elites not only began referring to them as diasporans and encouraging them to organize as such but also praised them as the new 'model diaspora' to be emulated. Reframing 'the diaspora' to include Armenians in the former Soviet space, especially the large and growing population in Russia, rhetorically diluted the pool of critical diasporans and recast state-diaspora relations in a more favourable light from the perspective of incumbents in Yerevan (Cavoukian 2016: 7–8).

A key institution in this identity gerrymandering effort was the Ministry of Diaspora, created in 2008 and headed by Hranush Hakobyan, a former *Komsomol*[5] official and loyal member of the ruling Republican Party of Armenia (RPA). With no prior expertise in diaspora affairs, Hakobyan began to assert herself as the central figure in the state-diaspora relationship. She and her staff expressed concern about the divisive and uncooperative nature of the Western diaspora and its organizations, and praised the model of organization emerging in the former Soviet space, and especially in Russia – hierarchical umbrella organizations, invariably led by wealthy businessmen, which claimed to represent all the Armenians living in a state. They depicted this model as less contentious and easier for the ministry to work with than the more partisan Western diaspora, indeed seeing any model of diaspora other than one that spoke with a single voice as undesirable.[6] They simultaneously highlighted the value to Armenia of the growing Armenian community in Russia, which was largely the product of a constant stream of labour migration to that country, much of which was temporary and circular. In fact, labour migrants often did not consider themselves to have 'left' Armenia in any meaningful sense (Cavoukian 2016: 116).

A tale of two diasporas: Western and post-Soviet

Most of what can now be considered the established or Western Armenian diaspora consists of survivors of the Armenian Genocide and their descendants, largely hailing from eastern Anatolia, a region located in present-day Turkey, and also known as Western Armenia. Three pre-existing political parties followed the genocide survivors into exile, and competed for the loyalty of the newly forming diaspora communities: the socialist and nationalist ARF (or 'Dashnak' Party), the Social Democratic Hnchakyan (or 'Hnchak') Party and the Armenian Democratic Liberal (or 'Ramgavar') Party. Each commanded enough loyalty that diaspora Armenian national identity became intimately associated with membership in these parties and their associated community organizations, such as the Ramgavar-associated Armenian General Benevolent Union (AGBU) and the ARF-affiliated Armenian Relief Society (ARS) (Panossian 2006: 297). Over time, the ARF emerged as the dominant party such that many diaspora communities were ultimately divided into ARF and anti-ARF camps, each with its own schools, churches, charities and newspapers. In the United States, powerful lobbying organizations also arose to represent each camp: the ARF-affiliated Armenian National Committee of America (ANCA), and non-ARF Armenian Assembly of America (AAA). The two shared similar goals in the pre- and post-independence periods, including genocide recognition, support for the self-determination of Nagorny Karabakh, Section 907 prohibitions on US aid to Azerbaijan and increased US aid to Armenia.

The institutions of the Western diaspora have been virtually absent in the post-communist world, with the exception of Bulgaria, where the ARS and the AGBU are both active (Papazian-Tanielian 2016: 201), and Georgia, which has a limited ARF presence (Siekierski 2016: 17). More common are relatively recent umbrella organizations claiming to represent all of the Armenians in the state, and often, as in the Union of Armenians of Russia and the Union of Armenians of Ukraine, led by prominent local businessmen (Siekierski 2016: 17). As Dyatlov notes, these businessmen-cum-community leaders are motivated by leadership ambitions, social acceptance and prestige, the opportunity to establish patron-client ties with co-ethnics, and access to political authorities in both host and home states. They also seek to regulate the behaviour of newcomers, who may damage the reputation of the group in the eyes of the host-state majority (Dyatlov 2016: 29). Like some of their Western counterparts, Russia's Armenian organizations also engage in a form of lobbying, which Dyatlov suggests is 'based on a significant intermediary resource': the ability to turn out co-ethnic voters for Putin and his preferred candidates (2016: 36).

The diaspora as a force for continuity

Since Armenia's population is less than three million, while estimates place the global Armenian diaspora at roughly double that, it comes as no surprise that discussions of the diaspora's role enter into virtually any discussion of Armenian politics, and much of this discussion pertains to the Western diaspora (Cavoukian 2013: 712). However, despite stereotypes and expectations to the contrary, the diaspora has played a limited and comparatively conservative role since the late Soviet period of Armenia's history, arguably doing more to curb regime resistance and change than to support it.

Perhaps most notable in setting the tone for the post-independence state-diaspora relationship was the October 1988 joint letter issued by the leadership of the three Western diaspora political parties, urging caution among Soviet Armenians demanding the unification of the Nagorno-Karabakh autonomous region with Armenia, and later, advocating independence from the Soviet Union. The letter argued that without Soviet military protection, there was no guarantee that Turkey and Azerbaijan would not attack Armenia, and even commit a second genocide. Although these were not entirely unrealistic fears, this unheeded warning was perceived by many in Armenia as evidence that the diaspora was out of touch with the realities they faced (Tölölyan 2007b: 226), and was even 'reinforcing the Communist line' (Shain 1999: 63–4).

As the Nagorny Karabakh conflict unfolded, the diaspora was overwhelmingly supportive, providing economic aid, lobbying their host-state governments for Armenia- and Karabakh-friendly policies, and, in some cases, even smuggling in guns and military supplies. However, despite viewing the conflict through the lens of a potential second genocide, few Western diaspora volunteers actually fought in the war. The handful of diaspora warriors that did, the most famous of whom was California-born Monte Melkonian, were lionized in the diaspora, and in Armenia itself (de Waal 2013: 219–20; Tölölyan 2007a: 116–17). However, they were ultimately the exceptions to the general rule of the diaspora preferring to contribute funds from a comfortable distance.

From the earliest days of independence, the diaspora's primary role in Armenia has been to prop up the regime financially. As Acemoglu notes, in its desire to see Armenia succeed and to defend its reputation internationally, the diaspora's tendency was to equate the Armenian state with the government of the day, to mute its critiques of its treatment of Armenian citizens, and to thus lend it legitimacy. He also suggests that the Armenian diaspora's resources have in some ways resembled the rents that elites in resource-rich states have fought one another over and that have ultimately hindered, rather than facilitated, economic, social and political development (Daron Acemoglu... 2016).

Diaspora-to-home-state financial transfers have attracted significant scholarly and political attention (King and Melvin 1998: 224), but Shain and Sherman differentiate between financial flows channelled to nascent state bodies, and characteristic of the struggle to achieve or consolidate statehood, and the redirection of these flows towards non-state bodies, such as civil society groups or opposition political organizations, once state viability has been established (Shain and Sherman 2001: 6–7, 18, 20–1). In Armenia, after a few years of ad hoc attempts at philanthropy and investment, in which numerous diasporans were swindled out of large sums of money in a chaotic legal environment, the state-dominated Hayastan All-Armenian Fund emerged to become the dominant form of giving for fraud-wary diasporans who wished to contribute to the home state's development. Not coincidentally, it was encouraged by, and in turn reinforced, the rent-seeking behaviour of elites in Armenia. Thus, while Shain and Sherman would expect to see a diversification of diaspora financial flows as Armenia's statehood solidified, diaspora support for Armenia largely remained in pro-regime 'life-support' mode (Cavoukian 2017), and 'qualitative engagement, such as, for example, between civil societies of both entities, did not occur' (Ghaplanyan 2017: 200).

The early years of Armenia's post-Soviet transition, in which the nascent state's institutions were malleable and its economy in dire need of assistance, were the ones in which the diaspora was most able to exercise stateless power (Tölölyan 2007b: 222). Indeed, the lengthy debate over whether to grant diaspora Armenians dual citizenship and the right to vote in Armenian elections included the notion that those living in more democratic host states might 'infuse Armenia's political culture with the new habits and skills of democratic participation' (Ohanyan 2004: 298), and the Ter-Petrossian and Kocharian regimes' attempts to keep the diaspora as distant as possible from Armenian politics, for as long as possible, was seen to reflect precisely this understanding.

By the Sargsyan era, however, the Armenian state could no longer be said to be in 'transition', having consolidated into a system best described as 'competitive authoritarianism', in which formal democratic institutions existed, but were so regularly undermined by the incumbent regime that they could not be said to meet minimum democratic standards (Levitsky and Way 2002: 52). Those in the diaspora who had hoped for a democratic home state were largely resigned to the existing regime that, in any event, appeared to be the tiny state's only bulwark against foreign aggression. Renewed hostilities with Azerbaijan, with whom Armenia had fought a war over Nagorny Karabakh, were a constant fear, and Turkey (Azerbaijan's ally) was seen as a perennial threat due to memories of the 1915–18 Armenian Genocide.

This grudging acceptance had led to ambivalent behaviour on the part of Western diaspora elites. On the one hand, they made regular statements in support of 'strong' statehood, and engaged in a fair degree of pandering to ruling RPA elites as leaders of the state, while on the other hand, they complained about the regime's corruption and criminality:

> You get diasporan leaders, for lack of a better word, who come to Armenia, and when they do so, they start taking pictures with corrupt officials, with the president, and they galavant with them, they hang out with them, they feel good, they receive medals from them, and the moment they come back to the West, they start criticizing them and talking about how horrible they are. (Zareh Sinanyan... 2018)

This Janus-like behaviour was in fact mirrored by Armenia's political elites who, while they regularly complained about the Western diaspora organizations that appeared to fracture, rather than unite host-state communities, in fact tended to reinforce the importance of these organizations by continually reaching out to them as official representatives of the diaspora, at the expense of unaligned individuals and smaller groups (Armenia's Government... 2018).

In its initial stages, the Velvet Revolution seemed like yet another instalment of what had by then become a well-worn repertoire of contention in Armenia, after the public protests of 1 March 2008 against electoral fraud, the 2013 'Barevolution', the 2013 bus-fare boycott (also known as the '100 dram' protest), the 2015 'Electric Yerevan' protests, and the 2016 *Sasna Tsrer* hostage crisis, which drew a sizeable protest in support of the hostage takers (see Chapters 2 and 4). Of all of those, the dramatic *Sasna Tsrer* episode probably captured the diasporic imagination most, since it came on the heels of a four-day re-ignition of the 'frozen' Nagorny Karabakh conflict, which cost Armenia 800 hectares of territory and many casualties. The perpetrators, veterans of the 1990s war with Azerbaijan, framed their seizure of a Yerevan police station in nationalist terms, invoking fears that Armenia's leaders would give up even more territory to Azerbaijan in a future peace agreement (Novikova 2017: 184–6).

But by and large, the diaspora was simply not relevant to these earlier movements in opposition to specific domestic policies, or the ruling elite in general (Arménie-Diaspora... 2018). Neither were Armenia's opposition parties. Indeed, the grassroots nature of these movements was such that, according to Andreasyan and Derluguian, individual activists, personal discussions at the local level, and 'growing networks of mutual obligation' were the decisive organizational factors (Andreasyan and Derluguian 2015: 42).

The Armenian diaspora's general lack of involvement in these domestic movements is unsurprising, given its resigned acceptance of the republic's ruling elites, and its tendency to focus on Armenian foreign policy at the expense of domestic politics. While it had always been a straightforward matter to rally diaspora support for conflicts with a clear external enemy, such as Turkey or Azerbaijan, the Velvet Revolution was not a struggle against an enemy 'other', but rather, against the domestic political elite. A nationalist case could as easily be made for supporting the regime as it could for opposing it, and diasporans with limited knowledge of Armenia's domestic politics may have had difficulty determining how seriously to take the opposition's arguments or resolve.

The Velvet Revolution: Limited diaspora involvement

The diaspora reaction to the unfolding events in Armenia in 2018 was ambivalent, with most – especially the established organizations – treading cautiously, while thousands of individuals and many smaller groups cheered on and supported the protests in the home state. The following section will first explore reactions in the Western diaspora, specifically in the United States, followed by reactions among Armenians in Russia.

It is important to specify first that diaspora *repatriates* to Armenia cannot be lumped in with those actually living in diaspora. While a mass repatriation movement has never materialized, a small number of Armenians from the diaspora have relocated to Armenia since its independence. Generally referred to as 'repatriates', the term is an awkward fit for many, especially Western diasporans, most of whose ancestors lived in what is now eastern Turkey, rather than the present-day republic, and many of whom still maintain residences in their host states.

The rate of repatriate involvement in the Velvet Revolution appears to have differed little from that of 'local' Armenians. Many took part in demonstrations alongside their neighbours, and some documented their experiences online (see for example Aharonian 2019). Repatriates were not, however, featured prominently in the movement. Even Armenia's most renowned repatriated diaspora politician, Raffi Hovannisian, essentially sat out the Velvet Revolution, neither appearing at the protests nor running as a member of his Heritage Party in the parliamentary elections that occurred afterward. This was unsurprising since, while Hovannisian had come in second in the 2013 presidential contest, by the 2017 parliamentary election, his party failed to garner enough votes to pass the required 5 per cent threshold to win seats in parliament (Iskandaryan 2018: 470). The Heritage Party did issue official statements in support of the movement, and against Pashinyan's arrest, however (Armenia in Crisis... 2018), and Hovannisian ran unsuccessfully for mayor of Yerevan in September 2018, in the first popular election held after Sargsyan's resignation (Heritage... 2018).

It is difficult to determine how many diaspora Armenians travelled to Armenia specifically to join the Velvet Revolution protests. Some diasporans describe deciding to drop everything and buy a plane ticket, overcome with emotion and hope (I Felt I Had To Be Here... 2018). However, the vast majority of diaspora Armenians experienced the Velvet Revolution from afar, engaging with it via various sources of media, social media and conversations with those on the ground.

Western diaspora engagement with the Velvet Revolution events was facilitated by the rise of high-quality media organizations in Armenia, founded and/or largely staffed by diasporans and repatriates, reporting in both Armenian and English. This included the more established online media organization *CivilNet*, and the newer online weekly magazine *EVN Report*, barely a year old in the spring of 2018. In addition to long-form reporting, *EVN Report* maintained a significant social media presence, whose following ballooned to ten times its size during the protests (Amos 2019).

The most visible manifestation of diaspora support took the form of solidarity demonstrations in various diaspora hubs, such as protests in Marseilles and other French towns, and a demonstration in the Los Angeles suburb of Glendale that had an estimated 5,000 attendees. Protesters repeated slogans chanted in Armenia, such as the iconic 'Take a step, reject Serzh' (Armenians of Marseilles... 2018; Thousands... 2018). But these small demonstrations were the exception to the much larger trend of diaspora inaction. One diaspora commentator in the United States described 'a sense of fatalism ... that nothing is going to change' (Armenia's Government... 2018). As another noted, regarding the absence of discussions of the Velvet Revolution during the genocide remembrance events in New York, Boston and Los Angeles,

> there were smaller pockets of supportive diasporans who separated from the traditional gatherings to rally support. And I genuinely appreciate the voices, no matter how few. But all of this made me wonder: where were our leaders? Where were our diasporan Nikols? Where were our supporting crowds?' (Armen 2018)

As Taline Papazian notes, the solidarity protests in the diaspora were by and large organized by individuals or smaller and newer organizations, such as Armenian Renaissance, a diaspora organization that had sprung up around the formation of the Founding Parliament political party in Armenia, and reportedly helped organize some of the US protests. No demonstrations were organized by the large, established organizations typically associated with the Western diaspora. Given that these events were attended by members of both older and newer 'waves' of diasporans, a large proportion of whom were youth, this may be evidence of a serious crisis in representation and relevance for these older organizational forms (Arménie-Diaspora... 2018).

Organizational inaction

As a general rule, the large, established Western diaspora organizations – including diaspora political parties, philanthropic organizations and lobby groups – exercised a high degree of caution regarding the Velvet Revolution, until its outcome was a near certainty. These groups either 'kept quiet or endorsed Sargsyan until his resignation' (Atanesian 2018). The following few examples of these silences illustrate the general organizational trend.

Considering the 'revolutionary' self-image of the ARF (Dashnaktsutyun or Dashnaks), which had engaged in armed struggle in the Ottoman and Russian Empires, and formed the government of the short-lived first independent Armenian Republic from 1918 to 1920 (Tölölyan 2007a: 111–12), its conservative approach to the Velvet Revolution merits specific attention. While the ARF has always commanded significant loyalty among the Western diaspora, since independence, it has also functioned as a political party in Armenia, competing in elections and, in recent years, serving as a junior coalition partner to the RPA. As such, the ARF's international Bureau and its Armenian branch have often had divergent interests. The organization's reaction to the events that precipitated the Velvet Revolution was thus both a 'diaspora' reaction *and* one coloured by its desire to increase its political fortunes in Armenia. The latter interest led the ARF to support the constitutional changes proposed in 2015 and ultimately implemented by Sargsyan's RPA (see the Introduction), which shifted Armenia's political system from a presidential to a parliamentary one. This came as little surprise since 'presidencies on the Yeltsin-Putin model, which weaken the parliament in which the Dashnaks have power, are, unsurprisingly, opposed by the Dashnaks' (Tölölyan 2007b: 230). The ARF's support for this reform came despite warnings that Sargsyan would use the move to stay in power, which he ultimately did. As the RPA's junior partner, the ARF also rightly perceived its fortunes to be tied to those of the ruling regime and realized that 'Velvet Revolutionaries' would treat the party as a regime collaborator. Indeed, while Pashinyan initially granted the ARF two ministerial posts in his interim government in May 2018, he dismissed both ministers in October, accusing them of continued collaboration with the RPA, and in the subsequent December 2018 election, the ARF failed to win a single seat (Dashnaktsutyun Leaders... 2019).

In the United States, the AAA made no statement on the events until Sargsyan had resigned and, then, only commented on the 'remarkable demonstration of democracy in action', saying nothing about the issues that had sparked that demonstration in the first place (Armenian Assembly... 2019). Aram Hamparian, Executive Director of the ANCA, likewise touted Armenia's democratic credentials, describing the Velvet Revolution's 'remarkable, peaceful and constitutional political transition' as a point of commonality between Armenia and the United States, and '[a] powerful display of democracy that has opened a new chapter in our longstanding bilateral friendship' (Hamparian 2018). While keen to translate the now-successful toppling of Sargsyan into evidence of Armenia's worthiness, these groups failed to make common cause with the protesters as the events unfolded.

To be fair, these two lobbying organizations rarely comment on domestic Armenian matters, and focus nearly entirely on advocating for genocide recognition, US aid for Armenia, and international recognition of the Nagorno-Karabakh (Artsakh) Republic. In fact, according to the mayor of Glendale, California, also known as 'Little Armenia' due to its large Armenian population, these organizations worried that solidarity demonstrations with the events in Armenia, which reached their crescendo right before Genocide Memorial Day (24 April), might result in an 'intermingling of messages', or that 'the genocide recognition message would be somehow hijacked' (Zareh Sinanyan... 2018). Still, the cautious silence of these large organizations contrasted with statements of support from smaller groups. A number of Armenian Student Associations across the United States, for example, wrote a joint letter in support of what they called Armenia's 'student-driven democratization movement', which they claimed to view through 'a non-partisan lens' (ASAs... 2018), an obvious reference to the political parties that commanded the loyalty of older generations of diasporans.

The reserve shown by the establishment organizations, while perhaps regrettable in hindsight, reflected several factors driving the hesitation felt by many diasporans with respect to the events unfolding in Armenia. First, like the diaspora warning to the Karabakh movement in the late days of the Soviet Union, reactions to the Velvet Revolution were shaped by significant foreign policy-related fears regarding the potential reactions of Armenia's neighbours. The threat that Russia might respond negatively was as obvious to diasporans as it was to Armenian citizens, and while ultimately successful, the deliberate framing of the protests as 'not a colour revolution' could easily have been derailed by careless media reporting or social media rumours about Western machinations. Former Georgian president and 'Rose Revolution' leader Mikheil Saakashvili's description of the events as a 'rebellion against Russia' was a case in point (Georgia... 2018).

Second, the possibility that Azerbaijan might take advantage of Armenia's momentary lack of leadership to launch an attack could not be discounted, especially given the renewed hostilities between Armenia and Azerbaijan just three years earlier. In Armenia, citizens may have considered their ruling elites responsible for the losses sustained and the apparent military weakness exhibited during the 'four-day war' (Iskandaryan 2018: 468–9). Viewing the conflict from a distance, however, many in the diaspora saw unity behind those same authorities as the only guarantee against even greater losses.

Third, there was the very real possibility that President-cum-Prime Minister Sargsyan would remain in power, and might use force against civilians to do so. As such, on the one hand, established diaspora organizations must have worried about appearing to condone protests resulting in bloodshed, and on the other hand, they likely feared losing influence (and face) should they back the losing side. Given that street protests had become a 'permanent and prominent feature of political life' in Armenia over the past decade without toppling the government (Iskandaryan 2018: 472; see also Chapters 2 and 3 in this volume), overseas observers had every reason to bet against, rather than for, the success of this most recent episode.

Fourth, at least during its early days, the Velvet Revolution was predominantly a youth movement that, while inspiring to diaspora youth, may simply have not been taken seriously by the largely middle-aged to elderly (and generally risk-averse) community members who typically ran the larger, more established diaspora organizations. As Sinanyan noted,

> This movement has been really remarkable in its large number of young participants. In reality it seems like it was a young movement and the youth were the leaders in the movement. And I think that captured the imagination of a lot of young people in the diaspora. (Zareh Sinanyan... 2018)

Diaspora celebrities play a supporting role

In recent years, a few diaspora celebrities with global name recognition, such as Armenian-Canadian actor Arsineé Khanjian and Armenian-American musician Serj Tankian, had become outspoken critics of Sargsyan's regime (on Tankian, see Chapter 3). Along with others such as filmmakers Atom Egoyan and Eric Nazarian, they had joined electoral observation missions and had been featured prominently in demonstrations that had taken place over the previous decade.

Neither Khanjian nor Tankian was in Armenia when the Velvet Revolution began, and as it began to escalate, there were calls for them to join the demonstrations, though neither did so until after Sargsyan's resignation. In the meantime, however, they responded to the events from a distance. Khanjian's 17 April 2018 open letter to Sargsyan called on him to avoid bloodshed, and included mention of a litany of misdeeds committed under his watch.

> Corruption, absence of rule of law, police violence, judicial straight jacketing, bribery and election rigging, poverty, depopulation, human and civil rights violations (violence against women, discrimination against LGBTQ communities), absence of freedom of speech have all been a signature daily outcome during your government. (Arsineé Khanjian... 2018)

Tankian's video message to protesters on 21 April suggested that the protests were supported by everyone in the diaspora, 'even those in organizations that oppose your efforts' (Serj Tankian... 2019).

Khanjian arrived in Armenia on 28 April, after Sargsyan's resignation, and despite a swirl of rumours regarding his presence in the country, Tankian only landed in Yerevan on 7 May. They both received heroes' welcomes, but arrived to find an Armenia whose revolutionary work had already largely unfolded. They simply added interest, star power and moral support to an already vibrant movement led and propelled by locals. Yet although their presence may not have been decisive for the revolution itself, their descriptions of their own experiences, along with the reports of repatriates and others, probably helped sway the minds of many in the diaspora. As Khanjian noted, her experience on the ground and in speaking to crowds in Gyumri and Ijevan showed her that the fear of speaking out had seemingly evaporated in Armenia, whereas fear still persisted in the diaspora (Diaspora and Armenia... 2018).

From Russia, with cautious neutrality

Perhaps more than that of any external force, it was Russia's reaction to the protests engulfing Armenia that threatened to derail the Velvet Revolution. That Putin did not react negatively, given his well-known disdain for revolutions of any sort, begs explanation. On the one hand, prior Armenian protests had, for years, carefully avoided the 'colour revolution' frame, and the importance of this strict discipline with respect to framing was recognized both in Armenia and among diasporans (Iskandaryan 2018: 466; Serj Tankian... 2019; Diaspora and Armenia... 2018). On the other hand, Russian elites had previously expressed alarm at the prospects of a Western-sponsored Euromaidan-style event in June 2015, during the 'Electric Yerevan' protests against electricity price hikes (Andreasyan and Derluguian 2015: 32). The Velvet Revolution, which brought down an entrenched state leader, and was admired by Putin rival Alexey Navalny, must have shaken to its core the view of Armenia as an obedient client state of Russia (Broers 2018). Moreover, the Velvet Revolution was a reaction against an event that observers have often compared to the Putin-Medvedev 'castling' move in Russia (Cavoukian 2018; Derluguian and Hovhannisyan 2018: 442), since Sargsyan slid from the president's chair into the prime minister's, just as his term limits would have precluded another presidential run. There was certainly ample reason to fear a negative Russian response.

Baev has posited that one explanation for Putin's non-intervention is to be found in Russia's military overstretch in Syria, and the inability of an essentially one-man regime to focus on too many external events at a time (2018: 22; see also his arguments in Chapter 7 of this volume). Whatever the reason, Putin's view of the events in Armenia did not appear to have been influenced in any meaningful way by Russia's large and oligarch-dominated

Armenian diaspora. This is unsurprising, given the culture of diaspora organizations in Russia, which exist at the pleasure of the regime, whose most prominent leaders derive their authority from connections to Putin's inner circle, if not Putin himself, and who avoid any public airing of differences with the government, preferring to 'solve problems' privately by way of personal connections (Cavoukian 2016: 25). Since Putin's reaction towards events in Armenia was to remain apparently neutral, it comes as no surprise that these groups followed suit, neither praising nor condemning the Velvet Revolution as it unfolded.

The Union of Armenians of Russia (UAR), which has always stressed its leader Ara Abrahamyan's personal connections to Putin, held an emergency meeting to discuss the unfolding events in Armenia, at which it expressed concern regarding the domestic potential for violence and Armenia's sensitive geopolitical environment (21 aprelya v Moskve … 2018). It then expended considerable energy refuting statements critical of the Velvet Revolution, which it claimed had been wrongly attributed to the organization (Atanesian 2018; Raz'yasneniya… 2018), before releasing a neutrally worded official statement on 28 April 2018, days after Sargsyan's resignation. In it, Abrahamyan called on Armenians to make a wise choice in the upcoming election and pledged to support whatever Prime Minister was elected in accordance with the constitution (Zayavleniye … 2018; Soyuz armyan Rossii … 2018).

Interestingly, despite the significant differences between the Russian and Western Armenian diaspora's organizations and culture, a similar dynamic could be seen in terms of the youth breaking with large, conservative organizations to support the Velvet Revolution. The UAR has claimed to represent the entirety of Russia's Armenian population of roughly two million, with a hierarchically arranged pyramid of state-level, regional and local community organizations, all subsumed under the UAR banner and effectively taking orders from Abrahamyan. Yet there were clearly some Armenians in Russia who openly supported the events unfolding in Armenia, and a few dozen youth activists even gathered publicly to demonstrate against Serzh Sargsyan outside the Armenian church in Moscow, before being detained by the police (Mkrtchyan 2018).

In the revolution's aftermath, if the Russian press was any indication, there were signs that despite Pashinyan's consistent reassurances (Armenia 'Committed…' 2018), the Kremlin worried that the new leader might take Armenia's foreign policy in a more pro-Western direction (Artsruni 2018; Kucera 2018; Russia Accuses US… 2018). Russian elites also expressed alarm at the prosecution of former president Robert Kocharian for his role in the events of 1 March 2008, in which ten Armenians were killed, as well as the arrest of Yuri Khachaturov, Secretary General of the Russian-led Collective Security Treaty Organization (Mughnetsyan 2019). However, in spite of these concerns, and a series of thinly veiled and overt warnings, Russia appears, at least publicly, to have largely refrained from interfering in Armenia's regime change, or accusing Western states of having done so.

Post-Revolution: Continuity or change in state-diaspora relations?

Once the events of the Velvet Revolution had successfully unfolded, the Armenian diaspora's reaction was generally positive, ranging from cautious optimism to immense pride in the bloodless events that garnered international accolades. However, in the following months, there would be much more negative reactions to institutional changes that might affect the Armenia–diaspora relationship.

As previously mentioned, the Hayastan All-Armenian Fund (hereafter, the Fund) had served, since its creation in 1992, as one of the most trusted institutions of the state-diaspora relationship. The Fund channelled diaspora donations towards development projects prioritized by the state, such as the Goris-Stepanakert Highway, completed in 1999, which linked the otherwise isolated de facto Nagorno-Karabakh Republic to Armenia. While more recently dwarfed by private remittances, diaspora charity and philanthropy had been vital during the early years of Armenian independence, and for many diaspora Armenians, donating to the Fund and 'helping Armenia' had become an identity-affirming activity. Part of the Fund's attraction was its claim to transparency and accountability, including regular audits, and it thus served as an alternative to unscrupulous local partners who might take advantage of gullible diasporans (Cavoukian 2016: 113–14).

In July 2018, the Fund's Executive Director Ara Vardanyan was arrested on charges of embezzlement, having apparently used Fund money to support his online gambling habit (Hayastan… 2018). Initial online reactions from the Western diaspora were understandably characterized by shock and anger. Yet less than a week later, diasporans appeared to be doing their utmost to rehabilitate the image of the Fund. Reactions by the established organizations, many of whom were members of the Fund's board of trustees ('Our Trustees' 2019), were to express concern and call for transparency but, simultaneously, to renew their commitment to the near-sacred mission of the Fund. While criticizing Ara Vardanyan's behaviour, Avedik Izmirlian, Political Chairman of the ARF Western US Central Committee, noted that 'the Hayastan All-Armenia Fund is an important part of the Armenian Nation and must be preserved and strengthened since its mission is far from over' (ARF Western US… 2018). Individual diasporans took to social media to defend their intentions to continue donating. One thread claimed that a particular US branch of the Fund was quasi-independent and had set its own funding priorities, such that it was still 'safe' to donate to that branch. In the wake of a scandal large enough to shake diaspora donor confidence to the core, rather than be shocked into reconsidering their approach to financial engagement with Armenia, many diasporans were seemingly desperate to restore a semblance of the status quo ante.

A similar level of Western diaspora shock greeted the announcement that Armenia's Ministry of Diaspora was to be eliminated, as part of a general restructuring by the Pashinyan government that would reduce the number of ministries. The ministry had been created in 2008, with a view to institutionalizing the largely ad hoc and often contentious relations between the Armenian state and the diaspora since independence in 1991 (Panossian 2003: 140). While its existence was widely praised in post-Soviet diaspora circles, it had faced considerable criticism among Western diasporans and Armenian citizens alike for its vague mission, tiny budget and Minister Hakobyan's complete lack of prior experience with the diaspora. Many diasporans saw it as a 'bureaucratically irrelevant, functionally dysfunctional, and structurally incoherent' ministry, which did little to serve or listen to diasporans and operated largely as a mechanism for milking the proverbial cash cow (Kopalian 2019). Over time, however, it came to be regarded as a regular feature of Armenian state-diaspora relations. Hakobyan, in turn, became a mouthpiece for RPA discourse, effectively equating the security of the Armenian nation with adherence to traditional values and support for the ruling party (Cavoukian 2016: 130).

Upon taking office, Pashinyan's initial decision regarding the Ministry of Diaspora was to simply replace Hakobyan. Diaspora reactions to this move were measured – Hakobyan had never been well-liked by Western diasporans and newly appointed minister Mkhitar Hayrapetyan's early remarks echoed their own critiques of the ministry. He indicated that he would encourage repatriation (potentially of 'millions of Armenians') by creating a 'country of law', and would staff the ministry with 'professionals' and younger people with 'new and creative ideas' (Arménie-Diaspora… 2018; One View… 2018). In early 2019, however, Pashinyan announced the planned dissolution of the Ministry of Diaspora as part of an overall reduction of government departments. The tentative new plan was to merge some of its functions with the Ministry of Foreign Affairs – a return to the arrangement under Sargsyan's predecessor, Robert Kocharian – and to have diaspora engagement sections within other ministries, as well as a special prime ministerial envoy for diaspora relations. Pashinyan personally defended the decision (using Facebook Live, one of his preferred methods of outreach) as an exercise in eliminating government bloat, noting that the Armenian public service was far larger than necessary, and that more government departments provided more opportunities for corruption (Pashinyan 2019).

The reaction to this more dramatic change was outwardly negative, and critiques of the decision poured in from around the diasporan world. As the Armenian Institutions of the Argentine Republic (IARA) noted in its statement, 'the existing and representative institutions in our Diaspora organized communities were ignored when making such a decision without consultation' (The Armenian Community... 2018). An Armenian newspaper editor in Istanbul referred to the decision to eliminate the ministry as 'painful' (Chief Editor... 2019); an Australian-Armenian writer referred to the 'significant psychological statement of commitment' the ministry's existence had provided to the diaspora (Kerkyasharian 2018) and His Holiness Aram I, Catholicos of the Great House of Cilicia, one of the Armenian Apostolic Church's highest officials, urged Pashinyan to reverse course because of the 'symbolic meaning', if not the practical value, of the ministry (Aram I... 2019). If there had been a lukewarm diaspora reception to the creation of the ministry, after ten years, there was downright hostility towards its dissolution.

A 'Velvet Revolution' in the diaspora?

The fact that the Armenian diaspora had little involvement the Velvet Revolution is relatively unsurprising. As noted earlier, the diaspora's attention had tended to be largely focused on foreign policy matters, and on conflicts in which there was a clear non-Armenian 'other'. Moreover, the diaspora's hesitation to become more involved in Armenian domestic politics had been reinforced by an attitude among Armenian political elites towards the diaspora, since independence, that actively sought to discourage that involvement:

> ...saying that, you know, you don't live here, so shut up. That's been basically the attitude of the Armenian government when it comes to being on the receiving end of diasporan criticism, but that issue never comes up when they ask for money for this project, that project. So, the relationship has always been insincere. (Zareh Sinanyan... 2018)

Still, certain aspects of the state-diaspora dynamic surrounding this event are noteworthy. The fact that the general non-reaction of the established Western diaspora organizations differed little from the non-reaction of diaspora institutions in Russia might suggest that, at least in part, Armenian elites' identity gerrymandering efforts, and their attempts to produce a pliant and compliant organized diaspora, had been successful. Yet it was also apparent that individual diasporans, smaller organizations and especially younger Armenians had broken from these organizations to express solidarity with the Velvet Revolution. And in the wake of the events, which the vast majority of the diaspora watched from the sidelines, many Western diasporans began contemplating change in their own host-state communities. Many saw the established diaspora organizations as clearly outdated and in need of either renewal or replacement, given the increasing alienation of their membership from the top brass (Serj Tankian... 2019). Their membership had been dwindling, with ever more diasporans no longer members of any traditional institution (Armenia's Government... 2018). One commentator lamented that diaspora life had often involved a plethora of activities geared primarily towards outwardly demonstrating one's Armenianness, and linked this tendency to the old establishment institutions. 'In Armenia, the Velvet Revolution saw a youth-driven initiative take power away from outdated forms of authority and unite as a nation. I think the Diaspora could also use a little more velvet' (Tchakmak 2018).

Moreover, regime change in Armenia inspired many diasporans to rethink their institutional links to the home state. Slow change had already begun in the Western diaspora over the previous decade. With public demonstrations against the Sargsyan government occurring with increasing regularity, some diasporans had realized there was a new role to be played in supporting civil society (Diaspora and Armenia... 2018). Papazian suggested that the proliferation of grassroots organizations in Armenia, and their appearance in the diaspora, opened up new possibilities for collaboration and mutual recognition. She noted that democratization was as necessary in the diaspora as in Armenia, and hoped to see new leadership emerge to renew the established diaspora organizations (Arménie-Diaspora... 2018).

Even within the old guard, the Velvet Revolution appears to have been a catalyst for some degree of renewal. It is telling that the ARF, at its February 2019 World Congress, adopted relative gender quotas for all future meetings and decision-making bodies (Kayserian 2019). While the party has progressive roots – it has historically had a social democratic orientation and is long-standing a member of the Socialist International – these had long since been effectively abandoned by the Armenia wing, which had become complicit in the government's corrupt and highly conservative misrule. The Velvet Revolution removed the ARF from Armenia's legislature, and this clearly prompted the party to take stock of its principles, if for no other reason than to better compete in future Armenian elections. While the ARF certainly lost face and prestige as a result of being on the 'wrong side' of the Velvet Revolution – especially given its claim to being a 'revolutionary' party – it will likely remain a significant force in the Western diaspora, where its role as a source of social solidarity and culture may never dissipate entirely.

Meanwhile, newer diaspora groups began to emerge, some directly inspired by the Velvet Revolution. A new progressive diaspora organization, *Zoravik*, formed in the Boston area about one month after the events in Armenia, with a view to forging direct links with activist civil society groups in the home state. It was unaffiliated with any diaspora party, church or other institution, though many of its members were also members of these older organizations as well, and saw maintaining that membership as a way to gradually bring positive change to the old guard. Co-founder Sevag Arzoumanian also insisted that *Zoravik* not be a new pro-regime organization. Now that Pashinyan had come to power, he saw their role as shifting to support progressive opposition groups in Armenia (Arzoumanian 2019).

A Velvet Revolution in state-diaspora relations?

Armenia's new government's jettisoning of the Ministry of Diaspora opened up space for a fulsome debate regarding the institutional underpinnings of the state-diaspora relationship, along with an acknowledgement that the way forward would undoubtedly involve trial and error. However, the specific institutional arrangement is arguably less important than a general attitudinal shift regarding roles and expectations.

Diaspora Armenians must finally accept that their role in the future of Armenia is a greatly diminished one, as compared with their ability to influence the republic's development in the early 1990s. This is not necessarily a negative development; a clear-eyed understanding that the diaspora and Armenia are not, and need not be, two sides of the same proverbial coin, could lead to positive change in both the home state and diaspora communities. Abandoning the ideal of transnational unity and the quixotic mission of 'influencing' Armenia might finally put to rest calls for the diaspora to be united and speak with one voice. There is simply no reason to pursue unity (especially hierarchical unity), and plenty to recommend the acceptance of diasporic diversity.

As more and more of the previous regime's corruption and criminality is made public, diasporans choosing to engage with Armenia financially ought to reassess the wisdom of supporting *any* ruling regime's official priorities, via official philanthropy vehicles such as the Fund. Armenia is no longer in 'life-support mode', and perhaps the time has come for diasporans to prioritize direct, unmediated engagement with individuals, intellectuals and civil society groups in the home state, who are working to build an Armenia in which diasporans can take pride.

Identity gerrymandering is deeply manipulative state behaviour (Cavoukian 2016: 274–5). The Velvet Revolution opposed and exposed the corruption of the regime towards its own citizenry, but its aftermath presented an opportunity to reassess the degree to which the state-diaspora relationship was itself problematic, and in turn facilitated the regime's corrupt practices. A new, and hopefully more responsive, regime may intend to establish more horizontal, non-manipulative and egalitarian relations, but close attention will be needed to overcome the inertia of existing patterns. The aim should be to emphasize a voluntary relationship in which, just as diasporans must accept a diminished role for themselves in the life of the Armenian state, the state must also accept that it is not the ultimate arbiter of diasporic identities, and will forever share with the diaspora the ability to define what it means to be Armenian.

Notes

1   Some members of the diaspora will no doubt take issue with this generalization. One commentator noted, for example, that 'no one with any consciousness can deny that the Diaspora played a significant role by providing a much-needed psychological and a degree of financial support to that "Velvet Revolution", as it was rightly named by its intrepid leader and visionary Nikol Pashinyan'. There was no specific evidence offered by the author (Kerkyasharian 2018).

2   Given that 'Tulip' is not a colour, and that Georgia's 'Rose' Revolution referred to the flower, not the colour, the classification of the Orange, Rose, and Tulip revolutions together as 'colour revolutions' can only be described as a regrettable linguistic absurdity.

3   The majority of Western diasporans were descended from survivors of the Ottoman Empire's Armenian Genocide (1915–18), spoke Western Armenian (as opposed to the Eastern Armenian dialect spoken in Armenia), and lived throughout the Middle East, Europe, and North America, with smaller populations in Latin America and Australia. Most had never lived in, and had no relatives in, Soviet or post-Soviet Armenia. Cold War ideological divisions had exacerbated the differences and social distance between the Western diaspora and Armenia's citizens. All this meant that Western

diasporans excitedly visiting post-Soviet Armenia often found a country dramatically at odds with their grandparents' descriptions of 'Armenia', one that did not actually include their ancestral territories, and one to which few would consider repatriating.

4   The controversy centred around the inclusion of a joint historical commission which would discuss the events of 1915. This was widely seen as an opportunity for Turkey to question the veracity of the Armenian Genocide. The Turkey-Armenia Protocols were never ratified by either state, but the ultimate sticking point was the Nagorny Karabakh conflict and Azerbaijan's opposition to the normalization of relations, rather than any interference by the Armenian diaspora.

5   *Komsomol* was the popular abbreviation for the Young Communist League, the Communist Party's leading youth organization in the Soviet Union.

6   The author conducted a series of interviews at the Ministry of Diaspora over a seven-month period, from September 2009 to March 2010. Interviewees included the minister and nine of her staff.

References

Aharonian, L. (2019) *The Revolution As We Lived It*. [Blog] Motherhood, Repatriation and Other Fictions. Available at: https://larajan.blogspot.com/2 019/01/the-revolution-as-we-lived-it.html?fbclid=IwAR0TstdZXe3z-0TgGr4 cWn1zGgNqZlgb-3oMTbYnwUfJ5ZRei_gyqKC0MuQ (accessed 1 February 2019).

Amos, H. (2019) 'It's Messed Up.' How One News Outlet Is Trying to Reshape the Media in Post-revolution Armenia. *The Calvert Journal*, 20 March. Available at: https://www.calvertjournal.com/articles/show/11077/evn-repor t-media-armenia-revolution (accessed 20 March 2019).

Anderson, B. (1992) *Long-Distance Nationalism, World Capitalism and the Rise of Identity Politics: The Wertham Lecture*. Amsterdam: Centre for Asian Studies.

Andreasyan, Z. and Derluguian, G. (2015) Fuel Protests in Armenia. *New Left Review*, 95 (September–October): 29–48.

Aram I Urges Pashinian to Keep Diaspora Ministry. (2019) *Asbarez*, 10 January. Available at: http://asbarez.com/177105/aram-i-urges-pashinyan-to-keep-dia spora-ministry/ (accessed 10 February 2019).

ARF Western US Calls for Transparency in Hayastan Fund Activities. (2018) *Asbarez*, 27 July. Available at: http://asbarez.com/174028/arf-western-us -calls-for-transparency-in-hayastan-fund-activities/ (accessed 28 February 2019).

Armen, S. (2018) The Diaspora, and What to do Next. *CivilNet*, 30 April. Available at: https://www.civilnet.am/news/2018/04/30/The-Diaspora-an d-What-to-do-Next/335558 (accessed 1 February 2019).

Armenia 'Committed To Further Integration' Within Eurasian Union. (2018) *Radio Free Europe/Radio Liberty*, 27 December. Available at: https://www.rfe rl.org/a/armenia-committed-to-further-integration-within-eurasian-unio n/29680038.html (accessed 1 March 2019).

Armenia in Crisis: Heritage Party Condemns Crackdown on Leaders, Citizens. (2019) Heritage Party, official website, 22 April. Available at: http://www.heri tage.am/en/news/583-220418-en (accessed 11 March 2019).

Armenian Assembly of America Statement on Democratic Developments in Armenia. (2019) Armenian Assembly of America, official website, 23 April. Available at: https://armenian-assembly.org/2018/04/23/armenian-assem bly-of-america-statement-on-democratic-developments-in-armenia/ (accessed 4 March 2019).

The Armenian Community of Argentina Expressed Its 'Concern' Over the Closure of the Ministry of Diaspora. (2018) *Prensa Armenia*, 24 December. Available at: http://www.prensaarmenia.com.ar/2018/12/the-armenian-co mmunity-of-argentina.html (accessed 5 February 2019).

Armenians of Marseilles Burnt Serzh Sargsyan's Photo. (2018) *Lragir.am*, 19 April. Available at: https://www.lragir.am/en/2018/04/19/38196 (accessed 2 March 2019).

Armenia's Government Must Reach Beyond Traditional Diaspora Institutions. (2018) Edgar Martirosyan, interviewed by Ani Paitjan, *CivilNet*, 3 October. Available at: https://www.civilnet.am/news/2018/10/03/%E2%80%9CArmeni a%E2%80%99s-Government-Must-Reach-Beyond-Traditional-Diaspora-Ins titutions%E2%80%9D/346079 (accessed 28 February 2019).

Arménie-Diaspora: la nécessité d'une relation horizontale. (2018) Taline Papazian, interviewed by Ani Paitjan, [Video] *CivilNet*, 3 June. Available at: https://www.civilnet.am/news/2018/06/03/Arm%C3%A9nie-Diaspora-la-n%C3%A9cessit%C3%A9-d%E2%80%99une-relation-horizontale/338434 (accessed 28 February 2019).

Arsinee Khanjian: Open Letter to Serzh Sarkisian. (2018) *Massis Post*, 17 April. Available at: https://massispost.com/2018/04/arsinee-khanjian-open-letter-serzh-sarkisian/ (accessed 1 February 2019).

Artsruni, S. (2018) V chem prichina rossiyskoy isterii: chto Moskva khochet ot Nikola Pashinyana? *Perviy Armyanskiy Informatsionniy*, 22 July. Available at: https://ru.1in.am/1232245.html (accessed 1 March 2019).

Arzoumanian, S. (2019) Personal Communication, 6 March.

ASAs Across the U.S. Voice Solidarity with Armenia's Student-Driven Movement. (2018) *Asbarez*, 30 April. Available at: http://asbarez.com/171989 /asas-across-the-u-s-voice-solidarity-with-armenias-student-driven-mov ement/ (accessed 28 February 2019).

Atanesian, G. (2018) In Wake of Armenia's Peaceful Uprising, Diaspora's Clout Is Questioned. *Eurasianet*, 24 April. Available at: https://eurasianet.org/ in-wake-of-armenias-peaceful-uprising-diasporas-clout-is-questioned (accessed 1 March 2019).

Baev, P. (2018) What Made Russia Indifferent to the Revolution in Armenia. *Caucasus Analytical Digest* 104 (23): 20–4. Available at: http://www.laender-a nalysen.de/cad/pdf/CaucasusAnalyticalDigest104.pdf (accessed 1 March 2019).

Boyarin, J. and Boyarin, D. (2002) *Powers of Diaspora*. Minneapolis: University of Minnesota Press.

Broers, L. (2018) In Armenia, a Constitutional Power Grab Backfires. Chatham House, 24 April. Available at: https://www.chathamhouse.org/expert/comm ent/armenia-constitutional-power-grab-backfires (accessed 1 February 2018).

Cavoukian, K. (2013) 'Soviet Mentality'? The Role of Shared Political Culture in Relations between the Armenian State and Russia's Armenian Diaspora. *Nationalities Papers*, 41 (5): 709–29.

Cavoukian, K. (2016) Identity Gerrymandering: How the Armenian State Constructs and Controls 'Its' Diaspora. PhD. Diss., University of Toronto, Canada. Available at: https://tspace.library.utoronto.ca/bitstream/1807/76371 /3/Cavoukian_Kristin_201611_PhD_thesis.pdf

Cavoukian, K. (2017) Can the Armenian Diaspora Bring a 'New Management Culture' to Armenia? *Policy Forum Armenia, PFA* Blog, 4 October. Available at: https://pfarmenia.wordpress.com/2017/10/04/management-culture/ (accessed 4 October 2017).

Cavoukian, K. (2018) 'Yerevan Spring': A New Day For Armenian Democracy? *LeftEast*, 1 May. Available at: http://www.criticatac.ro/lefteast/yerevan-spr ing-a-new-day-for-armenian-democracy/ (accessed 1 May 2018).

Chief Editor of Istanbul-based Marmara paper describes the decision to close Diaspora Ministry as 'painful'. (2019) *Aysor*, 5 February. Available at: https ://www.aysor.am/en/news/2019/02/05/marmara-editor/1522130 (accessed 6 February 2019).

Cohen, R. (1996) Diasporas and the Nation-State: From Victims to Challengers. *International Affairs*, 72 (3): 507–20.

Daron Acemoglu: The Positive and Negative Roles of the Diaspora. (2016) [video] *CivilNet*, 13 September, https://www.youtube.com/watch?v=Dvj 1UPzYSUs&t=4s (accessed 1 February 2019).

Dashnaktsutyun Leaders Meet Russian Envoy. (2019) *Azatutyun.am*, 26 April. Available at: https://www.azatutyun.am/a/29906306.html (accessed 27 April 2019).

Derluguian, G. and Hovhannisyan, R. (2018) The Armenian Anomaly: Toward an Interdisciplinary Interpretation. *Demokratizatsiya*, 26 (4): 441–64.

Diaspora and Armenia: Understanding Each Other. (2018) Salpi Ghazarian Interviews Arsinee Khanjian, *CivilNet*, 30 April. Available at: https://www.civ ilnet.am/news/2018/04/30/Diaspora-and-Armenia-Understanding-Each-Other/335470 (accessed 20 February 2019).

Dyatlov, V. (2016) Armenians of Contemporary Russia: Diasporic Strategies of Integration. In: Siekierski, K. and Troebst, S., eds, *Armenians in Post-socialist Europe*. Köln: Böhlau, 26–38.

Fujiwara, A. (2015) Canada's Response to Euromaidan. In: Marples, D. R., and Mills, F. V., eds, *Ukraine's Euromaidan: Analyses of a Civil Revolution*. Stuttgart: ibidem-Verlag, 199–215.

Georgia: Mixed Reactions over Armenia Protests. (2018) *Civil.ge*, 24 April. Available at: https://civil.ge/archives/231698 (accessed 26 March 2019).

Ghaplanyan, I. (2017) Diaspora: Armenia's Failed Marriage. In: *Post-Soviet Armenia: The New National Elite and the New National Narrative*. London: Routledge, 176–205.

Hamparian, A. (2018) ANCA Executive Director Aram Hamparian's Remarks at the U.S. Senate Centennial Celebration of U.S.-Armenia Friendship. *The Armenian Weekly*. Available at: https://armenianweekly.com/2018/06/27/hamparian-remarks-senate-100th/ (accessed 20 February 2018).

Hayastan All Armenian Fund Director Arrested for Embezzlement. (2018) *Armenian Weekly*, 3 July. Available at: https://armenianweekly.com/2018/07/03/hayastan-all-armenian-fund-director-arrested-for-embezzlement/ (accessed 3 February 2019).

Heritage Releases Election Platform. (2018) Heritage Party, official website, 4 September. Available at: http://www.heritage.am/en/news/612-040918-en (accessed 11 March 2019).

'I Felt I Had To Be Here': The Armenian Diaspora Who Joined The Protests. (2018) *Radio Free Europe/Radio Liberty*, 10 May. Available at: https://www.rferl.org/a/armenia-politics-society-protests/29219010.html (accessed 1 March 2019).

Iskandaryan, A. (2018) The Velvet Revolution in Armenia: How to Lose Power in Two Weeks. *Demokratizatsiya*, 26 (4) Fall: 465–82.

Kapur, D. (2007) The Janus Face of Diasporas. In: Merz, B. J. Chen, L. C. and Geithner, P. E., eds, *Diasporas and Development*. Cambridge and London: Global Equity Initiative, 89–118.

Kayserian, H. (2019) ARF Signals Return to Roots, Adopts Women's Quota at World Congress. *Armenian Weekly*, 4 February. Available at: https://armenianweekly.com/2019/02/04/arf-signals-return-to-roots-adopts-womens-quota-at-world-congress/ (accessed 4 February 2019).

Kerkyasharian, S. (2018) Ministry of Diaspora Must Stay. *ArmeniaOnline*, 30 December. Available at: http://www.armenia.com.au/news/Feature-Articles/English/63315/Op-Ed--Ministry-of-Diaspora-Must-Stay (accessed 3 February 2019).

King, C. and Melvin, N. J. (1998) Conclusion: Diasporas, International Relations, and Post-Soviet Eurasia. In: King, C. and Melvin, N. J., eds, *Nations Abroad: Diaspora Politics and International Relations in the Former Soviet Union*. Oxford: Westview Press, 209–27.

Koinova, M. (2009) Diasporas and Democratization in the Post-Communist World. *Communist and Post-Communist Studies*, 42: 41–64.

Kopalian, N. (2019) The Elimination of the Diaspora Ministry has Nothing to do With the Diaspora. *EVNReport*, 17 January. Available at: https://www.evn

report.com/opinion/the-elimination-of-the-diaspora-ministry-has-nothin
g-to-do-with-the-diaspora (accessed 20 February 2019).

Krasynska, S. (2015) Digital Civil Society: Euromaidan, the Ukrainian
Diaspora, and Social Media. In: Marples, D. R. and Mills, F. V., eds, *Ukraine's
Euromaidan: Analyses of a Civil Revolution*. Stuttgart: ibidem-Verlag, 177–98.

Kucera, J. (2018) Russian Press Portrays Armenia's Pashinyan as 'carbon copy'
of Poroshenko. *Eurasianet*, 23 July, https://eurasianet.org/russian-press-por
trays-armenias-pashinyan-as-carbon-copy-of-poroshenko (accessed 1
March 2019).

Levitsky, S. and Way, L. (2002) The Rise of Competitive Authoritarianism.
Journal of Democracy, 13 (2): 51–65.

Mkrtchyan, E. (2018) Moscow Armenians Gathered for a Protest in the
Courtyard of the Armenian Church, Ezras Called the Police. *Arminfo*, 22
April. Available at: http://arminfo.info/full_news.php?id=30807&lang=3
(accessed 1 March 2019).

Mughnetsyan, G. (2019) Russia Irked Over Developments in Armenia, Warns
of Consequences. *CivilNet*, 2 August. Available at: https://www.civilnet.am/
news/2018/08/02/Russia-Irked-Over-Developments-in-Armenia-Warns-of
-Consequences/342506 (accessed 21 February 2019).

Novikova, G. (2017) Armenia: Some Features of Internal (In)stability. *Caucasus
Survey*, 5 (2): 177–94.

Ohanyan, A. (2004) The Promise and the Perils of Dual Citizenship: The Case of
Post-Communist Armenia. *Diaspora: A Journal of Transnational Studies*, 13
(2): 279–305.

One View of the Diaspora. (2019) Mkhitar Hayrapetyan, interviewed by Mshak
Ghazarian. *CivilNet*, 14 May. Available at: https://www.civilnet.am/news/2
018/05/14/One-View-of-the-Diaspora/336868 (accessed 10 February 2019).

Our Trustees. (2019) Hayastan All Armenian Fund, http://www.himnadram.
org/en/our-trustees (accessed 1 March 2019).

Panossian, R. (2003) Courting a Diaspora: Armenia-Diaspora Relations since
1998. In: Østergaard-Nielsen, E., ed., *International Migration and Sending
Countries: Perceptions, Policies and Transnational Relations*. Hampshire and
New York: Palgrave Macmillan, 140–68.

Panossian, R. (2006) *The Armenians: From Kings and Priests to Merchants and
Commissars*. New York: Columbia University Press.

Papazian-Tanielian, S. (2016) The Community Life of Armenians in Post-
Socialist Bulgaria. In: Siekierski, K. and Troebst, S., eds, *Armenians in Post-
socialist Europe*. Köln: Böhlau, 193–204.

Pashinyan, N. (2019) Facebook Live [video], 18 January. Available at: https://
www.facebook.com/nikol.pashinyan/videos/293937011306023/ (accessed 19
January 2019).

Raz'yasneniya Press-sluzhby Soyuza armyan Rossii v svyazi s
poyavlyayushchimisya v armyanskikh SMI spekulyatsiyami ot imeni SAR.
(2018). UAR News: Union of Armenians of Russia, official website, 27 April.
http://sarinfo.org/sarnews/27-04-18.shtml (accessed 1 March 2019).

Russia Accuses U.S. Of Trying To Drive Wedge In Relations With Armenia. (2018) *Radio Free Europe/Radio Liberty*, 29 October. Available at: https://ww w.rferl.org/a/russia-accuses-u-s-of-trying-to-drive-wedge-in-relations-with -armenia/29570932.html (accessed 1 March 2019).

Safran, W. (2009) The Diaspora and the Homeland: Reciprocities, Transformations, and Role Reversals. In: Ben-Rafael, E., Sternberg, Y., Bosker Liwerant, J. and Gorny, Y., eds, *Transnationalism: Diasporas and the Advent of a New (Dis)order*. Leiden and Boston: Brill, 75–99.

Sanamyan, E. (2009) President Sargsyan Promotes Turkey Protocols in Diaspora Meetings (Updated): ARF Stages Street Protests in New York and Los Angeles. *Armenian Reporter*, 6 October. Available at: http://www.reporter. am/go/article/2009-10-06-president-sargsian-promotes-turkey-protocols-indiaspora-meetings (accessed 10 October 2009).

Serj Tankian to protesters: You've already won the cultural revolution. (2019) *CivilNet*, 21 April. Available at: https://www.civilnet.am/news/2018/04/21/ Serj-Tankian-to-protesters-You%E2%80%99ve-already-won-the-cultural-rev olution/334361 (accessed 25 February 2019).

Shain, Y. (1999) *Marketing the American Creed Abroad: Diasporas in the U.S. and Their Homelands*. Cambridge: Cambridge University Press.

Shain, Y. and Sherman, M. (2001) Diasporic Transnational Financial Flows and Their Impact on National Identity. *Nationalism and Ethnic Conflict*, 7 (4): 1–36.

Sheffer, G. (1994) Ethno-national Diasporas and Security. *Survival*, 36 (1): 60–79.

Sierkierski, K. (2016) Studying Armenians in Post-Socialist Europe: Problems and Perspectives. In: Siekerski, K. and Troebst, S., eds, *Armenians in Post-socialist Europe*. Köln: Böhlau, 13–25.

Smith, A. D. (2010) Diasporas and Homelands in History: The Case of the Classic Diasporas. In: Gal, A., Leoussi, A. S. and Smith, A. D. eds, *The Call of the Homeland: Diaspora Nationalisms, Past and Present*. Studies in Judaica 9. Leiden: Brill, 2–35.

Soyuz armyan Rossii soobshchil, chto ne delal zayavleniy o situatsii v Armenii. (2018) *RIA Novosti*, 28 April. Available at: https://ria. ru/20180428/1519660284.html (accessed 1 March 2019).

Tchakmak, S. (2018) The Diaspora Could Use a Little More Velvet. *Armenian Weekly*, 22 June. Available at: https://armenianweekly.com/2018/06/22/th e-diaspora-could-use-a-little-more-velvet/ (accessed 31 January 2019).

Thousands of SoCal Armenians Protest Election Results in their Homeland. (2018) *abc7 Eyewitness News*, 23 April. Available at: https://abc7.com/pol itics/socal-armenians-protest-election-results-in-their-homeland/3380671/ (accessed 1 March 2019).

Tölölyan, K. (2007a) The Armenian Diaspora and the Karabagh Conflict Since 1988. In: Smith, H. and Stares, P., eds, *Diasporas in Conflict: Peace-Makers or Peace-Wreckers?*. New York: United Nations University Press, 106–28.

Tölölyan, K. (2007b) Stateless Power and the Political Agency of Diasporas: An Armenian Case Study. In: Totoricagüena, G., ed., *Opportunity Structures in Diaspora Relations: Comparisons in Contemporary Multilevel Politics of Diaspora and Transnational Identity*. Reno: Center for Basque Studies, 215–34.

de Waal, T. (2013). *Black Garden: Armenia and Azerbaijan Through Peace and War*. Rev. edn. New York and London: New York University Press.

World Bank. (2019). Record High Remittances Sent Globally in 2018. [online]. Available at: https://www.worldbank.org/en/news/press-release/2019/04/08/record-high-remittances-sent-globally-in-2018 (accessed 2 June 2019).

Zareh Sinanyan on the 'Velvet Revolution' and the Roles of the Diaspora. (2018) Zareh Sinanyan interviewed by Mshak Ghazarian. *CivilNet*, 7 May. Available at: https://www.civilnet.am/news/2018/05/07/Zareh-Sinanyan-on-the-Velvet-Revolution-and-the-roles-of-the-Diaspora/336150 (accessed 28 February 2019).

Zayavleniye Soyuza armyan Rossii. (2018) UAR News: Union of Armenians of Russia, official website, 28 April. http://sarinfo.org/sarnews/28-04-18.shtml (accessed 1 March 2019).

21 aprelya v Moskve Soyuz armyan Rossii organizoval kruglyy stol, posvyashchyonnyy voprosam vzaimootnosheniy diaspory i Armenii v svete sobytiy, proiskhodyashchikh v Armenii. (2018) UAR News: Union of Armenians of Russia, official website, 21 April. http://sarinfo.org/sarnews/21-04-18.shtml (accessed 1 March 2019).

Conclusion

What's next for Armenia? Authoritarian reserves and risks in a democratic state

Anna Ohanyan

I am writing this chapter at the Silk Road hotel in Yerevan where the walls are covered with rugs, old and new. On a rug-making station, across from my table, a woman has been weaving, following an intricate chart in front of her. She will not be done in the three weeks that I am here, I am told, with some rugs taking over a year to make. Accustomed to the speed and immediacy in American culture, I find the slow pace of the rug-making to be incredibly therapeutic.

Armenia's current political moment and its democratic transition are hardly any different from the task ahead of the artisan woman working across from me. There is a clear base that has been established with Armenia's Velvet Revolution, but filling it in layer by layer, one individual, one organization, one community, one institution and one protest at a time, will take many years. As in rug-making, following the blueprint remains key: staying true and mobilized around the goals, in this case national unity around the values of liberal democracy (Ruston 1970), will be essential. The challenges are many, from local authoritarian reserves to global pressures on liberal values.

The contributions in this volume sought to explain the strategy of the Velvet Revolution, as well as the structural conditions that led to it. Chapters on the dynamics and indicators of authoritarian decline, the fabric and historical depth of traditions of civil resistance, and the challenges of a multipolar geopolitical order offer a holistic view on the Velvet Revolution. The authors collected here also examine the conditions and challenges of its consolidation, situating Armenia's democratic transition in a comparative global context. Analysing Armenia as a competitive yet enduring authoritarian regime, this volume approaches the Velvet Revolution as an opportunity to discuss non-violent civil resistance as an exit strategy from hybrid regime types. Once entrenched, authoritarian regimes can become resistant to societal pressure, as Armenia's two-decade-long struggle between regime and society demonstrated.

Scholars and practitioners alike have long pondered exit strategies from hybrid regimes stuck between democracy and authoritarianism, or the 'transition challenge'. Democratic transitions occur along a spectrum, from peaceful change through the ballot box, such as in Ghana, to mass uprisings vulnerable to securitization and violence, such as in the Middle East. Between these extremes, this volume has argued that Armenia's Velvet is an example of a third way, an institutional pathway grounded within state structures, yet with the targeted application of mass mobilization. This gradual and institutional approach has made a transition possible in a neighbourhood that is politically inhospitable to democracy and at a time of democratic backsliding worldwide. Yet while successful in dislodging a deeply entrenched authoritarian regime, whether this model of transition will result in a consolidated democracy still requires assessment.

Armenia's chances of democratic consolidation are highly dependent on four main factors. The first is the way that persistent, if expected, 'authoritarian reserves', meaning residual spaces, institutions and networks still operating by the rules of the previous regime, are handled. Authoritarian decline has not been terminal, and the peaceful transition of power within legislative and executive branches should not lull reformers into complacency: authoritarian reserves are a significant risk factor with the capacity to derail this democratic transition. Second, institutional weakness, particularly in party politics, can weaken and erode the vast democratic credentials of civil society. Converting social mobilization and civic engagement on a massive scale into more durable and institutionalized political mechanisms of engagement between society and government is a crucial task ahead. Third, the fractured regional fabric in the South Caucasus complicates the effective management of both of these risks. States in fractured regions, such as Armenia, have internal political fault lines that make them vulnerable to external manipulation by illiberal powers. Finally, the unfolding security dynamics in Armenia's long-term rivalry with Azerbaijan are another major risk factor. Resuming tensions, and any flashes of large-scale violence, may push the currently liberal government to the right. I now turn to discuss these four factors, concluding with a section on policy implications from the Velvet Revolution for the prospects of liberal rules-based world order.

Authoritarian decline, persistence and reserves

As I argued in Chapter 1, Armenia's Velvet Revolution shares little with either 'colour revolutions' in the post-Soviet space or the Arab Spring revolutions that started in late 2010. Using what I term the 'interactive framework', I argued that the 'colour revolutions' challenged relatively weak administrative states that had emerged from their Soviet shells, while the Arab Spring movements confronted organizationally entrenched authoritarian states in which civil society had been co-opted and marginalized. The political terrain and challenges confronting the Velvet Revolution were somewhat different: here the movement challenged a stable, if competitive, authoritarian regime, which had nevertheless conceded political openings over the past two decades for civil society to mature, and for some political institutions of state governance to emerge. In this sense, Armenia's Velvet, I argued, has more in common with some of the transitions from military rule in Latin America in the late 1980s.

This argument is rooted in the insight that the strategy and the mode of political transition create durable legacies for post-transition politics (Munck and Leff 1997). Local and contextual factors during and after a transition are significant in shaping the prospects of subsequent democratic consolidation in any given case. As many studies have argued, the degree of control by the incumbent regime over the transition process and the pathways of its exit shape the ability of reformers to enact a clean break with the previous regime, and shape incentives for genuine reform and constitutional change. Munck and Leff (1997: 346), for example, argue that

> the mode of transition affects the form of post-transitional regime and politics through its influence on the pattern of elite competition, on the institutional rules crafted during the transition, and on key actors' acceptance or rejection of the new rules of the game.

In this view, the identity of the agent of change (elite or counter-elite) and its strategy (accommodation, confrontation or a combination of both) is central. This framework is useful in delineating differences in the mode of transition among Brazil and Argentina, Chile, Czechoslovakia, Bulgaria and Hungary (Munck and Leff 1997). Some of these transitions produced a much cleaner break with the previous regime than others, explaining variable, and sometimes more favourable, conditions for the reformers in counter-elites to consolidate fragile democratic transitions.

Armenia's mode of transition folds easily into this framework, reflecting features of 'reform through rupture' exemplified by democratic transitions in Czechoslovakia and Argentina (Munck and Leff 1997: 346). In both cases, the transitions were initiated by counter-elites, with a mixture of confrontation and accommodation with the ruling elite. However, in Armenia, the 'rupture' was not as total, since the judiciary remained largely untouched by the revolution and, as I discuss further, became an authoritarian reserve for the previous elites. In an interview with the author, the newly elected justice of the Constitutional Court Vahe Grigoryan highlighted the following:

> The Republican Party tailored the Constitutional Court to its needs. The Court supported fraudulent elections in the past. After parliamentary elections following the Velvet Revolution swept aside the Republican Party, the constitutional crisis, expressed in terms of the gap between constitutional and political legitimacy of the Constitutional Court, was fully exposed. (Grigoryan 2019)

Still, the application of this framework to the Armenian case discounts one important dimension in Armenia's transition: whether or not the transition evolves within or against the existing constitutional order and state institutions. This institutional dimension, which I discussed in Chapter 1, was significant both in terms of the strategy of mass mobilization and in terms of managing bigger geopolitical rivalries between Russia and the West, while building a domestic democratic movement. As in Argentina and Czechoslovakia, Armenia's reformers succeeded in realizing a clean break in a relatively short period of about a year. And similarly to Chile, Armenia's reformers advanced their transition within the legal framework of the old regime. But while Chile's reformers failed to secure full control over the transition, Armenia's reformers were more successful. Utilizing mass-scale social mobilization throughout 2018, Nikol Pashinyan kept up the heat on the Republican Party of Armenia (RPA) forces in the National Assembly (parliament). He was able to secure the snap parliamentary elections he wanted, despite a slim political base in a parliament still dominated by the prior authoritarian elite at that time.

In short, Armenia reveals the combination of accommodation and confrontation, but also the value of working from below, from a wide social base, as well as from above, negotiating and transacting with the incumbent elites (Ohanyan 2018b). Throughout this process, however, reformers always left an institutional pathway for the incumbent regime to regroup and contest power through the ballot box. This enabled institutional continuity during the transition, while providing much-needed political stability, a strategic asset considering Armenia's location in Russia's fractured neighbourhood. Importantly, this approach built broader domestic support for the reformers, even as former incumbent elites crumbled. Sorely lacking in even a modicum of legitimacy, prior RPA and RPA-affiliated elites were unable to utilize the pathway provided to them. Prosperous Armenia, built up around the oligarchic power of Gagik Tsarukyan, was the only party that succeeded in passing the 5 per cent threshold in the 2018 December parliamentary elections, and that consequently succeeded in regrouping within the new political system.

Despite a clear institutional pathway for prior authoritarian forces to regroup and re-enter formal politics, most of them failed to do so. Left out of the parliament, former incumbents regrouped through the judiciary and the media, over which they maintained significant control. These two domains emerged as authoritarian reserves for the previous regime from which to attack Pashinyan's record in office. It could be argued that by removing the former elite from parliament, the new administration may have contributed to the instrumentalization of the judiciary and the media by the former elite. On the other hand, the absence of a coherent right-wing authoritarian presence in the parliament helped the reformers to maintain their organizational identity. This can be contrasted with the dilution of the reformist camp in Brazil as a result of the integration of the former sympathizers of the military regime, considered a major factor challenging Brazil's democratic transition in the mid-1980s (Munck and Leff 1997). In Armenia, authoritarian reserves are outside of parliament, often challenging the legitimacy of that institution. Indeed, while insignificant in formal politics, these authoritarian forces have opened up domestic cleavages that are ripe for exploitation by the Kremlin, as discussed further (Ohanyan 2018e).

Sustained civic activism, institutional erosion and the rebirth of political parties

Co-opted and eroded party politics under authoritarian regimes creates an important challenge for consolidating a democratic transition. Some parts of this problem are uniquely local, while others reflect more global challenges of democratic decline.

Legislatures in authoritarian settings can be deployed as instruments to neutralize threats from rival elites as well as pressures from society (Bonvecchi and Simison 2017; Gandhi and Przeworski 2007; Wright 2008; Wright and Folch 2012). Yet even when dominated by executive-affiliated political parties, legislatures in authoritarian regimes can be more than ceremonial, rubber-stamping institutions. They can emerge as theatres of genuine, if limited, political contestation, with variable credibility in constraining the executive (Wright and Folch 2012). Some may be vehicles of 'consultative authoritarianism' (He and Warren 2011) able to produce regime support, as in China (Truex 2017). Others, even in contexts of deep authoritarianism, such as in Brazil in 1970s–1980s, are able to push back against the executive when strategic conditions on the ground allow (Desposato 2001). The party system is credited with the consolidation of some fragile democracies, particularly in the context of Latin American transitions, because of its centrality in interest intermediation and administrative governance. States lacking institutionalized party systems, on the other hand, stand out with more erratic politics in which establishing legitimacy is more difficult (Mainwaring and Scully 1995).

Armenia shares with many parts of the world, including advanced industrialized regions (Marsh 2013), a weak political party system. Its transition comes at a time of growing challenges to institutionalization of party politics across the globe. Marsh (2013) identifies several challenges of this kind, including the drastic decline of party membership in Western democracies; disenchantment with Keynesian approaches to economic management; the overall retrenchment of the administrative state in the face of economic globalization; the growing differentiation of issues and forms of their articulation by the public; the rise of the celebrity politics; and short-term and populist orientations in policy-making, among others. These global challenges to the consolidation of party politics in democratic systems add to and deepen more local constraints on the development of an effective party system in Armenia.

While parties supporting Armenia's previous regime were deeply institutionalized and ingrained into the fabric of the competitive authoritarian system, parties were heavily personalized, failed to constitute genuine political platforms, and served to entrench a ruling elite driving a lack of public trust in parties as organizations and mechanisms of representative democracy (Iskandaryan 2018). Personalized and co-opted party politics pushed challengers into civil society. Despite this, however, the legislative efficacy of the Armenian parliament before the Velvet (and before Armenia transitioned to a parliamentary system) was also relatively functional. Opposition forces, even under conditions where the ruling party had a total majority, managed to push back, or at the very least to create an oppositional discourse, be it in challenging proposed constitutional changes to transition to a parliamentary system, or opposition to Armenia's membership of the Eurasian Economic Union (EAEU).

Alexander Iskandaryan rightly points out how Nikol Pashinyan's Civic Contract party was deliberately conceived as a new type of non-political protest:

A project publicly discussed in 2013-2015, Civil Contract institutionalized civil protests, in contrast to the fruitless political movements of the previous two decades. It strived to reformat opposition activity in a creative new form for a new generation. The widespread demand for new forms of protest was thus filled by the creation of a youth-driven movement clearly distinct from the old guard. (Iskandaryan 2018: 476)

Iskandaryan observes that decentralization, personification, networked organization and the absence of hierarchies were central in mounting an effective social movement, but that these very same features can also challenge the institutionalization of state-building processes. By washing away much of the institutional mechanisms of formal and informal interest intermediation between the people and the government, the Velvet tide left a gaping hole within the political system. This is being filled by the next generation of political parties, with many of its members coming from civil society. While successful in unseating the RPA regime, the grassroots, socially driven form of political participation devised by Pashinyan faced a challenge: it is unclear whether this approach to political participation can transform itself into credible and effective mechanisms of governance, by either becoming an institutionalized political party or offering an alternative political instrument of democratic statecraft. As elsewhere in the democratic world, Armenia is struggling to find effective means to mediate people, government and representation.

While continued civil society engagement has been credited as essential for consolidating democratic openings and preventing authoritarian backsliding (Linz and Stepan 1996), if unbalanced and unmatched by political party organization and activity, mobilization will not result in representation. Simply put, if party politics continues to lack credibility as an effective mechanism for administrative problem-solving and interest intermediation, and remains unable to fix fundamental policy problems (what I describe as Armenia's pothole-to-parliament gap), the democratic transition will remain vulnerable. A key challenge for Armenia's transition will rest in its ability to consolidate political parties as institutions of representative democracy, while also strengthening the role of opposition forces within the parliament. With decisive parliamentary dominance enjoyed by Pashinyan's bloc after its resounding victory in December 2018, its ability to self-restrain will ultimately determine the prospects of democratic consolidation in the country. It is crucial that the relatively recently formed opposition political parties strengthen and consolidate if legislative institutions are to play the role of restraining the executive.

The 'golden age' of democracy promotion in the post-communist world by Western powers is widely believed to have ended. While there is no consensus on whether Russia or China directly support the diffusion of authoritarian models, the existing scholarship has both firmly established that the Kremlin's crackdown on the NGO sector in Russia has been emulated by neighbourhood autocrats and has highlighted the coherent strategy of using conservative social values to challenge discourses and practices on human rights and liberalization. The Kremlin's search for global influence often manifests through indirect support of illiberal groups in the civic space of the post-communist world (Ohanyan 2018a). Positioning itself as the defender of conservative family values against 'decadent Western cultures of individualism, feminism, drug abuse, and gay activism' (Evans 2015; Ziegler 2016), the Kremlin's push for global hegemonic positioning is being waged as much as inside the societies of its peripheries as in global capitals on both sides of the Atlantic. In Armenia, as elsewhere in post-communist spaces, the institutional weakness of party politics makes the political system vulnerable to geopolitical intrusion from anti-liberal forces, such as the Kremlin.

Multipolarity, neo-imperialism and regional fracture

Armenia shares with neighbouring Georgia and numerous Eastern European states a struggle to consolidate democracy in a context of weak political institutions and external security pressures from much larger authoritarian neighbours, such as Russia and Turkey. The decline of a rules-based world order, and American reluctance to defend the hegemonic liberal order that it created, impose further constraints (Ikenberry 2015; Acharya 2018). The passing of the unipolar moment has opened the door to risks associated with the rise of multipolarity. These include neo-imperialism and a pre-Westphalian inclination in Eurasia, with both Turkey and Russia constantly pushing into their former imperial domains (Torbakov 2017; Ohanyan 2018a; Allison 2017; Colborne and Edwards 2018; Acharya 2018; Dunne and Flockhart 2013; Duncombe and Dunne 2018). Russia, in particular, stands out with its bifurcated stance on the international legal doctrine of state sovereignty: its statist stance in the international system in support of a Westphalian understanding of state sovereignty has been at odds with its policies in the post-Soviet space, where Russia claims privileged spheres of influence and sees itself as entitled to hegemonic and hierarchic arrangements with its former colonial peripheries (Allison 2017).

The challenge of multipolarity differs significantly from the era of ideological rivalry during the Cold War. The Cold War was characterized by considerable clarity between camps in a struggle waged between various superpowers and their clients. Contemporary geopolitical rivalry, some of it ideological, operates at multiple layers, sometimes transcending the clean political and territorial contours of the state system, sometimes undermining them from below. Regional and global geopolitical powers, often also neo-imperial ones, deploy political and administrative resources (Finkel and Brudny 2012), and media and sub-national non-state groups, in support of the authoritarian forces in a given country. Challenging the normative basis and legitimacy of the liberal world order, through diverse political and economic instruments operating at disparate levels, has become the new normal in world politics. In this sense, some of the challenges for Armenia's democratic consolidation are far from local, and they are shared, with no less urgency, by most integrated and advanced industrialized democracies across the globe. The challenges of democratization in a globalized context, ranging from rapid advances in communication technologies disrupting traditional institutions (whether democratic or authoritarian) to fragmented media spaces to new avenues of money laundering and global capital flight, collapse the distance between mature and transitional democracies.

Armenia's Velvet Revolution unfolded in the context of a highly fractured region – the South Caucasus (Broers 2018; Giragosian 2018). Regional fracture is characterized, to name just a few of its features, by internal cleavages within states, usually between governments and societies; divergent economic and security vectors pulling in different directions; and the capture of dividends from regional engagement by the narrow interests of elites and oligarchs (Ohanyan 2018a, c). Caught in the cross-hairs of overarching geopolitical rivalries, democratic transitions in such regions – when they emerge – face specific challenges. Yet while the Orange and Euromaidan Revolutions deepened existing geopolitical cleavages, with Russia and the West coalescing around status-quo players and reformers respectively, Armenia's Velvet Revolution succeeded – precariously – in averting further irritation of geopolitical competition between Russia and the West. As my fourteen-year-old daughter Isabelle observed, 'Armenia is the eye of the storm which is always calm.'

This is not to say that external geopolitical competition in an increasingly post-American world order has no effect on the prospects of democratic consolidation. But in contrast to more overt military interventions, such as war in eastern Ukraine, the annexation of Crimea and the punitive territorial takeover following the Russia-Georgia war in August 2008, the dangers confronting Armenia concern the exploitation of institutional fragility to enact institutional sabotage. Against the backdrop of a wider global crisis in the legitimacy of the ballot box as a mechanism of power contestation (Issacharoff 2018), fractured regions with internal political cleavages between governments and their publics (such as in pre-Velvet Armenia) or within elites (such as old regime versus Velvet revolutionary forces) offer ample opportunities for external and institutional sabotage of the democratization project by outside powers, most prominently the Kremlin.

One example is the support provided to Armenia's former president Robert Kocharian, currently under arrest in connection with charges that he illegally deployed Armenian army units against peaceful protesters in Yerevan after presidential elections on 1 March 2008. The Kremlin and Russian-linked businesses dealing with Armenia, connected to Kocharian, have portrayed his arrest as politically motivated. Not-so-tacit support was evident in a 13 June 2019 meeting between the Russian ambassador to Armenia, Sergey Kopyrkin and Kocharian; Kopyrkin was later summoned to the Armenian Foreign Ministry to give explanations (Ohanyan 2019).

Overt Russian support for Kocharian is a way to sabotage the claims at the core of Pashinyan's project to liberalize Armenia, by framing the Velvet simply as 'regime change' rather than a popular civilizational choice for human rights, self-governance and enhanced state sovereignty. The government views Kocharian's arrest as a lynchpin for a project to enact transitional justice in order to deal with legacies of corruption and human rights abuses. Vahe Grigoryan, the newly elected justice of the Constitutional Court after the Velvet Revolution, pointed out in an interview with the author:

> Not everything should be viewed from the transitional justice angle, from an angle of a single criminal case, such as the March 1st events. The court is dominated by a single party, and the judiciary reform is our number one problem. Otherwise, we face the risk of becoming Ukraine or Moldova, stuck in judicial reform for years. (Grigoryan 2019)

By contrast, the Kremlin's support for Kocharian inverts this to offer fodder for his supporters to portray him as a 'political prisoner'. Despite Kocharian's arrest, he was reappointed as a member of the board of directors in a large Russian corporation, AFK Sistema, with stakes in a wide range of sectors, such as telecommunications, energy and financial services, including Russia's leading mobile phone operator, MTS.

These strategies are echoed in neighbouring Georgia, where a diplomatic incident escalated into a major row between Moscow and Tbilisi in June 2019. Using economic instruments and exploiting political divisions inside states have become important in the Kremlin's toolkit in dealing with aspirant democratizers in the South Caucasus. Strategies of working institutionally, by co-opting elites and supporting right-wing movements and parties, are deployed with frequency by the Kremlin. While advanced industrialized states in Europe and across the Atlantic may have instruments with which to respond, nascent democracies with limited administrative resources, such as Georgia and Armenia, are significantly more vulnerable to such pressures from their bigger neighbour.

Overcoming the false choice between security and democracy

While it would be inaccurate to suggest that Armenia was a fully fledged 'garrison state' under military control (Laswell and Stanley 1997), it is nevertheless the case that over the two decades preceding the Velvet, national security was repeatedly leveraged as a source of political legitimacy and evoked as a justification for partial or incomplete democratic reforms (Ghaplanyan 2018). Conversely, opposition parties and politicians have been repeatedly undermined by the charge that they cannot provide for national security. Underpinning this distribution of symbolic and material power was a rhetorical dichotomy between democracy and security. In the mouths of many RPA officials and other establishment figures, a choice between security and democracy was founded as a primary structuring principle in Armenian politics. This choice suggested that the parameters of Armenian democracy must be circumscribed by national security needs; by implication, Armenia could not be both democratic *and* secure.

That understanding was overturned by the 'four-day war' in April 2016. Human and territorial losses sustained by Armenians disrupted the societal acceptance of the regime's claim to provide for security. But while the 'four-day war' may have galvanized mass mobilization for democratic change in Armenia, the fundamental security challenges remain. Armenia and Azerbaijan are now a 'divergent' dyad, two countries with different political systems whose governments draw their legitimacy from different sources. Assumptions and expectations that liberalization in Armenia will translate into unilateral concessions at the negotiation table underestimate the systemic nature of the power shift in the country. Such analyses see Armenia's transition as a 'regime change', with a more legitimate government at the helm being in a better position to make concessions, so the argument goes. In contrast, the liberalization of Armenia's domestic politics has been systemic, challenging the very foundations of the existing system around the conflict. The call for including the Nagorny Karabakh authorities into the negotiations as advocated by the Pashinyan government is only one step in a bigger and deeper process needed to enhance the legitimacy and inclusiveness of the peace process in general (Ohanyan 2018d). Broadening the peace process is opposed by Azerbaijan, and a resumption of constant, low-level violence is entirely possible. On the other hand, Hermann and Kelley (1996) and Kelley and Hermann (1997) suggest that democratization deters state aggression, and that democratic states are more effective in providing for external security of their statehood. Specifically, Hermann and Kelley (1996) have shown that democratic regimes are grounded in norms and institutions that favour the peaceful resolution of conflict domestically and internationally. Therefore, such states are more likely to push for diplomatic mechanisms of conflict resolution, and if a dispute or a conflict shifts to the field of negotiation and diplomacy, they are more likely to be trusted by their adversaries (Enterline 1998). In addition, they argue that democracies are less likely to be targeted by interventions by all regime types. In their research, democracies are shown to be more capable of defending themselves should violence materialize. Democratization, in and of itself, may therefore contribute to the capacity of democracies to defend themselves from foreign attack. Either way, possible conjunctures of variables leading to renewed large-scale violence between Armenia and Azerbaijan are impossible to predict.

A democratic dyad in the South Caucasus

The uncertain external security environment and shifting patterns of global polarity add additional pressures for the Armenian democratic opening, but they also present opportunities. The entry and stronger presence of China in the South Caucasus, combined to a lesser extent with the European Union and the United States, creates a political market of sorts, for smaller states to shop around for external patrons. This dynamic partly explains Russia's reliance on its regional organizations, the EAEU most notably (Ohanyan 2018a), in reasserting its role in areas it considers its spheres of influence. The rise of regional organizations, even hegemonic ones, creates new institutional spaces and mechanisms for these smaller states to push back against hegemonic players in more subtle ways, short of facing a geopolitical choice between Russia, the West and the rest. Emergent multipolarity may result in an increasing institutionalization of regional clusters and conglomerates or it may devolve into a pre-Westphalian feudal and neo-imperial order with regional powers challenging the international rules-based order in their neighbourhoods. This factor will be consequential in shaping domestic political developments in smaller states. While largely succeeding in keeping regional powers out during the Velvet Revolution, political vigilance and greater coordination with its neighbouring Georgia, another aspirant and fragile democracy, is needed.

While the drivers and strategies of democratic transitions in Georgia's Rose and Armenia's Velvet Revolutions were different (as discussed in Chapter 1), their chances of democratic consolidation are highly co-dependent. Armenia's Velvet Revolution created a democratic dyad in the South Caucasus, despite the divergent alliance structures that Georgia and Armenia have maintained. Georgia's push towards Euro-Atlantic institutions, combined with its strategic orientation towards Turkey and Azerbaijan (also conditioned by Georgia's Western orientation), has created a deep political fracture in South Caucasus, with Armenia orienting itself towards Russia and its regional institutions. But in meeting the challenge of democratic consolidation in a fractured neighbourhood, the utilization of political legitimacy and leverage stemming from the democratic dyad between Georgia and Armenia is essential for both countries. For regime trajectories, whether moving to or from democracy, the political fabric of the local neighbourhood matters (Gleditsch 2002; Cederman and Gleditsch 2004). Specifically, the local clustering of democracies has been shown to be an important factor in producing liberal outcomes at the global level. Global democratic waves towards and from democracy, are deeply local affairs, largely dependent on the capacity of democratizing states to adapt to their local, and often authoritarian, neighbourhoods.

A key mechanism in this local adaptation rests with democratizing states joining forces in collective security arrangements to protect their fragile democratic gains and the nascent political order, and in order to create 'peer pressure' on non-democratic neighbours:

> Our computational findings indicate that, together with collective security, democratization through locally dependent transition probabilities contributes strongly to the emergence of the democratic peace in systems with few initial democracies. Despite considerable fragility in the early stages of the democratization process, the geographical clustering due to adaptive regime change can make it easier for democratic states to survive in a hostile, non-democratic environment. Beyond a certain point, regionally operating regime change drives a positive feedback process that gives rise to Huntingtonian 'waves of democratization' capable of shifting the balance decisively in favor of the democratic peace. (Cederman and Gleditsch 2004: 604)

The divergent security orientations between Georgia and Armenia, towards the West and Russia respectively, have created a sense of fatalism and structural durability of alliances among policy-makers in the region. Policy choices with Russia for Armenia are often viewed in categorical and win-lose terms; Armenia is either with Russia or against it. This has led to divergent policy choices with neighbouring Georgia. The options of 'being with Russia' on some policy issues and not in others, receives little consideration thus far. One welcome departure from this stand was Armenia's June 2019 vote at the UN on a nonbinding resolution reaffirming the rights of Georgians displaced from South Ossetia and Abkhazia to return to their homes. Armenia abstained and did not vote against Georgian position, a marked departure from pre-Velvet years. And a much higher level of intergovernmental cooperation between the two countries also followed in the wake of the Velvet.

The development of regional organizations by Russia eases Armenia's options for building new institutional frontiers of diplomatic engagement and offers it a way out of all-or-nothing geopolitical choices and predicaments when it comes to Russia or the West. Maintaining the general contours of its security alliance with Russia, Armenia can now also integrate and coordinate policy choices with Georgia, despite being in opposite security camps in the region.

The second dimension of this democratic dyad refers to relatively recent research on the impact of stronger democratic poles in a region, in constraining authoritarian players and military/coercive approaches to unresolved conflicts. Indeed, the Velvet Revolution has shifted the balance from authoritarianism to democracy within the region: Armenia and Georgia now form a democratic dyad in South Caucasus. In doing so, it has strengthened the democratic pole in the region, creating opportunities for civil society and people-to-people contacts across conflict divides. It has strengthened Georgia's prospects of democratic consolidation (Gleditsch and Ward 2006), and increased the costs of aggression (McCallister 2016) in 'resolving' the Nagorny Karabakh conflict for Azerbaijan through military means. Recent studies have shown that with increasing democratic strength in a region, the probability of conflict and aggression tends to go down (McCallister 2016).

In short, a stronger democratic pole in the region enhances the chances of democratic consolidation for Armenia and Georgia, as well as chances for Azerbaijan to undergo a democratic transition. With stronger normative support for democracy and non-violence, and opportunities for deeper and more frequent transnational policy coordination between the two democratic states, Armenia and Georgia have a new opportunity to deepen their democracies in an otherwise authoritarian neighbourhood and a fractured region.

From crude to calibrated: the three 'Cs' in saving the liberal order

After the Cold War ended, democracy promotion strategies focused on support of the NGO sector, the promotion of human rights and liberal principles of market economics were ushered in through a top-down political framework. When democratic uprisings did present themselves, Western policy choices vacillated between too much intervention (often direct political, and at times military, support to reformer-elites) and too little intervention (often leaving mass-scale protest movements on their own, and at times siding with the authoritarian leaders the movements were trying to dislodge). This is the basis of the 'too much or too little', or 'Goldilocks dilemma', which has had an insidious effect on the credibility of democracy as a viable political and economic system. It led to democracy being identified with instability, collapse of state governance and regional disorder in many parts of the world.

Particularly with regard to US foreign policy, the West's 'Goldilocks dilemma', whether its response is too much or too little, played out in crude policy choices (Ratner 2009; Carothers 2000; Bouchet 2013), from overwhelming military intervention in Iraq to confusion and lacklustre responses in the case of grassroots social movements in Egypt or Tunisia. While democracy promotion was a dominant framework shaping American foreign policy in the twentieth century, its application has been semi-realist and inconsistent, always characterized by a crude separation between perceived national interests and human rights.

Partly associated with the Cold War–era foreign policy tool kit, these policies are premised on the assumption that change is top-down and elite-driven. They erroneously see change as being led by governments able to vector their countries to one or other side of an overarching ideological rivalry, and as such are now ill-equipped to handle liberal politics from below. Critical theorists have argued that in the immediate post–Cold War period, the West supported 'low intensity democracies', referring to the hybrid regimes arising in the post–Cold War period, as a way to thwart more radical changes that actually could have challenged neoliberal economic and largely oligarchic globalization (Hills and Gray 2012). The Arab Spring in particular exposed the limits of these Cold War–era policies. Similarly, the new elites within the post-communist world, and the wave of 'colour revolutions', can be viewed as facilitators for the gradual opening of political systems in these states, or, as critical theories have maintained, as a way to prevent the rise of radical movements calling for broad-based development, social justice and economic equality. Regardless of one's perspective on Western support of social change in the developing world since the early 1990s, the lack of Western strategy for providing meaningful support to grassroots democratic movements is striking. Confronted with their own domestic challenges of right-wing populism, consolidated democracies, most of whom contribute substantial foreign aid in the developing world, lack a strategy of meaningful democracy assistance.

The key policy implication stemming from this research is to call for a transition from crude to calibrated foreign policy responses in the democratic transitions unfolding in fractured regions. Calibrated strategy entails the recognition of 'people power' as a political factor, in contrast to state-centric geopolitical analysis that tends to obscure or minimize the strategic significance of social movements in shaping democratic transitions and altering geopolitical security landscapes in the process. The new tide of people power around the world, particularly in Africa with its entrenched authoritarians and dictators, is particularly important for this trend (Marks, Chenoweth and Okeke 2019). As Rocamora argues:

> People power is alive and well. It is sustained by the prodigious capacity of capitalism to produce victims; by the continuous production of educated, unemployed, bored youth; by the insults of autocracy; by the avalanche of information generated by the internet. Add to past generations of outbursts of people power in Tunisia, Egypt, Libya, Yemen, Syria; and we should make a point of including Greece, Spain, the UK and Israel. (Rocamora 2012: 201)

Armenia's Velvet Revolution has three basic policy implications for the Western world. Policy discourse in the West is dominated by the focus on geopolitical rivalries between the United States, China, Russia and the European Union. Much of the debate is driven by perspectives on 'rising China' and 'revanchist' Russia (Ohanyan 2019). A relatively more recent approach has been focused on American self-sabotage and on its unilateral and voluntary retraction of support for the very hegemonic world order it created (Ikenberry 2015). Instead, contemporary developments in Armenia (as well as in neighbouring Georgia) call for a new perspective in thinking about saving democracy and the global liberal world order. The South Caucasus calls for *clustered, conservative* and *consistent* responses by the West to socially driven democratic movements in fractured regions of the post-communist world.

The *clustered* approach, in the case of Armenia and Georgia, refers to recognizing the strategic significance of the democratic dyad established between these two countries. Rather than engaging with each state separately, more emphasis on strengthening and incentivizing transnational/trans-governmental ties between these two states is needed. As discussed earlier in this chapter, transitional democracies have a better chance of consolidation if surrounded by other democracies. The spatial-regional approach, therefore, is imperative in informing fresh foreign policies in South Caucasus. Since Armenia's Velvet Revolution, the pace of Armenia's collaboration with Georgia has intensified. The threat of new sanctions on Georgia from the Russian Duma, in response to heightened tensions between the two countries in the summer of 2019, illustrates the economic vulnerability of Georgia to Russia, but also the need to moderate the rivalry, by strengthening ties with Armenia, a member of the Russia-led EAEU. While Georgia can improve ties with Russia on its own, bandwagoning and coordinating with Armenia, and strengthening its democratic cluster with its neighbour, will enhance Georgia's (as well as Armenia's) bargaining power with the Kremlin.

The *conservative* approach is described and advocated for by Lind and Wohlforth (2019). They call for the United States and its partners to consolidate the gains of the liberal order that it has shaped, instead of expanding it to new places.

> The debate over U.S. grand strategy has traditionally been portrayed as a choice between retrenchment and ambitious expansionism. Conservatism offers a third way: it is a prudent option that seeks to preserve what has been won and minimize the chances that more will be lost. (Lind and Wohlforth 2019: 71)

This strategy bodes well for democratic transitions such as Armenia's Velvet. It requires the West to take a back seat on grassroots movements and local actors of social change, but remain engaged in supporting domestic as well as foreign policies of such states. Such policies could entail preferential trade packages to fresh forms of engagement with grassroots actors of democratic movements. This strategy will also require prioritizing domestic developments in democratizing states, with an eye to their democratic consolidation, even if it requires short-term and tactical changes in geopolitical calculations, which I discuss next.

The *consistent* approach is an organic continuation of conservative policies. Focusing on deepening the liberal gains achieved in many parts of the world will entail relaxing short-term geopolitical imperatives. A good example of an *inconsistency* in foreign policy responses to a democratic transition is the visit by John Bolton, National Security Advisor to the Donald Trump administration, to the South Caucasus in October 2018. In his visit to Armenia, Bolton, pursuing an international coalition to support the American sanction regime on Iran, insisted that Armenia should drastically reduce ties with Iran, one of the only two countries with whom Armenia has an open border. The economic calculations for such a policy, and the way they could stress Armenia's nascent democratic regime, failed to register with the senior US official. A consistent policy would be tailored and cognizant of the economic challenges faced by a nascent democracy. Tailoring and calibrating its Iran policy in the South Caucasus would be essential for the United States to sustain the solid gains in deepening democracy in the region. Similarly, there have been calls to de-couple American geostrategic interests from its democracy promotion initiatives (Ioffe 2013). For the Trump administration, this requires a consistently supportive approach to nascent democracies in South Caucasus that avoids entangling them into the US regime of sanctions on Iran. The long-term strategic benefits of such an approach in an era of global democratic decline are rather obvious.

The principles of consistency and conservatism in supporting the liberal order reflect the need to support those parts of that order that are under stress. Analysts point to the need to understand how different and specific elements of the liberal order are challenged, arguing that some are more stressed than others (Duncombe and Dunne 2018). Armenia's Velvet Revolution, and the emergence of the democratic dyad with Georgia, interrogate the view that the survival of that order depends on the willingness of hegemonic powers to defend it. Arguments pointing to a 'crisis of authority' (Ikenberry 2015), expressed in the American withdrawal from defending the hegemonic order, place disproportionate value on global levels and top-down approaches to supporting the liberal world order. These perspectives obscure and discount bottom-up support for liberal values, expressed in mass-scale social movements challenging autocrats in many regions, in parallel with democratic declines elsewhere. Moving forward, the conservative and consistent principles of supporting the liberal world order point to the importance of supporting democratic developments in regions like South Caucasus, without crude vacillation between forceful expansion and full disengagement.

In conclusion, Armenia's Velvet, with its geographical location in a fractured region, signals the need for fresh thinking in Western capitals at a time of strategic uncertainty and rising power of illiberal actors in world politics. It underlines the importance of understanding how competitive authoritarian/hybrid regimes evolve or decline in order to devise constructive strategies for engaging with them. There is a great deal of scholarship on modern authoritarianism, but very little on exit scenarios from these types of regime. The examination of the Armenian experience also offers paths to understanding what kind of mechanisms may be effective both in engaging with hybrid regimes prior to their collapse or consolidation and in supporting nascent democratic transitions when they displace such regimes. With the neoliberal rules-based order under stress and democracies in decline, effective engagement with aspirant democratizers stuck in-between competing geopolitical powers (Ohanyan 2018c) needs to be better understood. Mass uprisings and attempted democratic transitions in Syria, Libya, Ukraine, Georgia or Yemen have shown the vulnerability of such transitions to absorption by broader regional power rivalries. The survival of democracy in such contexts is consequently as much an existential concern for the wider liberal democratic world, as it is for Armenia.

References

Acharya, A. (2018) *The End of American World Order*. New York: Polity.

Allison, R. (2017) Russia and the Post-2014 International Legal Order: Revisionism and *Realpolitik*. *International Affairs*, 93 (3): 519–43.

Bonvecchi, A. and Simison, E. (2017) Legislative Institutions and Performance in Authoritarian Regimes. *Comparative Politics*, 49 (4): 521–39.

Bouchet, N. (2013) The Democracy Tradition in US Foreign Policy and the Obama Presidency. *International Affairs*, 89 (1): 31–51.

Broers, L. (2018) The South Caucasus: Fracture Without End? In: Ohanyan, A., ed., *Russia Abroad: Driving Regional Fracture in Post-Communist Eurasia and Beyond*. Washington DC: Georgetown University Press, 81–102.

Carothers, T. (2000) *The Clinton Record on Democracy Promotion*. Carnegie Papers no. 16. Washington DC: Carnegie Endowment for International Peace.

Cederman, L.-E. and Gleditsch, K. S. (2004) Conquest and Regime Change: An Evolutionary Model of the Spread of Democracy and Peace. *International Studies Quarterly*, 48 (3): 603–29.

Colborne, M. and Edwards, M. (2018) Erdogan Is Making the Ottoman Empire Great Again. *Foreign Policy*, June 22. Available at: https://foreignpolicy.com /2018/06/22/erdogan-is-making-the-ottoman-empire-great-again/ (accessed 8 July 2019).

Desposato, S. (2001) Legislative Politics in Authoritarian Brazil. *Legislative Studies Quarterly*, 26 (2): 287–317.

Duncombe, C. and Dunne, T. (2018) After Liberal World Order. *International Affairs*, 94 (1): 25–42.

Dunne, T. and Flockhart, T., eds (2013). *Liberal World Orders*. New York: Oxford University Press.

Enterline, A. J. (1998) Regime Change and Interstate Conflict, 1816–1992. *Political Research Quarterly*, 51 (2): 385–409.

Evans, A. (2015) Ideological Change under Vladimir Putin in the Perspective of Social Identity Theory. *Demokratizatsiya*, 23 (4): 401–26.

Finkel, E. and Brudny, Y. (2012) Russia and the Color Revolutions. *Democratization*, 19 (1): 15–36.

Gandhi, J. and Przeworski, A. (2007) Dictatorial Institutions and the Survival of Autocrats. *Comparative Political Studies*, 40 (11): 1279–301.

Ghaplanyan, I. (2018) *Post-Soviet Armenia: The New National Elite and the New National Narrative*. London and New York: Routledge.

Giragosian, R. (2018). Small States and the Large Costs of Regional Fracture: The Case of Armenia. In: Ohanyan, A., ed., *Russia Abroad: Driving Regional Fracture in Post-Communist Eurasia and Beyond*. Washington DC: Georgetown University Press, 103–17.

Gleditsch, K. S. (2002) *All International Politics Is Local: The Diffusion of Conflict, Integration, and Democratization*. Ann Arbor: University of Michigan Press.

Gleditsch, K. S. and Ward, M. D. (2006) Diffusion and the International Context of Democratization. *International Organization*, 60 (4): 911–33.

Grigoryan, V. (2019) Justice of the Constitutional Court of the Republic of Armenia; personal interview with the author, 13 July 2019, Yerevan, Armenia.

He, B. and Warren, M. E. (2011) Authoritarian Deliberation: The Deliberative Turn in Chinese Political Development. *Perspectives on Politics*, 9 (June): 269–89.

Hermann, M. G., and Kelley C. W., Jr. (1996) Ballots, a Barrier Against the Use of Bullets and Bombs: Democratization and Military Intervention. *Journal of Conflict Resolution*, 40: 436–60;

Hills, B. K. and Gray, K. (2012). Introduction: People Power in the Era of Global Crisis: Rebellion, Resistance, and Liberation. *Third World Quarterly*, 33 (2): 205–24.

Ikenberry, J. G. (2015) The Future of Liberal World Order. *Japanese Journal of Political Science*, 16 (3): 450–5.

Ioffe, G. (2013) Geostrategic Interest and Democracy Promotion: Evidence from Post-Soviet Space. *Europe-Asia Studies*, 65 (7): 1255–74.

Iskandaryan, A. (2018) The Velvet Revolution in Armenia: How to Lose Power in Two Weeks. *Demokratizatsiya: The Journal of Post-Soviet Democratization*, 26 (4): 465–82.

Issacharoff, S. (2018) Democracy's Deficits. *The University of Chicago Law Review*, 85 (2): 485–519.

Kelley, C. W., Jr. and Hermann, M. G. (1997) Putting Military Intervention into the Democratic Peace: A Research Note. *Comparative Political Studies*, 30: 78–107.

Laswell, H. D. and Stanley, J., eds (1997) *Essays on the Garrison State*. New Brunswick: Transaction Publishers.

Lind, J. and Wohlforth, W. C. (2019) The Future of the Liberal Order is Conservative: A Strategy to Save the System. *Foreign Affairs*, March/April.

Linz, J. and Stepan, A. (1996) *Problems of Democratic Transition and Consolidation: Southern Europe, South America, and Post-Communist Europe.* Baltimore: The Johns Hopkins University Press.

Mainwaring, S. and Scully, T. (1995) *Building Democratic Institutions: Party Systems in Latin America.* Stanford: Stanford University Press.

Marks, Z., Chenoweth, E. and Okeke, J. (2019) People Power is Rising in Africa: How Protest Movements are Succeeding Where Even Global Arrest Warrants Can't. *Foreign Affairs*, April 25.

Marsh, I. (2013) The Decline of Democratic Governance: An Analysis and a Modest Proposal. *The Political Quarterly*, 84 (2): 228–37.

McCallister, G. L. (2016) Beyond Dyads: Regional Democratic Strength's Influence on Dyadic Conflict. *International Interactions*, 42 (2): 295–321.

Munck, G. L. and Leff, C. K. (1997) Modes of Transition and Democratization: South America and Eastern Europe in Comparative Perspective. *Comparative Politics*, 29 (3): 343–62.

Ohanyan, A. (2018a) Theory of Regional Fracture in International Relations: Beyond Russia. In: Ohanyan, A., ed., *Russia Abroad: Driving Regional Fracture in Post-communist Eurasia and Beyond.* Washington DC: Georgetown University Press, 19–40.

Ohanyan, A. (2018b) Armenia's Democratic Dreams. [online] *Foreign Policy*. Available at: https://foreignpolicy.com/2018/11/07/armenias-democratic-dreams/ (accessed 31 July 2019).

Ohanyan, A. (2018c) The Regional Roots of Global Peace: The Problem of Regional Fracture. *Global Governance: A Review of Multilateralism and International Organizations*, 24 (3): 371–90.

Ohanyan, A. (2018d) At Long Last, Peace Might be Possible between Armenia and Azerbaijan. Here's What's Needed. [online] *Washington Post*. Available at: https://www.washingtonpost.com/politics/2019/03/20/long-last-peace-might-be-possible-between-armenia-azerbaijan-heres-whats-needed/ (accessed 27 August 2019).

Ohanyan, A. (2018e) Why Russia Starts So Many Conflicts on Its Borders. [online] *Washington Post*. Available at: https://www.washingtonpost.com/news/monkey-cage/wp/2018/09/12/russia-has-a-lot-of-conflicts-along-its-borders-thats-by-design/ (accessed 27 August 2019).

Ohanyan, A. (2019) How Old Courts Derail New Democracies. [online] *Foreign Policy*. Available at: https://foreignpolicy.com/2019/08/14/how-old-courts-derail-new-democracies/ (accessed 27 August 2019).

Ratner, E. (2009) Reaping What You Sow: Democratic Transitions and Foreign Policy Realignment. *Journal of Conflict Resolution*, 53 (3): 390–418.

Rocamora, J. (2012) Preface: People Power Is Alive and Well. *Third World Quarterly*, 33 (2): 201–4.

Ruston, D. (1970) Transitions to Democracy: Towards a Dynamic Model. *Comparative Politics*, 2 (3): 337–63.

Torbakov, I. (2017) Neo-Ottomanism versus Neo-eurasianism? Nationalism and Symbolic Geography in Postimperial Turkey and Russia. *Mediterranean Quarterly*, 28 (2): 125–45.

Truex, R. (2017) Consultative Authoritarianism and Its Limits. *Comparative Political Studies*, 50 (March): 329–61.

Wright, J. (2008) Do Authoritarian Institutions Constrain? How Legislatures Affect Economic Growth and Investment. *American Journal of Political Science*, 52 (April): 322–43.

Wright, J. and Folch, A. E. (2012) Authoritarian Institutions and Regime Survival: Transitions to Democracy and Subsequent Autocracy. *British Journal of Political Science*, 42 (April): 283–309.

Ziegler, C. E. (2016) Great Powers, Civil Society and Authoritarian Diffusion in Central Asia. *Central Asian Survey*, 35 (4): 549–69.

Index